Symbolism: The Manichean Vision

SYMBOLISM:

A Study in the Art of

the manichean vision

James
Conrad
Woolf
&
Stevens

by Daniel J. Schneider

University of Nebraska Press · Lincoln

A portion of chapter 2 first appeared under the title "Symbolism in Conrad's *Lord Jim*: The Total pattern" in *Modern Fiction Studies* 12 (Winter 1966–67): 427–38, Copyright (C) 1967 by Purdue Research Foundation, West Lafayette, Indiana. A portion of chapter 3 is reprinted with minor changes from "The Ironic Imagery and Symbolism of James's *The Ambassadors*," *Criticism* 9 (Spring 1967): 174–96 by permission of the Wayne State University Press, Copyright 1967 by Wayne State University Press.

Grateful acknowledgment is extended to Alfred A. Knopf, Inc. for permission to quote from the following copyrighted works of Wallace Stevens: *The Collected Poems of Wallace Stevens*, *Opus Posthumous*, edited by Samuel French Morse, and *Poems by Wallace Stevens*, edited by Samuel French Morse. Also to Faber and Faber Ltd. for permission to quote from these works. Grateful acknowledgment is extended to Macmillan Publishing Co., Inc. and to M. B. Yeats, Miss Anne Yeats, Macmillan of London and Basingstoke, and Macmillan Co. of Canada for permission to quote from *The Collected Poems of W. B. Yeats*.

Publishers on the Plains

UNP

The publication of this book was assisted by a grant from the Andrew W. Mellon Foundation.

Library of Congress Cataloging in Publication Data

Schneider, Daniel J.   1927–
  Symbolism : the Manichean vision.

  Bibliography: p.
  1. American literature—20th century—History and criticism.   2.   English literature—20th century—History and criticism.   3.   Symbolism in literature.   I.   Title.
PS228.S9S3   820'.9'15   74–12841
ISBN 0–8032–0847–2

To my Mother and Father

CONTENTS

PREFACE

Symbolism: The Manichean Vision traces its origin to a summer six-
teen years ago in which I attempted, for week after simmering
week, to ascertain the meaning of every symbol employed in the
poetry of Wallace Stevens, to classify the symbols, and to understand their structure—the principles of their generation and cohe-
sion. I sensed then that, however unique Stevens's symbolic scheme
and the accent he placed on each symbol, there was, in the breadth
and comprehensiveness of that "miraculous multiplex," a deep, organic relationship to the symbolic schemes found in such writers
as Joseph Conrad and Thomas Mann—and perhaps, it occurred to
me, to the symbolic schemes of most thoughtful writers. For the
generative source of the symbolism appeared to be the contrast
between mind and nature, or mind-art and life-nature, and it appeared that all symbolism, like all philosophy in Whitehead's view,
might be regarded profitably as a series of footnotes to Plato—to
the Platonic distinction between the world of forms and the corporeal world of change. When, still later, I studied Northrop
Frye's classifications of the iconography of the imagination—the
archetypal categories in which the artistic imagination has sought
to prehend experience—my excitement grew, and while the Platonic oppositions still seemed to provide the most general and the
most useful and congenial categories for the development of the
artist's imagination, I saw too that the sort of "Manichean" vision
I had been concerned with and the special developments of symbolism that occurred under the aegis of Manichean thought in the
nineteenth century constituted a separate chapter in the history of

the imagination's quest to grasp reality. And I began to explore the imaginative proliferations of that vision in a number of important British and American artists of the past century and a half.

Along the way I encountered some stubborn questions, of which perhaps the most important ones for future studies concern the interpretation of symbolist works. How does one identify the symbol *as* symbol, and how does one grasp its full significance—without falling into idle free association irrelevant to the image of life considered *as* image of life? Exactly how are symbols wedded to the image of life, and what are the limits of their implication? Or are there no limits? Now it is apparent to anyone acquainted with the learned journals that a great deal of arbitrary deciphering of symbols has gone on in our time. The formalist critic, astonished by the profligacy of critical assertions regarding the "meaning" of symbolist works, can only shake his head at the recklessness of interpretation: *Cosi è, se vi parè!*

Arbitrariness, if not falsehood, appears to have triumphed. And yet, when one's subject matter is a work of the imagination, when, as Gaston Bachelard has reminded us, "the value of an image is measured by the extent of its imaginary halo," how is any sort of responsible reading possible? Isn't it true, moreover, as Bachelard contends, that "it is nonsense to pretend to study the imagination objectively, since one only really receives the image if one admires it"? If one must be a poet to understand the reverberations of images, isn't criticism condemned to impressionism, to the Pirandellian *Cosi è?*

The problem is so complex that to solve it adequately requires the sort of patient and thorough analysis that Bernard Weinberg (for example) has exhibited in his study of French symbolist poems. But we may pause here to observe that to a degree the problem resolves itself into one question: at what point does the critic's reverie, his private associations generated by his reading, become irrelevant to the image of life in the work of art? And the answer would appear to be: they become irrelevant as soon as they cease to be intelligible as part of the *total structure* of the work; as soon, that is, as they can no longer be accounted for in terms of the scheme, whether of plot or of idea, that governs the creation of the artistic whole. Whatever is relevant to the whole is indeed implied by the work itself. Whatever is relevant only to a part of the whole is likely to be irrelevant. Thus to argue, as one critic does, that the garden of Gloriani in James's *The Ambassadors* is the Garden of Eden is to find an association with James's garden that the total structure of his novel finally makes irrelevant. To discern that the garden is a formal garden enclosed by walls and that it is rather like Spenser's Bower of Bliss is to come much closer to the mark: closer, that is, to an interpretation that accounts for the garden (and the actions therein) as elements in a thoroughly unified whole having to do with Lambert Strether's fate as a free spirit.

One of the major aims of my study thus has been to stress specific and thorough analysis of symbolism in relation to the shaping principle of the literary work. In studying the work of James, Conrad, Woolf, and Stevens, I have tried to do a complete analysis of the symbolism in one or two works by each author and to suggest how the symbolic scheme developed in these works reflects a total vision of life. My approach has been essentially inductive, although the form of my presentation may at times suggest that I have proceeded deductively. The truth seems to be that the critic tracing out the development of a symbolic system tends to follow the author's own process of creation: that is to say, he first discovers symbols in a few meaningful patterns, then begins to generalize, to extrapolate, from his initial discoveries. The imaginative development of a symbolic scheme is always the process of "elongating the cuts" that Wallace Stevens describes in "A Primitive like an Orb." And after a writer has developed his vision of life over two or three decades, it is possible virtually to predict the channels in which all his subsequent symbolism will flow. Hence criticism may seem to proceed deductively even when the critic has done his utmost to allow each new work to make its impression on him in all its uniqueness and has done everything possible to avoid preconceptions as to the meaning of the symbols. It goes without saying that the critic must insist on the unique meaning of the symbolism within a given work; but the discovery of a unique pattern of meaning in one work is ever the prelude to the apprehension of the great "poem within, and above, a poem" that the symbolizing imagination develops to extend its grasp of reality and its mastery of art.

It would seem that comprehension of the ways in which the symbolizing imagination creates its images of life—and its picture of reality—is just beginning to become clear. We may look forward over the next decades to the luxuriant development of criticism based on the work already completed. And future students of symbolism will, assuredly, build their new architecture on the solid foundations laid down by Charles Feidelson, Jr., Northrop Frye, Ernst Cassirer, Suzanne Langer, Mircea Eliade, Flanders Dunbar, and a host of scholars and critics whose researches have steadily enlarged our conception of man's symbolizing activity. It is with deep satisfaction that I acknowledge now my indebtedness to all these scholars and critics, without whose insights this study could not have been completed.

I also wish to acknowledge my debt to several scholars and teachers from whose advice and encouragement I have profited. I am particularly grateful to Maurice Beebe, former editor of *Modern Fiction Studies* and now editor of the *Journal of Modern Literature,* and to Bertram Sarason, editor of *The Connecticut Review,* for the encouragement they have given me in my work. Charles Fish of Windham College read most of a long, sprawling manuscript on the art of Henry James and gave me many invaluable suggestions. My work on symbolism began in the graduate schools of Northwestern University and the University of Chicago almost twenty years ago, and I was fortunate then to have studied under Wallace Douglas, Jean Hagstrum, Moody Prior, James Robinson, and William Keast. I take this opportunity to thank Richard Ellmann for the splendid advice and criticism he gave me when I began my work on Wallace Stevens, and for awakening my imagination to the imaginations of others. Finally, I would like to thank the editors of *Modern Fiction Studies* and *Criticism* for permission to reprint material which originally appeared in their periodicals.

DANIEL J. SCHNEIDER

Windham College
Putney, Vermont

I. THE MANICHEAN VISION AND THE READING OF SYMBOLIST WORKS

> The poetry is filled with tensions between stub-
> bornly recalcitrant contraries. Everywhere Yeats
> finds the drama of the antinomies.
>
> Cleanth Brooks

THE REMARKABLE DEVELOPMENT OF SYMBOLISM in the literature of the nineteenth and twentieth centuries is often traced to the growth of idealism and to the artists' revolt against the desert supremacy of positivistic and materialistic views of life. Symbolists, as the account goes, sought to depict a higher and truer reality than that dreamt of in the philosophies of Locke, Comte, Taine, Marx, or Loeb, and conceived that liberation from the dead end of scientific determinism lay somewhere along the road of correspondences, of mystic analogues, of the anagogic, the vague and suggestive. Coleridge, taking the hint from Kant, came to look upon nature not as a collection of brute particles jostled and jostling but as the veritable signature of the spirit, of the divine faculty of the imagination. Transcendentalism in America, taking the same hint, emphasized the reality inaccessible to science—the reality of the oversoul, of interconnectedness, of a unity existing beyond all atomized and factitious schemes of a reductionist science. "Science was false by being unpoetical," said Emerson. It was through poetry, and particularly through symbolism—the natural language of the spirit—that truth was to be attained if attained at all. The artist became the echo of the divine I AM, the universe became one with the mind, while the scientist, the mere material man of fact, was

doomed to the abyss of a philosophy that denied spirit altogether
or at least traced the origins of spirit to the concatenations of brute
matter.

   Such an account of the climate of opinion from which symbolism issued is clearly adequate to explain many of the developments
of symbolist art. Yet what is omitted from this description of the
movement is at least as important as what is included. In concen-
trating on the artists' reaction against positivism and in emphasizing their concern with the notion that words create the world,
historians of the symbolist movement have seldom, it seems to me,
made enough of the extent to which symbolists were *impressed* by
mechanistic and materialistic determinism and had already succumbed to the Lockean empiricism or Comtean positivism against
which they revolted. The poet might say,

> Death and life were not
> Till man made up the whole,
> Made lock, stock and barrel
> Out of his bitter soul,
> Aye, sun and moon and star, all.[1]

He might advise himself to be

> The unspotted imbecile revery,
> The heraldic center of the world
> Of blue, blue sleek with a hundred chins,
> The amorist Adjective aflame. . . . [2]

But as the child of his age, having witnessed all the triumphs of
positivism, tangible and intangible—both the conquests over nature
and the utterly convincing explanations of nature's operations—he
could scarcely doubt that science "worked" or that it would extend its conquests and its knowledge further as experimentation
and reasonings upon experiments proceeded. Whatever idealism
might say about the powers of the spirit, it was undeniable that
science had discovered certain truths about a world not even remotely responsive to the spirit, a world that conceivably had not
the slightest correspondence with the essences in which the spirit
dealt; and science had established a presumption, at least, that spirit,
being born in matter, might also be matter's slave, mere helpless
tenant in the attic of the material house, quaking under that tyran-

nical landlord the atom. Thus all talk about the transcendental reason or the transcendental forms of apperception or the primary and secondary imaginations could scarcely go unattended, from the start, by the dread that the noumenal world might well be staging the whole show, might be, in fact, the invisible puppetmaster pulling not only sticks and stones and planets but also the puny spirit across its grim and fateful stage. If scientists were wrong about material causation, how *was* it possible for them to predict the future? And even if their vaunted "laws" failed to take a great deal into account, who was to say that the scientists might not some day "fill in the gaps" and explain free will, the moral faculty, the entire inner life as purest mechanism?

I am suggesting simply that the dread was there—that it could scarcely not be there—and that its presence, the dark concession that the positivists and reductionists could be right, was inevitably to exert a powerful influence on the writing of symbolist works. Symbolism, as we know, grew up and reached maturity as faith in progress faded, as liberal optimism was struck blow after blow, both by developments in science and by such political events as the suppressions of 1848. The story of the assault upon romantic confidence is now of course an old one. Whitehead lists five major causes of the undermining of the "humanitarian ideal" which had been fostered by eighteenth-century humanitarianism and the religious sense of the kinship of men: Hume's criticism of the doctrine of the soul; the breakdown of unmitigated competitive individualism as a practical working system; the scientific doctrine of the elimination of the unfit as the engine of progress; Galtonian and Mendelian doctrines of heredity; and the rejection of the Lamarckian doctrine that usage can raise the standard of fitness.[3] To these five causes Joseph Wood Krutch, in his *The Measure of Man*, adds Freudian psychology and Marxist economics.[4] Krutch traces the profound loss of confidence that was apparent about the turn of the century (using H. G. Wells and Bernard Shaw to illustrate) to the growing conviction that man is the mere "product of forces outside his control": indeed, "it must seem that the Grand Strategy of nineteenth century thought had as its aim the destruction of man's former belief in his own autonomy." And: "Hobbes proves that man is an animal; Descartes proves that an animal is a machine. By a quasi-algebraical process one needs only to eliminate the term common to the two equations to get what by now most men seem to believe: Man is a machine." Jacques Barzun also identifies Darwin and Marx as the destroyers of the faith; and finds still another surrender to mechanism in Wagnerian music.[5]

Now it is precisely this growing doubt, distrust, and despair that give rise to what is, I think, the most interesting and artistically the most significant development of symbolist writing. Symbolism might have set out to convert the blank, colorless geography of the scientific world into a moral geography, to wed mind to nature. If thought is identical with being—if, as Wordsworth held in *The Prelude*, the world is fitted to the mind, or if, as Emerson thought, the mental order belongs to nature—the writer can be sure that whatever he says about nature, no matter how extravagant his poetic flights, is not entirely subjective. But when doubt intervenes —when the question arises whether one can, simply by taking thought, grasp anything more than *thought*—and when, in addition, there is on every hand evidence to suggest that all "hopeful" versions of experience may be sheerest delusion, there is no recourse for the poet—short of lapsing into Hart Crane's embittered conclusion that "in America the poet eats his own vomit"—but to develop a technique that confesses the doubt, the disbelief, in every line: no alternative, finally, to what Melville calls "the ambiguities."

The symbolist presentation of the ambiguities is, in one sense, a reinstatement of the old distinction between *natura naturans* and *natura naturata:* the distinction between the incorruptible essences and the world of corruptible matter. Yet in the nineteenth century the chief stimulus to such art is the clash between Christian or romantic and humanitarian views of experience and the new naturalism that, following Hobbes, undermines all Christian and romantic assumptions. Once the faith in nature as an emanation of God, or as a benevolent teacher, or as the source of innocence and goodness is called into question, once the assumption of the essential *trustworthiness* of the world is challenged, it becomes easy to swing to the dogmatic assertion that nature is basically cruel, hostile to man, or at least indifferent to him; or if nature is still held to be the signature of God, then God is altered—is certainly no God of Love, is at best a being of mixed qualities, at worst a monster. The sense of "the ambiguities" is however characteristically bound up with a sort of Manicheanism; at least it is bound up with that special and virulent form of irony that a Manichean hypothesis might be expected to foster. The Manicheanism, the sense of "dualities in unities," of a "dubious, uncertain, and refracting light," is of course everywhere in Melville. Charles Feidelson, Jr., has observed:

> Melville parodies the Emersonian "marriage of mind and nature," wherein "all this Earth is Love's affianced." He doubts the Emersonian doctrine that "from each successive world, the demon Principle is more and more dislodged . . . by every new translation." On the contrary, if there is no "Ultimate of Human Speculative Knowledge," it is because of the "barbarous hordes which Truth ever nourishes in the loins of her frozen, yet teeming North," and which overturn every synthesis. The evolution of thought is a series of revolutions, and it is the Devil who puts his shoulder to the wheel.[6]

It is the doubt that most prolifically generates the symbolism. The white whale—what is it? A brute that kills, yet gives the oil to light the lamps: both destroyer and preserver, Ormazd and Ahriman. And all parts of Melville's world exhibit the dualism, the ambiguity. The sea is lovely, and it is a horror: "its most dreaded creatures glide under water, unapparent for the most part, and treacherously hidden beneath the loveliest tints of azure."[7] "The calm is but the wrapper and envelope of the storm." The "graceful repose" of the whale line "carries more of true terror than any other aspect of this dangerous affair" (p. 282). And "who would think . . . that such fine ladies and gentlemen should regale themselves with an essence found in the inglorious bowels of a sick whale! . . . Now that the incorruption of this most fragrant ambergris should be found in the heart of such decay; is this nothing?" (p. 407). Ishmael is "married" to the terrifying savage with the harpoon; the mild Bildad and Peleg are "Quakers with a vengeance." "Butchers we are, that is true," says Ishmael of the whalers, yet "I freely assert, that the cosmopolite philosopher cannot, for his life, point out one single peaceful influence, which within the last sixty years, has operated more potentially upon the whole broad world . . . than the high and mighty business of whaling" (p. 107). Melville finds "the ambiguities" everywhere; and it is not surprising that his Ahab should feel the exultation of the power to convert fact into "meaning": "O Nature, and O soul of man! how

far beyond all utterance are your linked analogies! not the smallest
atom stirs or lives in matter but has its cunning duplicate in mind."
The obsession with the problem of the ambiguities, the awareness of the admixture of the light and the dark, of how virtues
spawn vices and how the highest aspiration and spirituality can
cause the most monstrous and perverted conduct, was eventually
to permeate literature in the second half of the nineteenth century.
Hawthorne's sense of the embeddedness of ambergris in corruption, for example, becomes as acute as Melville's. In *The Marble
Faun* (1859) a pattern of ironic deflation, reminiscent of Melville's
ubiquitous reminders of the terror lurking in the loveliest tints of
azure, is luxuriantly developed:

> We know not how to characterize, in any accordant and compatible
> terms, the Rome that lies before us; its sunless alleys, and streets of
> palaces; its churches, lined with the gorgeous marbles that were
> originally polished for the adornment of pagan temples; its thou-
> sands of evil smells, mixed up with fragrance of rich incense,
> diffused from as many censers; its little life, deriving feeble nutri-
> ment from what has long been dead. Everywhere, some fragment
> of ruin suggesting the magnificence of a former epoch; everywhere,
> moreover, a cross,—and nastiness at the foot of it. As the sum of all,
> there are recollections that kindle the soul, and a gloom and langour
> that depress it beyond any depth of melancholic sentiment that can
> be elsewhere known.[8]

The soul, in its attachment to the divine essences, may be kindled
by churches, rich incense, and the cross; but what man must face
unflinchingly is that these tokens of the ideal are embedded in the
world of corruption—of pagan temples, evil smells, and nastiness.
In a hundred analogous passages the cold perfection of art and the
cold purity of conduct are viewed as inextricably linked with the
world of imperfection and impurity. Thus in the chapter entitled
"The Suburban Villa" we find Hawthorne very carefully constructing a double world, composed of both marble and faunlike
elements, the ideal and the material so closely conjoined as to be
inseparable: an "ideal landscape," "a woodland scene that seems to
have been projected out of the poet's mind":

> In the openings of the wood there are fountains splashing into
> marble basins, the depths of which are shaggy with water-weeds; or

they tumble like natural cascades from rock to rock, sending their murmur afar, to make the quiet and silence more appreciable. Scattered here and there with careless artifice, stand old altars bearing Roman inscriptions. Statues, gray with the long corrosion of even that soft atmosphere, half hide and half reveal themselves, high on pedestals, or perhaps fallen and broken on the turf. Terminal figures, columns of marble or granite porticos, arches, are seen in the vistas of the wood-paths, either veritable relics of antiquity, or with so exquisite a touch of artful ruin on them that they are better than if really antique. At all events, grass grows on the tops of the shattered pillars, and weeds and flowers root themselves in the chinks of the massive arches and fronts of temples. . . . The result of all is . . . a scene that must have required generations and ages, during which growth, decay, and man's intelligence wrought kindly together, to render it so gently wild as we behold it now. [P. 631]

The world, in truth, is both gentle and wild. High and low, pedestal and turf, marble and weeds—all commingle, and there is nothing in man's intelligence that may be separated from growth and decay. The whole burden of *The Marble Faun* is to dramatize that great insight. The idealists, the men of marble, the artists who, as Hawthorne observes, are "lifted by the ideality of their pursuits a little way off the earth," must learn that the spirit, in its mongering for perfection, in its vision of "things too high for mortal faculties to execute," may so pitilessly abjure the flesh, the Faun, that life becomes poisoned at its very center, afflicted by a morbid obsession with sin and shortcomings, vitiated by the cruel dedication to rectitude and purpose. The spiritual men must learn, then, to accept the natural conditions of life—imperfection, corruption, the depredations of time, "the meanest necessities of to-day." For, spiritualize life as we will, we find the airy and unsubstantial always intermixed with "the commonest stuff of human existence." The Rome of washerwomen and bakers and organ-grinders, of tailors and merchants and jugglers and soldiers—the Eternal City built over its own grave—is a thoroughly real and a thoroughly ideal world: it is the ideal and the material in one—in short, the symbolic world of the Manichean vision.

As the century wore on the sense of the ambiguities deepened. Irony becomes commonplace, becomes virtually the whole stance of such writers as Hardy and Conrad. Conrad's development of the symbolism of ambiguity is particularly rich, and it springs, like

Melville's, from an acute dread that the Devil may be turning the wheel. We know what Conrad wished to affirm: like his Lord Jim, he wanted to affirm lordship, transcendent nobility, "the sovereign power enthroned in a fixed standard of conduct." But the dream of nobility is inexorably shattered by the reality of life: no man is "good enough," as Marlow observes, and in a crisis the best of men may panic like rats deserting a sinking ship. The Lord becomes Jim —just Jim, "a nobody." We see the underlying pessimism most clearly perhaps in Conrad's letters:

> There is a—let us say,—a machine. It evolved itself (I am severely scientific) out of a chaos of scraps of iron and behold!—It knits. I am horrified at the horrible work and stand appalled. I feel it ought to embroider,—but it goes on knitting. You come and say: "This is all right: it's only a question of the right kind of oil. Let us use this, —for instance,—celestial oil and the machine will embroider a most beautiful design in purple and gold." Will it? Alas, no! You cannot by any special lubrication make embroidery with a knitting machine. And the most withering thought is that the infamous thing has made itself: made itself without thought, without conscience, without foresight, without eyes, without heart. It is a tragic accident,—and it has happened. You can't interfere with it. The last drop of bitterness is in the suspicion that you can't even smash it ... it is what it is,—and it is indestructible!
>
> It knits us in and it knits us out. It has knitted time, space, pain, death, corruption, despair, and all the illusions,—and nothing matters. I'll admit however that to look at the remorseless process is sometimes amusing.[9]

All the virtues, all presumption concerning "moral" conduct becomes—mere presumption. The age's faith in progress and reform is but a beautiful pipe dream:

> The fate of a humanity condemned ultimately to perish from cold is not worth troubling about. If you take it to heart it becomes an unendurable tragedy. If you believe in improvement you must weep, for the attained perfection must end in cold, darkness and silence. In a dispassionate view the ardour for reform, for improvement, for virtue, for knowledge, and even for beauty is only a vain sticking up for appearances, as though one were anxious about the cut of one's clothes in a community of blind men. [*Life and Letters*, 1:222.]

"A vain sticking up for appearances": much of the Manichean

vision is in that phrase. And the root of the trouble may be, once again, that old sneer of the Devil, *There is no free will:*

> I like the worthy folk who will talk to you of the exercise of free will "at any rate for practical purposes." Free, is it? For practical purposes! Bosh! How could I have refused to dine with that man [Almayer]? I did not refuse simply because I could not refuse. Curiosity, a healthy desire for a change of cooking, common civility, the talk and the smiles of the previous twenty days, every condition of my existence at that moment and place made irresistibly for acceptance; and, crowning all that, there was the ignorance, the ignorance, I say, the fatal want of foreknowledge to counterbalance these imperative conditions of the problem.[10]

The clanking machine does its work thoroughly, if crudely; and nothing the spirit can do, nothing the mind can conceive, will change its unalterable course. Poetry changes nothing; the mind changes nothing. All thought, all moral pretensions must be admitted to be rationalizations, lovely fictions entertained to make tolerable a physical geography otherwise intolerable. Stein's dream, his beautiful butterfly soaring in the azure heaven (the wings that sustain it have yellow spots at the edges), comes to rest, at last, on a pile of dung.

The pessimism that issues from the recognition that the will is not free is deepened by the corollary that thought does not correspond to being. The fictions swarm in the mental world, but only in the mental world; they are "subjective," not "real." They have no analogues in the flux. Hence the motif of the dream in so much symbolist writing of the period: the beautiful, the incorruptible, the Platonic perfection exists—in air, not on earth. But once that concession has been made ("We dreamed that we dreamed we dream," says Melville; and Conrad: "There is no morality, no knowledge and no hope: there is only the consciousness of ourselves which drives us about a world that, whether seen in a convex or a concave mirror, is always but a vain and floating appearance."),[11] the world of value and spiritual significance becomes pure fake, a sort of paint or veneer spread over an immitigable horror. Action in the name of The Good becomes a pious make-believe; only desperation compels us to affirm the moral significance of our conduct. And this is Henry James's conclusion no less than Conrad's. In a letter to Henry Adams, James writes:

I have your melancholy outpouring of the 7th and I know not how
better to acknowledge it than by the full recognition of its unmitigated blackness. *Of course* we are lone survivors, of course the past
that was our lives is at the bottom of an abyss—if the abyss *has* any
bottom; of course, too, there's no use talking unless one particularly
wants to. But the purpose, almost, of my printed divagations was to
show you that one *can*, strange to say, still want to—or at least can
behave as if one did.[12]

James is no less disillusioned than Conrad. "I have the imagination
of disaster," he writes to E. C. Benson, "and see life indeed as
ferocious and sinister." In his darkness he can say, with Conrad,
that the only consolation is that the spectacle, the dime museum
of the world, is interesting or amusing. After 1890 his ironies
become devastating, he spares no one, not even his heroes and
heroines. Yet he was not "absolutely and exclusively condemned to
irony": such a position, in Flaubert, he rejects unequivocally. He
refuses to accept the abyss as the final truth. Or at least he affirms
that one can behave *as if* there were a point in living, as if progress
and reform were possible. (Vaihinger's philosophy of *As If* is recurrent in the work of Manichean symbolists.) To accept passively the
ferocious and the sinister is, for the ineluctably moral creature,
intolerable. Action—even though one knows that action may only
exemplify the ferocious and the sinister—is necessary. One must
pretend that action may be productive of good. One must tell the
"true lie"—such a lie as Marlow tells Kurtz's fiancée, who wishes
to believe in the dream of love and fidelity.

Now in the creation of images of life which are stamped by the
"dubious, uncertain and refracting light," the Manichean symbolists have inevitably been led to stress what Cleanth Brooks refers
to, in the epigraph to this chapter, as "stubbornly recalcitrant
contraries" and "the drama of the antinomies." Their sense of the
paradoxical character of experience indeed *necessitates* their employment of antinomies—their insistence upon the admixture of
opposites. We shall see the importance of the point in the following chapters. The Manichean vision is neither simply tragic nor
simply comic, but tends always toward a kind of tragicomic apprehension of experience—toward "irony *and* pity." What life *is*, the
modern Manichean, given his epistemology, cannot say; but that it
is, as apprehended, a mixed affair, full of contradictions, he cer-

tainly does affirm. And because his vision is complex, is mixed, his symbolism must be mixed.

To grasp the scope and structure of this complex symbolism is the chief aim of this study. We would understand how the imagination, prompted by a Manichean vision of life, selects and orders its materials, how it seeks to make every part of its image of life expressive of the Manichean idea. What categories, we may ask first, best describe the vision of the modern Manichean? What are the chief symbols—the "generative" symbols which breed the great progeny of lesser symbols that modern Manicheans find most useful and expressive? What are the "breeding lines" that the imagination tends to follow in extending and completing its vision? And then: how exactly does the imagination deploy its symbols when it seeks to prehend life under the aspect of "the ambiguities"? What forms or structures are needed adequately to present the Manichean vision? For our final concern is practical criticism, and we would account for the inclusion and the mode of deployment of every detail in the work of art; we would trace every symbol to its source in the total structure of the work, the concrete whole with which all generalizations about literary symbolism must begin.

Now in attempting to describe the iconography of the literary imagination, the student of symbolism can scarcely find anywhere more useful and comprehensive categories than those employed by Northrop Frye, who traces images back to their source in human desire and repugnance. From the extremes of desire and repugnance arise two fundamental visions of life—the archetypal vision of the apocalyptic and the opposite vision of the demonic: or, by extension, the comic vision and the tragic, the Eros vision and the Deros.[13] These mighty contraries in the imagination (returning always to our basic human preoccupation with survival, with life or death) generate opposed images or symbols at all levels of experience. The symbolism comprehends the divine, the human, the animal, vegetable, mineral, and, finally, the "unformed" worlds. The comic vision, as realized in depictions of the human world, for example, is a vision of community, communion, friendship, love, and marriage; in the tragic vision the human world becomes a tyranny or an anarchy, a world of isolated individuals, of the harlot, the witch, or Jung's "terrible mother." The comic vision as embodied in imagery of the animal world is of a community of domesticated animals (sheep, lambs, doves), while the tragic vision issues in imagery of beasts, birds of prey, dragons, etc. The vegetable world, in the comic vision, consists of a garden, grove, or park, a tree of life, a rose, a lotus; in the tragic vision it becomes a sinister forest, a heath or wilderness, a tree of death. The mineral world, in the comic vision, is the city, the temple, or some other geometric or architectural structure; in the tragic vision it is the desert, a place of rocks and ruins, etc. The unformed world, in the comic vision, is the river; in the tragic vision, the sea or flood.

Apocalyptic and demonic imagery issues from the visions of "extreme worlds"; but since most imagery in poetry deals with worlds lying between heaven and hell, Frye expands his iconography of the imagination by describing the "analogical imagery" that arises characteristically in "romantic, high mimetic, and low mimetic modes." It will not be necessary here to review his detailed descriptions of analogical imagery, and we may content ourselves with a simplified version of the entire scheme, to be found in Frye's little study of T. S. Eliot:

> Youth and age, spring and winter, dawn and darkness, rain and sea, form two contrasting states. Blake calls these states innocence and experience, and his terms are useful even for Eliot. For poets with a religious imagination, there are also heaven and hell, the paradisal and demonic realities underlying the mixture of good and evil in human life. Heaven and hell can be represented in poetry only by images of existence, hence images of innocence, the garden, perpetual spring, eternal youth, are closely associated with heaven or paradise, and images of repugnant experience, the desert, the sea, the prison, the tomb, are associated with hell. But for any poet who follows this structure of symbolism, including Eliot, there are four worlds, and heaven and innocence, hell and experience, are distinguished as well as associated.[14]

So Frye focuses on four key places, sources of major imagery: paradise, the inferno, the fallen world of experience, and the mountain of the Purgatorio.

It is, to repeat, a very comprehensive and useful scheme. And while some readers of *Anatomy of Criticism* may share M. H. Abrams's fear that "systems which are too elaborately symmetrical tend to keep order by tyrannizing over the unruly facts" or David Daiches's concern that Frye's archetypal criticism "becomes a technique of description by categorization and reduction . . . subsuming different works in a class, defining by showing the kind, not the quiddity," [15] not the least of the virtues of Frye's scheme is that in tracing imagery or symbolism back to *dianoia* in its undisplaced forms, it makes image-patterns intelligible in a new way and gives to the study of imagery a new dignity. Instead of tracing images back to circumstances in the lives of poets (for example) we see them as originating in the effort of the human soul to grasp reality and come to terms with it. Frye's iconography of the imagination thus corrects and complements biographical and historical criticism, and becomes a valuable adjunct to formalist criticism.

Yet, like Abrams and Daiches, I feel to a degree the constraint of Frye's categories and find myself searching for more flexible terms to describe the actual peregrinations of highly generalizing, philosophical intelligences seeking to contemplate accurately the dilemma of the divided self and the paradoxical character of existence. The danger of Frye's categories, as used in the explication of symbolist works by critics less perceptive than Frye himself, is that a traditional symbolism drawn from nonliterary contexts may be substituted for a poetic symbolism created by a mind seeking not to embody traditional meanings but to discover new meanings. As J. Christopher Middleton has said in a perceptive article dealing with symbolic style, "a confusion occurs between making meaning and knowing it":

> It is one of the truisms of the idealist theory of symbolism, where the confusion does arise, that (to quote Philip Sherrard) "the poet, through his use of myth and symbol, seeks to give expression to certain archetypal patterns of experience and to certain universal truths in terms of the particular time and place in which he finds himself." But these stereotype terms, "use of," "give expression to," and "in terms of," show how shakily such argument is yoked to fallacious expression theory. . . . when Sherrard pre-establishes his self-evident universals, he smothers the question of making, and gives a very shallow and schematic picture of the relation between traditional symbols, as registers of the "inner nature of life," and the moment-to-moment life of the imagination in the midst of concrete experience.[16]

Especially in seeking to describe and understand "the life of the imagination" as revealed in works created by highly generalizing intelligences, and to grasp the unique logic by which symbolic proliferations occur in such works, the critic finds himself, willy-nilly, driven beyond the categories of archetypal criticism or the dramaturgy of the tragic and comic visions. He is led, finally, I think, beyond the unconscious to a contemplation of the operation of very highly conscious and disciplined thought. Indeed, the critic seeking the generative principles of symbolism "in the midst of concrete experience"—to use Middleton's phrase—is drawn inevitably to a consideration of philosophical categories that have been central in Western thought ever since Plato. He is driven, in fact, in his search to understand the life of the imagination, to conclude that what Whitehead said about philosophy may also be applied to the symbolist writing of the Manicheans in the past century and a half: that it is but a series of footnotes to Plato. For the comprehensive "platonic" insight to which these symbolists return again and again is, as we have seen, that man dwells simultaneously in two worlds, an incorporeal world of the spirit and the corporeal world of matter moving in space and time. Man, as both spirit and animal, "participates in" both the divine and the created world. (As men in the Renaissance said, man is the microcosm, partaking of the total cosmos, from the most ethereal to the meanest and lowest.) Insofar as man lives in the realm of spirit he is confronted with unchanging essences, eternal images, Yeats's "flames that no faggot feeds," "flames begotten of flame." It is a world of art, of mind, of the ghostly forms known only by a ghost; it is thus in a sense a nonexistent world, a nothingness, as nominalists have held; and to live in such a world may be a kind of death—unless the unchanging paradise of essences is the *only* true home of man. Insofar as man lives in nature, on the other hand, he is immersed in the flux, in chaos, in the wild and elemental, the primitive, the amoral or pagan. This world in motion is destructive—an abyss—but it is also "creative" and "alive," and if it is hostile to the spirit, it is perhaps congenial to the life- and pleasure-affirming animal.

Now idealists may affirm that spirit is all, materialists that matter is all, but whatever one's philosophy, the world man encounters is, *as experienced,* a sort of embodied contradiction, a radical paradox. It is, and is not, ideal; is, and is not, corporeal. It is a world of

normal love and pleasure, beneficent; and it is a world of pain and
death, hostile, maleficent. Confronted by "the ambiguities" in experience, the symbolist, according to his moods at various times, is led
to choose among three alternatives. He may decide that the corporeal world is a prison or a hell and that his only hope or refuge
lies in transcending corporeality—fleeing, ascending to the world
of bloodless essences, of dream, of the divine. (This strategy is
employed particularly by traditional religious poets such as Donne,
Hopkins, and Eliot, but one may also find the basic plot—exposure
to materiality followed by a turning to the ideal—in certain poems
of Paul Valéry, Wallace Stevens, W. B. Yeats, Hart Crane, and
others.) On the other hand, he may decide that the ideal world is
sterile, cold, lifeless, and may feel that his hope or health lies in a
return to the world of passion, blood, corporeality. (The attack
upon the reason as "an instrument of constraint, of instinctual
suppression" [to use Herbert Marcuse's phrasing], has of course
issued in any number of poems and novels in which the liberation
of instinctive energies, the "resurrection of the body," has been
hailed as a virtually unqualified good. But one may also find artists
not presumably in the antirationalist camp choosing, from time to
time, to dwell in the mire of corporeality, preferring sensual liberation and license to being imprisoned in a world of cold abstractions
—the intolerable superhuman. Yeats, in "A Dialogue of the Self
and Soul," makes this choice. Wallace Stevens makes it in several
short lyrics.) Finally, one finds symbolists refusing to choose one
extreme or the other, and seeking some symbol of a healthy rapprochement or marriage of the ideal and the real in life. This
choice—the choice of "wholeness"—has dominated Western literature for many centuries. It is found in an especially well-developed
form in the satiric tradition—in the ridicule both of excessive
intellectuality and of excessive corporeality. With its animating
notion of proportion, its stress on the right balance of head and
heart, satire tends implicitly to oppose the Christian ideal of
etherealization as well as the naturalistic reduction of man to a pure
corporeality of brute particles jostled and jostling according to
immutable law. It speaks for good sense, for a reality-principle, a
recognition of the complexity of experience and the difficulty of
achieving proportion. It says: "Only connect." This idea of proportion and connecting, uniting the opposed halves of the human

personality and the contraries in the world, takes the form, in symbolist literature, of a remarkable search for the symbols of unity of being. Most of Yeats's work is concerned with this problem; all of Stevens's is. D. H. Lawrence, Virginia Woolf, and Henry James struggle with the problem. And, needless to say, it is the preoccupation of Baudelaire, Mallarmé, Valéry, and other French symbolists.

Now the division within the self is most easily, and most dramatically, represented in five major—and, I think it is fair to say, five "generative"—symbolic contrasts. These are the oppositions of (1) heights and depressions; (2) elevated and degraded creatures on the chain of being; (3) art and nature (including the oppositions of artifice and spontaneity, coldness and warmth, sterility and generation, immobility and motion, order and disorder, restraint and "freedom"); (4) light and dark (as well as various colors associated with heaven and earth, spirit and instinct); and (5) sickness and health, death and life (categories overlapping those under the heading of "art and nature").

The five categories, as presented, are vulnerable of course to all the charges brought against Frye's categories. The slots do not give us "the life of the imagination." But when we see families of symbols as generated by the artist's struggle to deal with the "stubbornly recalcitrant contraries" of experience; when we see them as reflecting a whole vision that seeks to realize itself in all parts of the work; when we see the imagination operating synecdochically, breeding from the generative symbols, using newly bred symbols to generate still other symbols, we realize that categories may be used, not to limit and schematize "meaning" in the work of art, but rather to expand our conception of meaning, to enrich and deepen it—and to make it more exact. For to understand the proliferation of a symbolic scheme from its generative oppositions is to grasp also the limits of implication, to realize that there is a moment, in the reading of symbolist works, when the reader's inferences from the symbol can legitimately proceed no further without doing violence to the nature of the whole as a whole of a determinate kind. To study the major categories in which the Manichean imagination realizes its vision is thus to arm oneself against "loose and baggy" explication (to borrow a phrase from Henry James); it is to promote responsible and focused reading of symbolist works. But more on that point later.

The pattern of heights and depressions is of course generated by the opposition of heaven and hell or between heaven and the sublunary sphere—the fallen earth. The divine or the ideal has usually been conceived as standing above the real, and so it is associated with the blue heaven, the stars, mountain tops, towers, balconies, and so on. To climb a mountain or ascend a staircase is often (as in Yeats and Eliot) to cast off the flesh and to advance toward a condition of pure spirituality. To move downward, into a pit, marsh, mire, or jungle, is to fall into the corporeal world, usually sinful, often terrifying. A jump into the sea or into the dark waters may become a dangerous (or rejuvenative) plunge into the domain of the instincts, the unconscious. Usually such low places are frightening; but of course the pure freezing atmosphere of a mountain top may also prove threatening, especially to the warm-blooded, sun-loving animal. Hawthorne's Hilda, in her high tower, is cold, and her morality is cruel. Hemingway's leopard dies on Kilimanjaro. Stevens reminds us: "It is fatal in the moon and empty there." And Yeats on occasion prefers the ditch of irrationality to the inhuman air of the tower.

The origins of the symbolism of heights and depressions may be traditional religious ideas (the ancient myth of the sun-god rising above us in the empyrean; the symbolism of a mountain-top paradise found in the cosmoramas of Sumer, Babylon, Iran, and the East).[17] But it seems reasonable, too, to assume that the human experience of gravity, our resentment at being pulled downward by our weight and the weight of the earth, also accounts for the frequent employment of the heights-depressions symbols. To free oneself from earth, to levitate, to float off as in a dream, is a "natural" correlative of the release from the corporeal burden. In *The Great Gatsby* the symbolism of buoyancy and of flight is thus used to suggest a fairy-tale world of the dream. Similarly, the myth of Icarus's flight has usually been associated with the aspiration to reach the ideal, the unattainable (the sun-god?), and his plunge into the sea is, of course, a return to nature, the primordial. Conrad's Lord Jim tries to throw off the burden of the material earth and fly through the air; his Jewel has wings like a butterfly's; and James's Maggie Verver becomes a "trapeze artist."

An important extension of the heights-depressions pattern is the symbolism of the north and south. The north, being cold, is associated with spirit, intellect, will; the south, with its burning sun, its somnolent animals, its jungles and tropical rivers, is associated with animality, instinct, the unconscious. Such symbolism is found in artists as diverse in their interests as Thomas Mann, Wallace Stevens, E. M. Forster, and D. H. Lawrence. Blake's use of the north to symbolize imagination and the south to symbolize the commonsense world *untransformed* by imaginative vision has clearly an affinity to the schemes employed by these others. Symbolic schemes are expanded through association. Whatever is high or is northern, if it is also expressive of the qualities the poet wishes to stress, may symbolize the ideal, the dream, the world of thought; whatever is low or southern may symbolize the real, the corporeal, the world of flesh and instinct. Henry James speaks of "high, imposing shadows of objects low and mean." Conrad uses the "foretop" or the bridge of the ship, which he contrasts with the ship's hold, its bowels; or he likes to use stovepipe hats or turbans to betoken the ideal. Wallace Stevens uses all sorts of high or elongated objects to symbolize the imagination or spirit: hats, columns, domes, steeples, clouds, pediments, etc.—objects belonging, of course, to the domain of art, in contrast with nature.

Most symbolists also create a host of personnae who symbolize the ideal or the real. Pure thought or spirit is inevitably represented by gods, angels, ghosts, or by the pure woman, a Beatrice, Eliot's "lady" of *Ash Wednesday*, Conrad's Jewel. Spiritual men, such as a bishop or a rabbi, may betoken the ideal or the imaginative; and since any titled person may suggest "elevation" above the common or ordinary, almost any rank in the aristocracy or in political or military life may symbolize participation in the realm of the spirit: Conrad uses the lord and the gentleman as opposed to the "poor beggar" and the "nobody"; Wallace Stevens uses lords, captains, emperors, etc., and contrasts them with such plain and corporeal creatures as the Johannesburger Hans and "the MacCullough." Certain animals may also symbolize the spirit: thus birds or butterflies, which, being airborne, belong naturally in the heaven of the ideal; also, occasionally, a northern or arctic creature such as the polar bear, contrasted with the tiger in Mann's *Tonio Kröger*. D. H. Lawrence associates the spiritual will with the bird of prey, the hawk; and Henry James seems to be working with a similar symbolism in his creation of such names as Madame Merle and Maria Gostrey.

The personnae associated with corporeality, on the other hand, are often fat or sensual: swine, elephants, etc. Almost any undomesticated animal may serve as a symbol of the participation in nature, in unthinking bestiality, but the symbolist who wishes to stress the gulf between mind and matter may be driven to use some such animal as the beetle or the snake as a symbol of mindless and earthbound activity. Or he may use dragons, wolves, and serpents to stress brutal predation, as in *King Lear*. The human beings associated with the corporeal realm are often fat men (see especially Conrad's fiction, passim) and, because darkness betokens a world devoid of the ideal, the black man. We may note, too, that because symbolism operates synecdochically, any creature of the south may symbolize the material world, as well as any vegetation that is charged with the implication of gross physicality—like the vines, the mangoes, the watermelons, and all the juicy and "gobby" fruits in the poetry of Wallace Stevens.

Various personnae associated with logic, art, or any human ordering or perfecting of nature may also become symbolic. Stevens (whose symbolism provides virtually a dictionary for students of the Manichean schema) uses the "doctor of Geneva" or the "logical lunatic" to represent the abstractive intellect which is hostile to a sensuous and erotic physical life. The artist—poet, painter, musician, sculptor—is often a symbol of imagination. In contrast, a giant may symbolize brute nature, stubborn fact in all its hulking ugliness. Emily Brontë contrasts the bookish Lintons with the fiery, dynamic Earnshaws. Stevenson contrasts Jekyll and Hyde.

The symbolism of order and disorder, of art and nature, is clearly congenial to the imagination seeking to grasp the human condition. Nature is associated with freedom or lawlessness, spontaneity, unrestraint, life, flow, motion, warmth; art and civilization with control or restraint, rigidity or fixity, imprisonment, coldness, stillness, immobility, etc. Spenser found the antithesis between the Bower of Bliss and the Garden of Adonis stimulating to his imagination. And with the imagery of artifice, illusion, and deceiving fair appearances, the artist may create a whole world in which (as in *Hamlet* or *Lear*) darkness and evil are half-concealed, half-exposed—the world of "the ambiguities" par excellence. In Hawthorne and in Henry James the art-nature theme becomes obsessive, and enormous families of symbols proliferate by clado-

genesis to form totally ambiguous worlds. What appears to be
natural and spontaneous may be no more than a trap, such as
Acrasia employs to attract her prey and to turn men into swine.
James's fiction is full of such attractively baited traps—the fair
exteriors and exquisite forms and *objets d'art* that seem to testify
to a largeness, liberality, and completeness of spirit but in fact are
symbolic of sheer greed, the money- and power-lust. Conrad, too,
loves to dwell on the ambiguous appearance—the attractive young
lord, for example, who may be in truth a yellow dog, a beetle. It
is Hamlet's world, this world of appearances: a paranoid's world,
as some would say. All great expectations are undercut, all fair
seemings are exposed for what they are: not an Ophelia, not a Lord
Jim, not a Mme de Vionnet who is not exposed as monstrous
deceiver. All the open and lovely vistas for the romantic soul,
which would expand to infinity, become dungeons or cages in
which the soul withers and dies. And here we touch on the great
symbolic families having to do with sickness and health, sterility
and potency, mechanism and vitalism.

When the fair appearances are stripped away, what is often
revealed is a skeleton, a carcass, or a frighteningly inhuman mechanism, an automaton—in short, the mechanistic world of nineteenth-century science. Instead of living, healthy human beings,
one beholds a world of puppets pulled by strings, "the human
engine," corpses whose motions are determined by the terrible
knitting machine of time and matter. Or one beholds a world of
people crippled or enfeebled by their allegiance to matter and
mechanism. Thus in D. H. Lawrence there is a host of sick people
who fear life, bloodless, abstracted people who move rigidly, with
a strange fixity of the hips, or are maimed or diseased or paralyzed
below the waist. The symbolism of paralysis is found in any number of novels and poems, and it harkens back, perhaps, to the
prototype of the drugged and imprisoned knight, the moral agent
rendered incapable of independent action. From the point of view
of the psychologist, we may refer symbolism of imprisonment and
automatism to the paranoid or schizoid fear of "engulfment," "im-
plosion," and "petrification"—to use R. D. Laing's vocabulary. The
threatened soul feels itself unable to move; it is fixed; it becomes
a "still life" (as in James's *Portrait of a Lady*). Losing his humanity,
the person becomes a thing, an "it"—either because he has denied

the spirit (as in Conrad) or because he has denied nature and the flesh (as in Hawthorne and D. H. Lawrence). The search for an adequate symbolism of health (usually connected with a search for unity of being) is perennial, and the old tag "mens sana in corpore sano" lies back of such examinations of neurosis as one finds in most of the symbolists we shall be studying. We may note, in passing, that it is not quite true to say, as Norman O. Brown does, that contemporary artists like Lawrence are calling for a total release from repression, a new resurrection of the body, a new eroticism. Lawrence, like most of the other symbolists of our time, wants "wholeness"—affirms the ancient idea of the mean, a wise reconciliation of the demands of the "upper centers" and the "lower centers." Not the pleasure-principle but the reality-principle is affirmed—at least by the symbolists whose work I study here.

Finally, there is the immemorial symbolism of light and dark. Most readers are fully aware of this symbolism when they encounter it, but color-symbolism is often far more complex than casual readers take it to be. Spirit or mind has for centuries been associated with light, but in Lawrence and many other modern writers the light of the spirit is not the primal light, as in Christian symbolism; it is, on the contrary, only a cold, icy, reflected light—the light of the moon. Lawrence associates the moon with a feminine and spiritual principle, as Wallace Stevens associates it with the imagination. The primal light, however, is the light of the sun, which Lawrence associates with "the heat of the blood" and which Stevens associates with "reality." The moon presides over the world of the spirit, the ghostly world, cold and insubstantial; the sun presides over the world of flesh and blood, the sensual world, hot, marshy, primordial. Again, in such novels as Woolf's *Night and Day*, Hesse's *Narziss und Goldmund*, and Frisch's *Homo Faber*, we find daylight associated with the male and with reason and intellect, whereas night is associated with the female, with feeling, imagination, and poetry.

Frequently the colors of heaven and of earth are employed to symbolize the ideal and the material. Mallarmé's *azure* is certainly clear enough; so is Wallace Stevens's *blue* guitar. But one wonders whether many readers have noted the conjunction of blue and brown, heaven and earth, in the serapes woven by the men of Quetzalcoatl in Lawrence's *The Plumed Serpent*. Or whether many have understood Conrad's use of yellow, black, and brown, or F. Scott Fitzgerald's use of white to symbolize the dream, of yellow to symbolize materialism, and of cream to symbolize the admixture of dream and reality. How many have noted that Mme de Vionnet's gray or silvery dress symbolizes a similar admixture, or that Isabel Archer, when we first see her, sits with white hands folded on her black dress? Again, the student of the imagination may find fascinating the gray-red combinations in the fiction of Thomas Mann, or the spectrum of color from celestial blue to blood-red in Lawrence's *The Rainbow*. Red and yellow are used symbolically by Henry James to suggest the lust of the eyes and materialism; they are used by Virginia Woolf, I suspect, to betoken life and death —the red of passion and generation, the yellow of old bones. Green of course symbolizes nature in most symbolic works, but in *The Great Gatsby* it looks very much like a fusion of blue and yellow, dream and reality.

To trace many a color-symbol back to its roots in the antithesis between ideas and things, essence and existence, is to realize that what appears often to be a mere image *is* a symbol, and that the imagination, in its effort to make all parts of a symbolic work expressive, misses no opportunities to convert the casual and accidental into the necessary and inevitable. It is my hope that one of the benefits of this study will be to promote the recognition of the completeness and precision of the symbolizing process and thus to enhance our sense of the mastery and control that the symbolizing imagination is capable of displaying in its creation of images of life. Perhaps we had better—because the study of symbolism is so full of snares—turn our attention to some of the problems of interpretation that our analysis of symbolism is likely to raise.

Contemplating the uniqueness of any work of art, one may be tempted to reject out of hand Northrop Frye's assertion that "all poets speak the same symbolic language"—a language that they use "unconsciously" or learn from other poets.[18] Is it not reductionist to claim that even in a homogeneous culture a common symbolism lies behind the aberrant adventures of the imagination in its process of creation? Is it not—to return to Daiches's remark—to substitute the kind for the quiddity, the category for the living, concrete whole? What categories define the uniqueness of the rocking horse in Lawrence's "The Rocking-Horse Winner"? Or the uniqueness of the pear tree in Mansfield's "Bliss," or of the red pony in Steinbeck's story of that name? What common symbolism underlies Kafka's imagery in "A Country Doctor," "The Hunger Artist," or "The Penal Colony"?

Now it goes without saying that a literary symbol, absorbing associations and implications from all parts of the total context in which it participates (usually by a logic of "identifications," positive and negative), often becomes charged unexpectedly with meaning. Eliseo Vivas's description of "the constitutive symbol" in his study of Lawrence describes this process of meaning-absorption and shows how, in a specific scene, meanings tend to expand and reverberate.[19] Indeed the dilation of meaning is sometimes so extraordinary that one finds critics defining a symbol as an "infinitely suggestible" concretization.

Yet literary symbols characteristically exist in families defined through the polarizing operations of the imagination.[20] Indeed, polarization is inevitable in literary symbolism, for symbols are generated from the very center of the literary work—from plot, from conflict or struggle. And conflict, whether embodied in extended images of life or in very short ones, is defined and dramatized by setting sympathetic agents against unsympathetic, or desirable things against undesirable, good fortune against misfortune, etc. Images arising from conflict thus tend to fall into antithetical patterns and when they do this they may become symbols. A literary symbol, indeed, as it is most frequently encountered, is nothing less than a term or phrase that, by virtue of its existence in a pattern of antithetical terms, absorbs a meaning larger than its ordinary meaning—a meaning whose limits are defined by the whole pattern of terms of which the symbol is a part. The symbol assimilates meaning—usually by a process of association or, as I have said, by the sort of negative or positive identifications to which Kenneth Burke has called attention. But the symbol is not, after all, infinitely suggestible—only finitely. Its meaning is limited by the central pattern of oppositions in which it participates and is always qualified by action, characterization, and other elements of the work.

That is to say, the symbol acquires meaning in two ways: first, dynamically, or as Vivas might say, "constitutively," by absorbing such meaning as the particular scene in which the symbol appears makes relevant. Thus the figure whom Gustav von Aschenbach sees standing near the mortuary chapel has a "snub nose" because he partakes of the character of death—he has the skeleton's snub nose. The symbolic meaning of *snub nose* arises through assimilation of the idea of death suggested by the mortuary chapel. Second, symbols acquire meanings by virtue of their participation in coherent patterns of terms—families, kiths. Thus the fact that the figure before the mortuary chapel has "rusty" eyelids and hair is not explained by the scene in which Aschenbach sees him for the first time, but *is* explained later when we see red and rust used in conjunction with the symbols of passion and carnality—the strawberries, the flaming sun, the rouge, etc. The full symbolic meaning of this menacing figure whom Aschenbach observes is, therefore, death in the form of unrestrained passion. At least that is the core of symbolic meaning that Mann obviously wishes us to grasp. And failure to grasp that core of meaning would render the details of the scene gratuitous, trivial, meaningless as art: elements of the accidental and arbitrary that a scrupulous critic like Henry James categorically rejects. If the image is to be charged with maximum expressiveness, it often *must* become symbolic. And failure to incorporate small details in a work of art into a symbolic system is one of the marks of the unseasoned writer.

There are those who resist such readings, however—who argue that such extensions of meaning are probably only in the mind of the critic, not really in the work itself or in the artist's "intention"; and who hold that symbol-hunting is the queer diversion of obsessive personalities, a silly game not worth the average reader's time. But in reading works composed by abundant and highly generalizing imaginations, the price we pay for ignoring symbolic patterns may be far greater than we, as intelligent readers, can reasonably afford. For the presence of symbolic terms is bound to influence our judgment at every point in the action, to condition all of our responses, to determine the exact degree of our sympathy and apprehension as the image of life unfolds. Insensitivity to symbolism can result not only in failure to grasp the full "meaning" of the work, but even in failure to receive a just impression of the work's felt life.

We may try to imagine, for example, how those readers of *The Ambassadors* who fail to respond to the ironic symbolism of that novel will interpret Strether's encounters with Maria Gostrey. Maria, by any nonsymbolic reading of the novel, certainly seems "sympathetic" and charming; her relationship with Strether seems quite as pleasant and wholesome as any relationship between mature adults can be, and indeed the two seem so compatible, so much alike in their wit and sensibility, that the prospect of their marriage must loom (to such a reader) as particularly inviting and desirable. But suppose that the reader is receptive to symbolic structure in poetic works and grants from the beginning the possibility that both parts of the name *Maria Gostrey* may be symbolic (especially in a novelist known to have worked symbolically); and suppose further that he notes with an eye on their possible implications the phrases employed by James in his first presentation of Maria:

> [Her eyes] had taken hold of him straightway, measuring him up and down as if they knew how; as if he were human material they had already in some sort handled. Their possessor was in truth . . . the mistress of a hundred cases or categories, receptacles of the mind, subdivisions for convenience, in which, from a full experience, she pigeon-holed her fellow mortals with a hand as free as a compositor handling type. She was as equipped in this particular as Strether was the reverse. . . . [21]

Suppose then that he takes note of the passage in which Strether reflects that Waymarsh must view Maria Gostrey as

> a Jesuit in petticoats, a representative of the recruiting interests of the Catholic Church. The Catholic Church, for Waymarsh—that was to say the enemy, the monster of bulging eyes and far-reaching quivering groping tentacles—was exactly society, exactly the multiplication of shibboleths, exactly the discrimination of types and tones, exactly the wicked old Rows of Chester, rank with feudalism; exactly in short Europe. [21:41]

Suppose, finally, that he takes special note of the imagery used to describe Maria's apartment:

> Her compact and crowded little chambers, almost dusky, as they at first struck him, with accumulations, represented a supreme general adjustment to opportunities and conditions. . . . The life of the occupant struck him, of a sudden, as more charged with possession even

than Chad's or than Miss Barrace's; wide as his glimpse had lately become of the empire of "things," what was before him still enlarged it; the lust of the eyes and the pride of life had indeed thus their temple. It was the innermost nook of the shrine—as brown as a pirate's cave. In the brownness were glints of gold; patches of purple were in the gloom; objects, all, that caught, through the muslin, with their high rarity, the light of the low windows. Nothing was clear about them but that they were precious. [21:119–20]

All these passages suggest a view of Maria Gostrey which is at variance with the received view of her, the view taken by readers who have declined to read James as symbolist. Taken together, the passages suggest: (1) that Maria is named after the Virgin because she is, in some sense, a representative of the recruiting interests of the Catholic church; (2) that she gets hold of people and handles them as if they were things; (3) that she is thus a citizen of the empire of things, Europe; (4) that she is thus a worshipper of appearances, of whatever takes the "bulging eyes" or expresses "the lust of the eyes"; (5) that she is in some sense a pirate—a thief, a marauder; (6) that she is not what she appears to be—she is as ambiguous as her chambers in which high and low, light and dark commingle.

Now one of the standard objections to a symbolic reading is that it takes us away from the dramatic image of life; but the fact is, as our illustration shows, that it brings us closer to the drama of the novel: it intensifies our sense of apprehension, it reminds us *everywhere* that Strether is threatened and ought to be on his guard. And scenes that might read as pleasant conversation become, on this approach, charged with dangers: possible slips, dangerous concessions, errors of judgment. We see *drama* where before we had seen only "conversation." Thus when Maria—with such exquisite charm and good humor!—asks Strether to "give himself up" to her, James's method of hinting at the terrible through his symbols compels us to respond with such apprehension as we might phrase in this way: "Better not; better wait; what is she up to? What if he *does* surrender to her—what will she *do* with him? Add him to her collection?"

The novel becomes thus more dramatic than a nonsymbolic work, and *the very quality of the life represented changes* for us—acquires a darker tone. Moreover, the novel becomes more beautiful to us in that every detail is seen to function dramatically and meaningfully in relation to the central conflict, the conflict between Paris and Woollett, the two rival empires that seek to "get hold of" Strether and to deny his freedom. The full subtlety and beauty of the symbolizing process can be appreciated only when we observe the peregrinations of every symbol throughout the work. Now the observation that Maria Gostrey's apartment is "as brown as a pirate's cave" spreads out in three directions: in imagery of color, of piracy, and of caves or enclosed places (as contrasted with open or elevated places). And every recurrence of a symbol calls to mind all the *relevant associates* of the symbol: as we have noted, meaning is absorbed by virtue of the symbol's participation in a family of related terms. Thus when James describes the cathedral at Chester as "red-brown" and Chad as "brown," we might well suspect that Maria, Chad, and the cathedral have something in common—something dusky, perhaps ominous, not in any case light and clear. The presumption of many critics is that it is possible to ignore such extensions of meaning without doing violence to the "felt life" of the novel. But our whole understanding of the amount of sympathy to which Maria Gostrey or Mme de Vionnet is entitled, is based to a degree upon our recognition of the ironic symbolism. And the sad truth is that some of the finest students of James's work have viewed Maria Gostrey and Marie de Vionnet—the two Mary's of Paris—with far more sympathy than a close reading of the symbolism would warrant.[22]

To demonstrate that a given image or symbol has such-and-such a meaning, by virtue of its participation in the pattern of oppositions that constitutes the *dianoia* of the work, is not always easy. I have suggested that a sound theory with respect to the "meaning" of a poetic work is one that explains everything in the work. But sometimes a sixth sense is needed by the critic if he is to see the relationship between a particular image and the informing principle of the work. Ideally, an imagination as highly generalizing, as penetrating, as the artist's own is desired. One must *become* the poet, the novelist; one must re-create the act of composition in which the imagination reaches out for exactly the right, the most expressive image: the image that reinforces everything else in the work, that establishes connections, deepens ironies, heightens contrasts, consolidates, fuses; the critic must learn the habits of the author's mind as it composes—the habits of association and extrapolation. Only the closest observation of every detail in his work will permit comprehension of the "logic of the imagination"—that miraculous reason that, as Wallace Stevens says, the imagination promotes. But the critic must insist that there *is* a logic of symbolic manipulation. Not to insist upon that is to relegate some of the most extraordinary artistic achievements of our age to what James has termed "the accidental and the arbitrary."

Granting then that meaning arises often, and characteristically in symbolist works, through a symbol's participation in a family of terms not always evident in the immediate context—in what Wallace Stevens refers to as a "poem above, and beyond, the poem"— one must still question whether there is a universal symbolism that "all poets speak." If such a symbolism exists, what, precisely, is its origin? If poets learn the common symbolic language "by instinct or unconsciously," one must of course postulate a sort of collective unconscious as the source of symbols. And that postulation has been very widely accepted by critics in our time. For the expressions of the unconscious, found in ancient vegetation myths, in myths of the sun-god, etc., are certainly universal; and symbols of generation, of heights and depressions, of motion and immobility, of light and darkness, of life and death may all be referred to myths of the solar year. The Manichean symbolism we have glanced at arises, then, presumably, from the poet's receptivity to the voices of the unconscious, and the literary critic would seem to be entirely justified in speaking of "elementary rapports welling up in the poet demonstrating their basic nature through the very unconsciousness of their eruption, intuited rather than worked out." [23] Now there is unquestionably much to recommend this view of the creation of symbols by "intuition" or by a sort of "unknowing"— to use J. Christopher Middleton's term. But in an age in which psychoanalytic perspectives have assumed such importance as to blur the significance of other perspectives, it may be well to recall, at this point, that poets themselves, in discussing their creative activity, often remark the significance of rational analysis and deliberation as the means of working out their poems. Thus we may remember Wallace Stevens's remark that the poet, once he has "found his subject," "becomes as deliberate in his own way as the philosopher" [24]—or Stevens's interest in Valéry's remark, "Man . . . fabricates by abstraction." [25] Or we may recall his essay "Imagination as Value," in which, analyzing the relationship between the imagination and reason in the composition of poetry, he asks, pointedly,

> Is there in fact any struggle at all and is the idea of one merely a bit of academic junk? Do not the two carry on together in the mind like two brothers or two sisters or even like young Darby and young Joan? Darby says, "It is often true that what is most rational appears to be the most imaginative, as in the case of Picasso." Joan replies, "It is often true, also, that what is most imaginative appears to be most rational, as in the case of Joyce." [26]

Again, in "The Relations between Poetry and Painting" Stevens questions "the dogma that the origins of poetry are to be found in the sensibility," and concludes that

> we find that the operative force within us [when a poem or painting is made] does not, in fact, seem to be the sensibility, that is to say, the feelings. It seems to be a constructive faculty, that derives its energy more from the imagination than from the sensibility. I have spoken of questioning, not of denying. . . . What these remarks seem to involve is the substitution for the idea of inspiration of the idea of an effort of mind not dependent on the vicissitudes of the sensibility. . . . [p. 164]

There is "a laborious element" in the creation of a poem, he goes on to say, and the poet's work is done "by imagination or by the miraculous kind of reason that the imagination sometimes promotes" (p. 165). Thus it may be misleading to speak of the eruptions of the unconscious; at least it is misleading to speak of them as if they entered poetry without being filtered through the screen of the reason, subjected to rational analysis: to a calculation, for example, of the bearing of one image upon the other images in the work, and of the role of the images in producing the final effect of the work.

Like Stevens, I would stress—as a corrective to the current emphasis on the origins of poetry in the unconscious—the "laborious element" in the creation of poems, the reason as generative source. The mind, in its constructive, synthetic activity, may seek to assimilate more materials than reason can easily manage, but this is not to say that its assimilations occur "irrationally." The "Platonist" oppositions I have traced in this chapter may be regarded as reflecting an effort of the mind to penetrate to the most basic contradictions within experience, and somehow to resolve those contradictions. To understand reality and the human place in the world, the mind *must* deal with the problem of essence and existence, being and becoming. It cannot, without contenting itself with a superficial grasp of reality, avoid tracing experience to the basic categories of thought found in the Platonic scheme. In "the construction and organization of human experience"—to use Cassirer's phrase—the imagination is not "escapist"; it is not seeking to evade the problems of life, but to grasp the full meaning of the phenomena it encounters. And the "eruptions" from the unconscious are the symbols that the mind *requires* to define the problems of existence. As the dreamer who, having visited his dentist (who has left a small pad of wool wedged between two molars), dreams of a mass of wet moss between two rocks, and thus in dreaming tries to objectify a problem,[27] so the symbolist, meditating on his situation in the world, searches for the symbols that would permit him to define the world as he encounters it, to understand it, and to come to terms with it. Symbolism is thus—like art itself in Cassirer's view—"one of the ways leading to an objective view of things and of human life. It is not an imitation but a discovery of reality."[28]

This is not, certainly, to deny the artistic functioning of symbols. In art they function in a variety of ways. They create drama, they raise apprehensions, they sharpen oppositions, underscore ironies, intensify emotions. But while formalist critics are certainly right to insist upon the dynamic functioning of symbols, symbolists themselves—and indeed most serious writers of our time—have often stressed that it is not merely artistic effects but a kind of truth that they are trying to create. Thus the breeding of images, as Dylan Thomas describes the process, is both a technique of composition—a means of getting a poem written—and a technique of cognition: a means of understanding reality. Thomas's description of his method, stressing "the creative, recreative, destructive and contradictory nature of the motivating centre, the womb of war," is so suggestive an analysis of the unfolding of a Manichean vision that it is worth quoting in full:

A poem by myself *needs* a host of images, because its centre is a host of images. I make one image—though "make" is not the word; I let, perhaps, an image be "made" emotionally in me and then apply to it what intellectual and critical forces I possess—let it breed another, let that image contradict the first, make, of the third image bred out of the other two together, a fourth contradictory image, and let them all, within my imposed formal limits, conflict. Each image holds within it the seed of its own destruction, and my dialectal [dialectical?] method, as I understand it, is a constant building up and breaking down of the images that come out of the central seed, which is itself destructive and constructive at the same time.

What I want to try to explain—and it's necessarily vague to me —is that the *life* in any poem of mine cannot move concentrically round a central image; the life must come out of the centre; an image must be born and die in another; and any sequence of my images must be a sequence of creations, recreations, destructions, contradictions. I cannot either—as Cameron does, and as others do, and this primarily explains his and their writing round the central image— make a poem out of a single motivating experience; I believe in the simple thread of action through a poem, but that is an intellectual thing aimed at lucidity through narrative. My object is, as you say, conventionally "to get things straight." Out of the inevitable conflict of images—inevitable, because of the creative, recreative, destructive and contradictory nature of the motivating centre, the womb of war—I try to make that momentary peace which is a poem. I do not want a poem of mine to be, nor can it be, a circular piece of experience placed nearly outside the living stream of time from which it came; a poem of mine is, or should be, a watertight section of the stream that is flowing all ways, all warring images within it should be reconciled for that small stop of time.[29]

Thomas's explanation of the war of images as the inevitable product of the seed which is "destructive and constructive at the same time"—"the womb of war"—stresses, I take it, what Whitehead and other philosophers of our time have tried to tell us: that process and interconnection are the laws of life. A poem must not perpetuate some "myth of isolation" but must reveal the "stream that is flowing all ways." In *Modes of Thought*, Whitehead reminds us of Emerson's truth that "science was false by being unpoetical."

Connectedness is of the essence of all things of all types. It is of the essence of types, that they be connected. Abstraction from connectedness involves the omission of an essential factor in the fact considered. No fact is merely itself. The penetration of literature and art at their height arises from our dumb sense that we have passed beyond mythology; namely, beyond the myth of isolation.[30]

It is tempting to claim that the symbolic oppositions of the Manichean vision constitute, in their intermingling, just such a vision of reality, of "interconnectedness," as Whitehead here refers to. For the warring symbols of the Manicheans tie man firmly to actual contradictions in his experience. They force him to acknowledge his ineluctable bondage to the conditions of the corporeal world and to recognize that the ideal must never masquerade as the final truth. They force upon him the significance of Wallace Stevens's contention that the imagination must not detach itself from reality. They remind him that his opinions are mere fragments of the whole truth and lead him to see the wisdom of Meister Eckhardt's admonition "Foresake opinions. God despises ideas."

In the last analysis, symbolism may lead us to grasp the mystical idea of the unity of all things. Since it operates, as Coleridge saw, by a kind of "participation mystique"—since all things partake of one another, or "participate in" the divine world-stuff—all things become one. Symbolism, because it is synthetic, keeps returning to that idea. The saint is the sinner, the slayer the slain. Once the doors of perception are cleansed, Blake maintained, "everything appears to man as it is, infinite." But even if one sets aside this mystical view of things, one may grant that symbolism, by awakening an awareness of interconnectedness and patterns of relationship, leads or can lead to what Allen Tate has called "the wholest knowledge" of things accessible to man. This, at least, is the view of such profound students of symbolism as Flanders Dunbar and Mircea Eliade. Both would have us restore the symbol "to its status as an instrument of knowledge"—thus returning to a point of view that "was general in Europe until the eighteenth century." [31] As Flanders Dunbar points out in his comments on Dante's "insight symbol,"

> It is of the character of insight symbol to look beneath a datum of experience to its relationships in the universal pattern and in consequence to set forth, not only the particular fact, but also that fact in its fundamental relationships. Thus it came to seem the closest possible approach to the expression of truth. [32]

Observing that modern biology "has pointed out the unity underlying all forms of life, and now it discloses the organism partaking of its environment and the environment interpenetrating the organism," and recalling John Fiske's statement that the whole universe, in modern physics, is but "differentiated sunshine," Dunbar argues that the insight symbol awakens awareness of man's participation in the primal energy. For symbols refer to things, and the study of an event's "relationship in the pattern of the universe" may disclose, not merely the soul of the poet or the associative processes of the poet's mind, but objective relationships in the universe itself. To study the patterns of symbols is to study "fundamental relationships in the universe long before [men] can express them in the language of science. The frequent anticipation of the findings of science as it were by instinct, in some apparent fairy tale or bizarre symbol of primitive man, is a source of constant comment" (*Symbolism in Medieval Thought*, pp. 453, 457–58).

It is an act of faith, of course, to affirm that any system of symbols is capable of presenting a vision of reality itself. Do symbols correspond to being? But without pressing the argument for the "truth" of symbolic imagery as used by the Manicheans, we cannot fail to observe that all the artists in the Manichean school have made a considerable effort to see life steadily and see it whole. Detachment and impersonality are as much a part of their work as of the work of scientists and philosophers. The artists we shall be looking at in this study—Stevens, James, Conrad, and Woolf— were determined to resist partial perspectives. James, rejecting as narrow both French pessimism and English optimism, was determined to see the veritable admixtures in life. The endings of his stories were thus, characteristically, "mixed," and a complex fusion of irony and sympathy marked his examination of his characters. Impersonality and detachment were, for him, the *sine qua non* of any rounded and deep impression of life. As he says in a letter to H. G. Wells, "There is, to my vision, no authentic, and no really interesting and no *beautiful*, report of things on the novelist's, the painter's part unless a particular detachment has operated, unless the great stewpot or crucible of the imagination, of the observant and recording and interpreting mind in short, has intervened and plays its part . . ." (*Letters*, 2:189). The operation of the imagination —in its "particular detachment"—gives a "precious effect of perspective" which is "indispensable" to "beauty and authenticity." The aim of the lover of the image of life is to catch "the very note

and trick, the strange, irregular rhythm of life. . . . In proportion
as in what she offers us we see life *without* rearrangement do we
feel that we are touching the truth; in proportion as we see it *with*
arrangement do we feel that we are being put off with a substitute,
a compromise and convention." [33] As Ellen Leyburn has shown in
her excellent study of James, his aim was to "reflect for us, out of
the confusion of life, the close connection of bliss and bale, of the
things that help with the things that hurt, so dangling before us
forever the bright hard medal, of so strange an alloy, one face of
which is somebody's right and ease and the other somebody's pain
and wrong." [34] There is a "terrible mixture in things," and all of
James's greatest work presents that mixture. As we shall see, his
symbolism is one of his chief means of capturing the mixture—the
"tragic, comic, pathetic, ironic *note*" which is "most characteristic
and essential" in life.[35]

James's emphasis on the truthfulness of his fiction is matched by
Joseph Conrad's. "The artist," says Conrad in his preface to *The
Nigger of the Narcissus,*" . . . like the thinker or the scientist, seeks
the truth and makes his appeal." His job is to capture "a passing
phase of life"—"to hold up unquestioningly, without choice and
without fear, the rescued fragment before all eyes in the light of
a sincere mood. It is to show its vibration, its color, its form; and
through its movement, its form, and its color, reveal the substance
of truth. . . . " Since his task is to disclose the truth, the artist must
reject "the temporary formulas of his craft": realism, romanticism,
naturalism, even "the unofficial Sentimentalism" must be aban-
doned; what should abide is "the truth which each imperfectly
veils." Thus Conrad, like James, can defend his work not by appealing to aesthetic canons but by the appeal to "nature" and
"truth." Speaking of *The Nigger of the Narcissus* in a letter to Edward Garnett, he writes: "As to lack of incident,—well, it's life.
The incomplete joy, the incomplete sorrow, the incomplete rascal-
ity or heroism—the incomplete suffering. Events crowd and push,
and nothing happens. You know what I mean. The opportunities
do not last long enough. Unless in a book of boy's adventures"
(*Life and Letters,* 1:197). Like James, Conrad thus works to create
a "strange alloy." Using Marlow as narrator, he preserves objectivity and achieves exactly that complex blend of irony and sympathy, that "precious effect of perspective," that James wished to

infuse into his stories. Marlow sees the angel and the devil in men: sees the soul—and the liver. Jim's occupation as a waterclerk is "beautiful and humane." "Later on a bill is sent in." Fyne's dog displays an excess of "incomprehensible affection" for Marlow; "this was before he caught sight of the cake in my hand." Captain Anthony may be motivated, in marrying Flora de Barral, by "pity"; he may also be motivated by an egotistical desire to get hold of the girl and to make her his possession. Both James and Conrad characteristically see both sides of the coin and see, too, I think, the same motive-forces at work within the human soul. And both of them use symbolism to render the admixture in things, to express their detachment and their Manichean vision.

Virginia Woolf's view of her fiction is an extension, and an amplification, of the views held by her great predecessors in realistic fiction. Like Conrad and James, she fears the tyranny of convention, the artificiality of plot, the simplifications of a single vision. In her effort to grasp the truth of life, she is willing, however, to go much further than James or Conrad. She drops plot. She eschews the convention of making sympathetic and unsympathetic characters, and discerns the fragmentation in personality, what Wallace Stevens calls "the milleman"—"so many selves, so many sensuous worlds, / Merely in living as and where we live." Life, she asserts, is neither economics, nor buttons and shoes, nor ideas, but a "semi-transparent envelope."

> Look within [she writes] and life, it seems, is very far from being "like this." Examine for a moment an ordinary mind on an ordinary day. The mind receives a myriad of impressions—trivial, fantastic, evanescent, or engraved with the sharpness of steel. From all sides they come, an incessant shower of innumerable atoms; and as they fall, as they shape themselves into the life of Monday or Tuesday, the accent falls differently from of old; the moment of importance came not here but there; so that, if a writer were a free man and not a slave, if he could base his work upon his own feeling and not upon convention, there would be no plot, no comedy, no tragedy, no love interest or catastrophe in the accepted style, and perhaps not a single button sewn on as the Bond Street tailors would have it. Life is not a series of gig lamps symmetrically arranged; life is a luminous halo, a semi-transparent envelope surrounding us from the beginning of consciousness to the end. Is it not the task of the novelist to convey this varying, this unknown and uncircumscribed spirit,

> whatever aberration or complexity it may display, with as little mixture of the alien and external as possible?
>
> Let us record the atoms as they fall upon the mind in the order in which they fall, let us trace the pattern, however disconnected and incoherent in appearance, which each sight or incident scores upon the consciousness.[36]

Not a word in all this about art and the beauty doctrine. Her whole concern is life, reality, truth. The disconnected, the erratic, the incoherent must be welcomed, for life *is* disconnected, erratic, and incoherent. Woolf's symbolism arises naturally from this sense of fragmentation, from a nominalist's awareness of the ever-changing appearances in the flux. But she has the realist's desire for a reality solid and enduring, and it is in the dramatization of the tensions between the nominalist and the realist that her fiction acquires much of its vitality.

Her vision of imperishable-perishable essences in the destructive winds and fires of the flux is essentially one with that of Wallace Stevens. Like Stevens, she knows that the lovely integrations, the beautiful circles that represent wholeness, the supreme fictions, are shattered by the flux. Like Stevens (and like James and Conrad), she has a sense of a terrifying noumenal world of inexplicable energy moving according to its own laws—the terrible time-machine of *Between the Acts* that says, "Dispersed are we, dispersed are we." Caught in time, man is enslaved, condemned to act out the roles which fate has assigned him. But there is always the vision of eternity and freedom, of spirit freed from time and conditions, creating a just world in which free men and women may realize the possibilities of their freedom. There are these fictions. But they are embedded in a flux that seems to deny their possibility, and the artist who would present the truth of things must see the idea in the flux, in the process of the universe—in what Thomas refers to as the "womb of war."

The great virtue of symbolism, from the point of view of all of these writers, who seek relentlessly to get at the truth of life, is that it permits the artist to integrate his materials without distorting reality—doing violence to its complexity. For symbols, as Thomas has suggested, grow from actual facts; they are "made" in the artist by life itself, arrived at (in the finest artists) a posteriori, not a

priori. They are discovered in the subject matter, not imposed
upon it. Moreover, the symbolist is enabled by his method to
comment on life without offering his comment as a final truth. His
symbols are offered frankly as fictions, in the atmosphere of doubt
that generates the Manichean vision, in the realization that thought
may never correspond to being, that whatever the abstractive intellect imposes upon reality may be false—a mere structure of ideas
inadequate in the last analysis to the structure of things. Thus
Manichean symbolists may show that beautiful detachment which
Eliot has praised so highly in the work of Henry James: the possession of a mind so fine that no idea can violate it. At their best the
Manicheans we shall be studying in the following chapters show,
with James, an absolute mastery over, an absolute escape from,
ideas. They are too intelligent to permit themselves to be encaged
by partial views or perspectives. It is a conviction irresistible to this
writer that their detachment is the finest fruit of liberal education.
And the highest praise of these symbolists, these students of recalcitrant contraries, is that they recognize the penetration of E. M.
Forster's "Only connect—."

NOTES

1. William Butler Yeats, *The Collected Poems of William Butler Yeats*
(London: Macmillan & Co., 1950), p. 223.
2. Wallace Stevens, *The Collected Poems of Wallace Stevens* (New York:
Alfred A. Knopf, 1954), p. 172.
3. Alfred North Whitehead, *Adventures of Ideas* (New York: New
American Library, Mentor Books, 1955), p. 43.
4. Joseph Wood Krutch, *The Measure of Man* (New York: Grosset and
Dunlap, Universal Library, 1954), pp. 34–36.
5. Jacques Barzun, *Darwin, Marx, and Wagner* (New York: Doubleday & Co., Anchor Books, 1958), passim.
6. Charles Feidelson, Jr., *Symbolism and American Literature* (Chicago:
University of Chicago Press, 1953), p. 202.
7. Herman Melville, *Moby-Dick* (New York: Random House, Modern
Library College Books, 1950), p. 275. All subsequent citations are to this
edition.
8. Nathaniel Hawthorne, *The Complete Novels and Selected Tales of Nathaniel Hawthorne* (New York: Random House, Modern Library, 1937), p.
653. All subsequent citations are to this edition.

9. Joseph Conrad, *Joseph Conrad, Life and Letters,* ed. G. Jean-Aubrey, 2 vols. (London: William Heinemann, 1927), 1:216.

10. Joseph Conrad, *Some Reminiscences* (London: Eveleigh Nash, 1912), pp. 155–56.

11. Conrad, *Life and Letters,* 1:226.

12. Henry James, *The Letters of Henry James,* ed. Percy Lubbock, 2 vols. (New York: Charles Scribner's Sons, 1920), 2:373.

13. See Northrop Frye, *The Anatomy of Criticism: Four Essays* (Princeton: Princeton University Press, 1957); also *Fables of Identity: Studies in Poetic Mythology* (New York: Harcourt, Brace & World, Harbinger Books,1963).

14. Northrop Frye, *T. S. Eliot* (New York: Barnes and Noble, 1963), p. 50.

15. These comments are quoted in Peter Cummings's article "Northrop Frye and the Necessary Hybrid: Criticism as Aesthetic Humanism," in O. B. Hardison, Jr., ed., *The Quest for Imagination* (Cleveland and London: Press of Case Western Reserve University, 1971), pp. 267–68.

16. J. Christopher Middleton, "Two Mountain Scenes in Novalis and the Question of Symbolic Style," in Helmut Rehder, ed., *Literary Symbolism: A Symposium* (Austin and London: University of Texas Press, 1965), pp. 103–4.

17. See Mircea Eliade, *Images and Symbols* (New York: Sheed and Ward, 1969), for an illuminating study of the symbolism of the cosmic tree and of the communication between heaven and earth by means of this pillar. Eliade's study strikingly illuminates the whole significance of the symbol as "an autonomous mode of cognition" and is of the greatest value to all students of symbolism.

18. Northrop Frye, "The Top of the Tower: A Study of the Imagery of Yeats," *The Southern Review,* Summer 1969, p. 850.

19. Eliseo Vivas, *D. H. Lawrence: The Failure and the Triumph of Art* (Evanston, Ill.: Northwestern University Press, 1960).

20. See Edwin Honig's *Dark Conceit: The Making of Allegory* (New York: Oxford University Press, Galaxy Books, 1966), especially the chapter entitled "Polarities: The Metamorphosis of Opposites": "Fundamental polarities gradually gather to themselves clusters of parallel oppositions, so that on one level dark and light are synonymous, say, with animal and human, lust and love; on another level, with seeming and being, mutability and permanence; on still another level, with doubt and will, despair and faith" (p. 63).

21. Henry James, *The Novels and Tales of Henry James,* 26 vols. (New York: Charles Scribner's Sons, 1907–17), 21:10. All subsequent citations are to this edition.

22. In chapter 3 I attempt to document this assertion.

23. Henry H. H. Remak, "Vinegar and Water: Allegory and Symbolism in the German Novelle between Keller and Bergengruen," in Rehder, ed., *Literary Symbolism: A Symposium,* p. 40.

24. Wallace Stevens, *Opus Posthumous* (New York: Alfred A. Knopf, 1957), p. 197.

25. Ibid, p. 272.

26. Wallace Stevens, *The Necessary Angel: Essays on Reality and the Imagination*, (New York: Alfred A. Knopf, 1951), p. 142; also cited in the next two quotations.

27. See Jean Piaget, *Play, Dreams and Imitation in Childhood*, trans. C. Gattegno and F. M. Hodgson (New York: Norton, 1962). Piaget's discussion of dream-symbolism stresses the constructive activity of the mind, as contrasted with "spontaneous, non-directed thought" (pp. 190 ff).

28. Ernst Cassirer, *An Essay on Man* (New York: Bantam Books, 1969), p. 158.

29. Dylan Thomas, quoted in Elder Olson, *The Poetry of Dylan Thomas* (Chicago: University of Chicago Press, 1954), pp. 34–35.

30. Alfred North Whitehead, *Modes of Thought* (Cambridge: At the University Press, 1938), p. 13.

31. Eliade, *Images and Symbols*, p. 9.

32. Flanders Dunbar, *Symbolism in Medieval Thought and Its Consummation in the Divine Comedy* (New York: Russell and Russell, 1961), p. 17.

33. Henry James, *Partial Portraits* (London and New York: Macmillan & Co., 1888), p. 398.

34. Henry James, *The Art of the Novel: Critical Prefaces by Henry James*, ed. Richard P. Blackmur (New York: Charles Scribner's Sons, 1934), p. 143.

35. Henry James, *The Notebooks of Henry James*, ed. F. O. Matthiessen and Kenneth B. Murdock (New York: Oxford University Press, 1947), p. 176.

36. Virginia Woolf, *Collected Essays*, 2 vols. (New York: Harcourt, Brace & World, 1966), 2:106.

II. THE DREAM
AND THE KNITTING MACHINE

Joseph Conrad's Symbolism

THE MACHINE OF THE UNIVERSE, having "evolved itself . . . out of a chaos of scraps of iron," performs "without thought, without conscience, without foresight, without eyes, without heart," its "horrible work." "It knits." Idealists, wishing the machine to embroider, apply their "celestial oil" and look for the machine to produce "a most beautiful design in purple and gold." But the machine goes on knitting: "It knits us in and it knits us out. It has knitted time, space, pain, death, corruption, despair, and all the illusions,—and nothing matters." [1] But man cannot endure that knowledge. His spirit embroiders endlessly its design in purple and gold, the beautiful fictions of truth, beauty, virtue. He lives in a dream, his very humanity is defined by his participation in the dream. But he lives, too, in the world of the knitting machine, that clanking mechanism which contradicts every article of faith and hope. It is in the dramatization of that great tension in man's existence that Conrad's fiction acquires its remarkable vitality, its wonderful blend of sympathy and irony, belief and disbelief, warmth and detachment.

He was preoccupied with the conflict between the machine and the dream even in his earliest work—so preoccupied with it, in fact, that his facile contrasts between illusion and reality exposed him to Max Beerbohm's deadliest parody. The antitheses that marked that early vision were frequently banal. The sea was faithful—and treacherous. Sailors lived "by its grace" or died "by its will." In *An Outcast of the Islands* Conrad's penchant for paired oppositions is indulged everywhere, and the result is a style faintly bombastic, artificial, full of easy polarities—easy because obvious, employing all the ancient but stale significance of light and dark:

> He had been baffled, repelled, almost frightened by the intensity of that tropical life which wants the sunshine but works in gloom; which seems to be all grace of colour and form, all brilliance, all smiles, but is only the blossoming of the dead; whose mystery holds the promise of joy and beauty, yet contains nothing but poison and decay.[2]

Or one encounters such deliberate and studied passages, with their automatic pairings of opposites (reminiscent of the antitheses of Augustan satirists), as these:

> To her [Aissa] the ex-clerk of Hudig appeared as remote, as brilliant, as terrible, as necessary, as the sun that gives life to these lands: the sun of unclouded skies that dazzles and withers; the sun beneficent and wicked—the giver of light, perfume, and pestilence. . . . [P. 248]

> . . . he [was] aware of some emotion arising within him, from her words, her tone, her contact; an emotion unknown, singular, penetrating and sad—at the sight of that strange woman, of that being savage and tender; strong and delicate, fearful and resolute, that had got entangled so fatefully between their two lives. . . . [P. 249]

Conrad remarked that *An Outcast of the Islands* was "never very near my heart. It engaged my imagination more than my affection."[3] And the remoteness of the story from the deepest springs of his affection perhaps accounts for the artificiality of the symbolism. Aissa, Willems, Lingard, Almayer, Babalatchi—these creatures never meant enough to their creator; they could not generate the rich and complex imaginative proliferations that one witnesses when an author taps the deepest sources of memory and imagination. Thus Conrad falls back, again and again, upon an obvious, melodramatic symbolism of light and darkness, and neither his characters nor his situation and its development are sufficiently vital to generate far-reaching complications of his vision. "Then she smiled. In the sombre beauty of her face that smile was like the first ray of light on a stormy daybreak that darts evanescent and pale through the gloomy clouds: the forerunner of sunrise and of thunder" (p. 71). How predictable this imagery is, how stale, at bottom, and how unimaginative! And while there is considerable energy of thought behind the novel, the intellectual complexity is impoverished by the melodramatic presentation, the artificial blocking out of action and scene, the easy oppositions.

By the time Conrad wrote *The Nigger of the Narcissus,* however, —having hit on a subject that engaged his affection decisively—he was able to release everything that had been held in. An astonishing exfoliation of the symbolism occurs. No longer confined to a few categories—the light and the dark, life and death, perfume and decay—Conrad suddenly finds himself in possession of fifty. What has happened, simply, is that what was loose, scattered, only latent in the early work has now, suddenly and opulently, become consolidated, concentrated. The vision is not essentially different from that of the early fiction. It is still Manichean: sun and shade commingle everywhere. But the perception of the commingling has become a daily habit of Conrad's mind. Darkness and light still dominate, as in the first sentence, when we learn that "Mr. Baker, chief mate of the ship *Narcissus,* stepped in one stride out of his lighted cabin into the darkness of the quarter-deck" or, at the end, when we see "the dark knot of seamen [drifting] in sunshine" and "the sunshine of heaven" falling "like a gift of grace on the mud of the earth." [4] There is the white *Narcissus,* there is the black Jim Wait, the Burden, the Weight, the Delayer, the Darkness. But while the old color-antitheses dominate, the Manichean vision has found its way into so many new channels that a new style, virtually, has been created.

What gave impetus to the luxuriant development of the symbolism was, precisely, the focusing of Conrad's vision. He saw all aspects of human behavior now as reflections of a Nietzschean will to power, a fierce desire for omnipotence, coupled with a desire for absolute peace, ease, and repose—the desire to be one with the Nigger, the prince of darkness, to lie in a bunk (very like a coffin) shirking all duty and danger. In his portrait of Willems in *An Outcast* Conrad had examined the will to power in all its ferocity —the egotist's dream of sovereign and absolute dominion; and he had seen the dream of omnipotence associated with another wish: "death is better than strife," Willems reflects (p. 81), and it is easier to "fall back into the darkness," to "[give] up as a tired swimmer gives up" than to endure the "warlike conditions of existence." But what was in Willems, that mediocrity, was in all men. All men failed: the dream of becoming singular, of achieving personal greatness, was condemned to end in disillusionment. All men "fell" and far from being "great" became mere "nobodies"—garbage, dirt. Then, unable to endure the condemnation and rejection of the world, and the failure of their dreams, men turned to opiates. In one way or another they surrendered, like Willems, to "the darkness"—perhaps to a woman who is "a complete savage," perhaps to whiskey or narcotics.

Thus the crew of the *Narcissus* are uniformly escapists:

> "Did you bring a bottle, any of you shore toffs? ... Give us a bit of 'bacey. ... I know her; her skipper drank himself to death. ..."
> [P. 3]

Or they escape into dreams of the "splendor and poetry of life":

> The popularity of Bulwer-Lytton in the forecastles of Southern-going ships is a wonderful and bizarre phenomenon. ... Mystery!
> ... are those beings who exist beyond the pale of life stirred by his tales as by an enigmatical disclosure of a resplendent world that exists within the frontier of infamy and filth, within that border of dirt and hunger, of misery and dissipation, that comes down on all sides to the water's edge of the incorruptible ocean ... ?
>
> By the foremast a few discussed in a circle the characteristics of a gentleman. [Pp. 5, 35]

Conrad saw now that every detail in his image of life had symbolic significance. The white and the black commingled, but were joined densely to symbols of heights and depressions, spirituality and animality, fixity and the flux; of work, duty, and discipline, in contrast with sloth, ease, irresponsibility; of manhood and life contrasted with the inorganic and the dead. The prose bristles with significances:

> The short black tug gave a pluck to windward, in the usual way, then let go the rope, and hovered for a moment on the quarter with her engines stopped; while the slim, long hull of the ship moved ahead slowly under lower top-sails ... the ship became a high and lonely pyramid, gliding, all shining and white, through the sunlit mist. The tug turned round short and went away towards the land. ... She resembled an aquatic black beetle, surprised by the light, over-whelmed by the sunshine, trying to escape with ineffectual

effort into the distant gloom of the land. She left a lingering smudge of smoke on the sky, and two vanishing trails of foam on the water. On the place where she had stopped a round black patch of soot remained, undulating on the swell—an unclean mark of the creature's rest.

The *Narcissus* left alone, heading south, seemed to stand resplendent and still upon the restless sea, under the moving sun. . . . The august loneliness of her path lent dignity to the sordid inspiration of her pilgrimage. [Pp. 29–32]

There is no cheap atmosphere in the writing; there is no "willing" of significance onto the facts—of the sort Allen Tate has condemned in contrasting a poetry of the will with a poetry of the imagination. The image of life is round and dense and thoroughly persuasive; it is "done," as Henry James would have said. But it is a totally symbolic world which Conrad has created.

We can see how complete his symbolic scheme is when we examine what is, perhaps, his most thoroughly "imagined" early novel, *Lord Jim*. The pattern of the symbolism in this remarkable novel, a pattern deriving from the central conflict, extends finally to hundreds of details that criticism, in its penchant to isolate and abstract only a few of the major symbols, has scarcely begun to notice. Why, we might ask—to take one trivial example—does Conrad mention in chapter 5 the Tamil driver of the gharry who has "given himself up to the inspection of his sore toe"? There ought to be a reason, in a thoroughly symbolic work, for the existence of that kind of observation. But so far, in focusing on isolated instances of the symbolism rather than on the whole pattern of it, criticism has failed to provide an explanation, as it has failed to account for hundreds of other pertinent details in the novel. So we had better study the whole pattern carefully.

The central conflict in *Lord Jim*, from which the symbolism derives, is a conflict between dream and reality, between Jim's (and man's) dream of a "sovereign power enthroned in a fixed standard of conduct"—his dream that he is able to serve that sovereign—and the appalling reality of his jump, his faithlessness, his animal desire for self-preservation. The dream, the "destructive element" of which Stein speaks, is, or may be, a pure fiction, one of the lies that human beings affirm in order to endure, and to transcend, "the warlike conditions of existence"; for men cannot *live* the dream: at a critical moment even the apparently invulnerable, such as Brierly, must "jump," defect, betray their fellow men and the fixed standard of conduct. No man, as Marlow says, is "good enough," and all men bear, in their souls and on their bodies, the marks of their defection from rectitude. But if man is condemned to jump, he is also condemned, in so far as he *is* man, to follow the bodiless, ghostly ideal, or, in the language of Stein, to submit himself to the destructive element. Indeed, man's participation in ideality may be far more "real" to him than his participation in the material world; and so the novel works extensively with the paradox that the real is unreal and dead, whereas the unreal is alone real and alive.

The symbolism that issues from the conflict between dream and reality is carefully introduced in the first paragraph of the novel, in which Conrad begins with a characteristic juxtaposition of opposites: "He was an inch, perhaps two, under six feet, powerfully built, and he advanced straight at you with a slight stoop of the shoulders, head forward, and a fixed from-under stare which made you think of a charging bull. . . . He was spotlessly neat, apparelled in immaculate white from shoes to hat. . . ." [5] Four enormous families of contrasting symbols are generated from this opening paragraph: the symbols of heights and depressions, animality and spirituality, color, and straightness and crookedness or malformation.

The important height-depression cluster springs from Conrad's conception of Jim as an elevated being—a Lord—and from the antithetical notion that he is, in reality, "just Jim—nothing more." *Lord Jim* is thus a kind of contradiction in terms, an oxymoron, as if one were to speak of *spiritual matter, high lowman,* or *royal commoner*—precisely the same contradiction as we encounter later in names like Gentleman Brown or Mohammed Bonso. As spiritual being, as dreamer, Jim is quite naturally at home in Heaven; and so it is that he comes "from a parsonage"—a "little church on a hill." Moreover, when he becomes a seaman, "his station was in the fore-top, and often from there he looked down, with the contempt of a man destined to shine in the midst of dangers, at the peaceful multitude of roofs cut in two by the brown tide of the stream, while scattered on the outskirts . . . the factory chimneys rose perpendicular against a grimy sky . . . belching out smoke like a volcano" (p. 6). He is above the brown and black filth and violence of the material earth, or at least appears to be above them. But Conrad has already told us that Jim is an inch, perhaps two, *under* six feet, and in chapter 2, after being disabled by a falling spar (the accident is symbolic, as I shall show later), Jim, perceiving the "unintelligible brutality of an existence liable to the agony of such sensations," feels "tormented as if *at the bottom* of an abyss of unrest" (p. 11; italics mine). This first glimpse of the horror of the material world and first intimation of his vulnerability as a creature of the flesh is quickly forgotten, however, and, sent to a hospital which stands "on a hill," Jim is able to taste once more the "gift of endless dreams," dreams that remain for him the only reality in life, while the cynical seamen he meets in the hospital seem to him "more unsubstantial than so many shadows." A short time later he becomes mate on the *Patna*, that symbolic vessel containing within itself both dreaming pilgrims and cynical sailors, the high and the low, heaven and hell: "*Above the mass of sleepers* a faint and patient sigh at times floated, the exhalation of a troubled dream; and short metallic clangs bursting out suddenly *in the depths of the ship* . . . exploded brutally, as if the men handling the mysterious things below had their breasts full of fierce anger. . . . 'Hot is no name for it down below,' said a voice" (pp. 19, 22; italics mine). Standing in an elevated position, "on the bridge" of the *Patna*, Jim feels secure in his ideal world, "penetrated by the great certitude of unbounded safety and peace that could be read on the silent aspect of nature like the certitude of fostering love upon the placid tenderness of a mother's face." Then disaster strikes. From his lofty ideality he jumps into an "everlasting deep hole." His animality betrays him, and it becomes necessary to restore himself to ideality by crawling out of the hole. And this, of course, is *literally* what happens. Arriving in Patusan (whose physical contours symbolize the division in the soul of man) Jim must pull himself up from the mud of his guilt and animality. Taken prisoner, he scales a palisade, attempts to leap over a muddy creek ("he took off from the last dry spot, felt himself flying through air"), and falls short. Then, unlike the mighty Brierly, who dies by refusing to support himself in the destructive element of the dream, Jim "made efforts, tremendous sobbing, gasping efforts . . . to crack the earth asunder, to throw it off his limbs—and he felt himself *creeping feebly up the bank*

... he arose muddy from head to foot. ... He swerved between two houses *up a slope,* clambered in desperation *over a barricade* of felled trees. ... He remembers being half-carried, half-rushed to the top of the slope ..." (pp. 254–55, italics mine). Heroically, Jim throws off the taint of the earth: he rises, he very nearly flies, into the arms of that spiritual animal Doramin. And Jim's ascent does not stop here. Sherif Ali must be defeated, and to defeat him Jim must scale another hill, must do what to the natives seems impossible, raise his cannons to the very top of the highest peak in Patusan, from which he dominates "the forest, the secular gloom, the old mankind." Jim is restored to his former height; he and Marlow can look down upon the forest and the jungle as though they had never crawled upon earth.

Of course Jim is not secure. It is always possible that he will again fall, show cowardice, betray the community of men; and Cornelius stands ready to do what he can to drag Jim down into the everlasting deep hole, for, like Chester, he cannot bear the childlike souls who are "too much in the clouds" and who "trample on me till I die." Out of guilty envy and hatred he would pull Jim down to the dirt and the dung, to the guano of Chester's inhuman island or to the level of Cornelius's house: "He bolted out, vermin-like, from the long grass growing *in a depression of the ground.* I believe his house was rotting somewhere near by, though I've never seen it, *not having been far enough in that direction*" (p. 323, italics mine). (Later Marlow observes: "there was plenty of mud around the house.") When Brown arrives in Patusan, he too joins in the attempt to reduce Jim to animality: "... you talk as if you were one of those people that should have wings so as to go about without touching the dirty earth. Well—it is dirty. I haven't got any wings" (p. 383). But despite Brown's efforts, Jim never again falls: he *has* got wings and is not condemned to crawl like a beetle in the dung.

And this brings us to the remarkable animal symbolism informing the novel, a symbolism which, like that of heights and depressions, proliferates from the basic antithesis of ideality and materiality: the division between *Lord* and *Jim.*

Even the casual reader is probably conscious of the significance of Stein's collection of beetles and butterflies. Conrad is in fact very careful to define the meaning of his symbols:

"This magnificent butterfly finds a little heap of dirt and sits still on it; but man he will never on his heap of mud keep still. He wants to be so, and again he wants to be so. ..." He moved his hand up, then down. ... "He wants to be a saint, and he wants to be a devil —and every time he shuts his eyes he sees himself as a very fine fellow—so fine as he can never be. ... In a dream...." [P. 213]

Man, in so far as he remains human, is a dreaming "romantic," wedded to the pitiless "shadowy ideal of conduct," aspiring to be the angelic butterfly. But it is not as if man can ever throw off the chains of the flesh: man belongs to the devil or to the devil's secular analogue, the jungle, the irrational, the "warlike conditions of existence." He belongs to both heaven and hell; or, as Marlow says at the beginning of his tale, "I am willing to believe each of us has a guardian angel, if you fellows will concede to me that each of us has a familiar devil as well" (p. 34). The real difficulty for man is to remain "romantic"—that is, to remain human. If he loses faith in the ideal, he becomes nothing but animal—mere flesh consigned wholly to the devil.

So it is that the German captain, who leads the leap from the *Patna* and is "the incarnation of everything vile and base that lurks in the world we love," is represented in such symbolic terms as the following: "He made me think of a trained baby elephant walking on hind-legs. He was extravagantly gorgeous too—got up in a soiled sleeping-suit, bright green and deep orange vertical stripes. ... His thick carcass trembled on its legs. ... I waited to see him overwhelmed, confounded, pierced through and through, squirming like an impaled beetle ... the whole burrowing effort of that gaudy and sordid mass ... a voice harsh and dead ..." (pp. 21, 37, 42, 47). He is dressed in a sleeping-suit, as the sailors whom Jim observes in the hospital are dressed in pajamas, because he is determined to "lounge safely through existence" and because he is morally asleep. He is fat and fleshy because he *is* only flesh; a carcass because he is dead, the ghost having departed long since. His sleeping-suit is gaudy and striped because he is a creature from the jungle, perhaps a very common green-and-orange beetle. And he is driven away, finally, by a "Tamil driver afflicted by a sore foot" (p. 47), because the sore-footed devil has got hold of him and is bearing him to—where? "I did not hear the precise address," Marlow says, but the reader will supply the correct answer.

The captain's cohorts are with equal severity condemned as animals. "They were nobodies," Marlow remarks, and he means of course that having betrayed the ideal of conduct they have ceased to exist as men. Thus the second engineer, "plucked ... off a garbage heap," lying in the hospital, would appear to be human—to retain his human devotion to duty and his childlike purity: "His lean bronzed head, with white moustaches, looked fine and calm on the pillow, like the head of a war-worn soldier with a child-like soul ..." (p. 50). But a few moments later, suffering from "D.T.'s of the worst kind" and imagining that millions of pink toads from the *Patna* are trampling him, he begins to howl like an animal. Indeed, they are all animals, these betrayers of mankind: "Then three voices together raised a yell. They came to me separately: one bleated, another screamed, one howled." In the lifeboat after the jump (p. 118) their "filthy jargon" goes like this: "Yap! yap! Bow-ow-ow-ow-ow! Yap! yap!" Brown addresses his men as "hounds" and is answered by "low growls" (p. 401). And even the majestic Brierly cannot shake off the yellow-eyed dog "that was always at his heels whenever he moved, night or day" (p. 61).

Jim, like Brierly, is not really one of the pack, but of course he is taken to be. During the trial he overhears somebody (referring to a "yellow dog") say, "Look at that wretched cur," and spinning around, Jim asks Marlow (p. 70): "Did you speak to me?" His cowardice, his "yellowness," has temporarily reduced him to the level of the undreaming brute, the yellow dog; but because he still follows the dream he must be considered not one of Stein's beetles, but a higher animal. Note that he weds himself not only to the pitiless shadowy ideal of conduct but also to one of those who, as Marlow says, "manage to put at times into their love an element just palpable enough to give one a fright—an extra-terrestrial touch" (p. 277). The trusting Jewel is in fact the perfect mate for Jim: "... the ghostly figure swayed like a slender tree in the wind ... two wide sleeves uprose in the dark *like unfolding wings* ... the girl, in a trailing white gown, her black hair falling as low as her waist, bore the light. Erect and swaying, *she seemed to glide without touching the earth*" (pp. 308, 303; italics mine). She is the butterfly, an extraterrestrial rather than a terrestrial animal; and her belief that Jim is "fearless" is one of the signs of her utter submission to the destructive element.

As for the other minor characters, they all have a place in the chain of being ranging from beetle to butterfly. Cornelius, of course, is at the bottom of the scale: "He reminded me of everything that is unsavoury. His slow laborious walk resembled the creeping of a repulsive beetle ..." (p. 285). Brown, as I have indicated, hasn't "got any wings," and after the treacherous massacre he ceases to live as a man, becomes a "tortured skeleton." As for Stein, he is both animal and spirit. Ironically, he captures his prize butterfly shortly after murdering three men—that is, after behaving like a brute. This "shadow prowling" among the collection of beetles and butterflies is heard to emit a "sympathetic growl" (p. 212); for though he is the shadow following the dream of the butterfly, he cannot help being the prowling beast, the growling dog. A similar association of spirit and prowling dog is observed by Marlow in Patusan: "More than once I saw her [Jewel] and Jim ... two white forms very close, his arm about her waist, her head on his shoulder. Their soft murmurs reached me, penetrating, tender, with a calm sad note in the stillness of the night. ... Later on, tossing on my bed under the mosquito-net, I was sure to hear slight creakings, faint breathing, a throat cleared cautiously—and I would know that Tamb' Itam was still *on the prowl*" (pp. 284, italics mine). The reader will find similar admixtures of spirit and flesh in a number of other passages and in connection with many other characters, including Doramin, the French Lieutenant, and a few others whom I shall discuss under another heading.

The color symbolism of *Lord Jim* is equally pervasive, and far more complex than most readers have taken it to be. We have already seen that Jim's leap from the *Patna* is a jump into the heart of darkness. ("It was black, black," Jim says before he jumps [p. 102], and in the rowboat [p. 113]: "They saw no lights. All was black.") We have seen, too, that various gaudy and violent colors, like green and orange, are strongly associated with—and hence may come to symbolize—jungle animality; and that the yellow associated with cowardice is the color of the treacherous dogs who betray the pilgrims. Conrad is in fact fairly explicit about the meanings of yellow, brown, and black: he has Marlow recall, in his letter to his friend, "You said also—I call to mind—that 'giving your life to them' (*them* meaning all of mankind with skins brown, yellow, or black in colour) 'was like selling your soul to a brute' "

(p. 339). Given clues like this, the reader will have little difficulty interpreting the fascinating handling of the colors in every paragraph of the novel, especially if he remembers that the ideal and the material are likely to be represented as existing side by side, like beetles and butterflies, or as commingling in a universe which may seem "safe" but may actually be "without pity."

It is no accident, for example, that the *Patna*, ship of both the faithful (led by an Arab "handsome and grave in his white gown and large turban") and the faithless, is described as follows: "The *Patna*, with a slight hiss, passed over that plain luminous and smooth, unrolled a *black ribbon of smoke* across the sky, left behind her on the water a *white ribbon of foam* ..." (p. 16, italics mine). Equally appropriate are the admixtures of color in Patusan, closely linked with the symbolism of heights and depressions and corresponding, of course, to the precarious existence of eternal ideals in a world of moral darkness and death. In the following passage, in which Marlow broods upon the spirit's inability to free itself from the ugliness of matter, the eternal ideals, the white abstractions, seem to have lost all vitality, all power to "rebound" and to enter the world of becoming. In their eternal fixity, they are in a sense dead, and it is as if the sole reality had become the death-dealing flux, the world of matter and animal instinct—the jungle.

"Nothing on earth seemed less real now than his [Jim's] plans, his energy, and his enthusiasm; and raising my eyes, I saw part of the moon *glittering through the bushes at the bottom of the chasm.* For a moment it looked as though the smooth disc, *falling from its place in the sky* upon the earth, had rolled *to the bottom* of that precipice: its ascending movement was like a leisurely rebound; it disengaged itself from the tangle of twigs; the bare contorted limb of some tree, growing on the slope, made a *black crack* right across its face. It threw its level rays afar as if *from a cavern,* and in this mournful, *eclipse-like light* the stumps of felled trees uprose *very dark,* the *heavy shadows* fell at my feet on all sides, *my own moving shadow,* and across my path *the shadow of the solitary grave* perpetually garlanded with flowers. In *the darkened moonlight* the interlaced blossoms took on shapes foreign ... as though they had been special flowers ... destined for the use of the dead alone. Their powerful scent hung in the warm air, making it thick and heavy like the fumes of incense. The lumps of *white coral* shone around the *dark mound* like a chaplet of bleached skulls, and everything around was so quiet that when I stood still all sounds and all movements in the world seemed to come to an end.

"It was a great peace, as if the earth had been one grave. . . ." [Pp. 322, 323; italics mine]

The admixtures of colors in Stein's house are even more interesting. His Japanese servant appears "in a sort of livery of *white jacket* and *yellow sarong*," like a "*ghost* only momentarily *embodied*" (p. 204, italics mine). One corner of the vast dining room is "strongly lighted," but the rest "melted into shapeless gloom like a cavern" (p. 204). There are "catacombs of beetles" and there is the butterfly with "dark bronze wings . . . with exquisite *white veinings* and a gorgeous border of *yellow spots*" (p. 205, italics mine). We learn that Stein, besides collecting butterflies and beetles, "had an office with *white* and *Chinese* clerks" (p. 207, italics mine). His wife, whom he called the "princess"—another one of the royal company of those who follow the dream—"had on a *white jacket, gold pins* in her hair, and a *brown leather belt* over her left shoulder with a revolver in it" (p. 209, italics mine). Idealized as princess, she has, like Jewel, a touch of the extraterrestrial; but she is also of the warlike earth —hence the brown belt for the revolver.

Once the imagination is alerted to these touches, it is easy to understand why the gentleman who murders Dain Waris is a Brown and why he stares at Marlow "with his yellow eyes out of a long, ravaged brown face." He has "a pepper-and-salt matted beard" (p. 345), however, because he retains, by virtue of his "near conversion" (or simply by virtue of having once been an innocent child and the son of a baronet), a trace—the white salt—of his former glory. It is also easy to see why Cornelius appears "swallowed up, totally lost, in a suit of black broadcloth" and with a "sour yellow little face" (p. 324)—though he, too, like Brown, bears the colors of a sullied purity: "his feet, shod in *dirty white shoes*, twinkled on the dark earth" (p. 323). By the same token he wears "a *tall* stove-pipe hat" though he emerges from "a *depression* of the ground" (p. 323).

A multiplication of instances is unnecessary. The reader will find hundreds of unexpected proliferations of this symbolism, like the following casual observation in the courtroom: "The plaintiff, who had been beaten, an obese *chocolate-coloured* man with shaved head, one fat breast bare and a bright *yellow castemark* above the bridge of his nose, sat in pompous immobility. . . . The head of the magistrate was half hidden by paper, his brow was *like alabaster*" (pp. 158, 159, italics mine). Or the description of Captain Robinson, opium smuggler and reputed cannibal: "An emaciated patriarch in a suit of *white drill*, a solah topi with a *green-lined rim* on a head trembling with age, joined us. . . . A *white beard* with *amber streaks* hung lumpily down to his waist" (p. 163).

We turn finally to the symbolism of straightness and crookedness, a symbolic kith which, like the others I have been tracing, derives from the antithesis between dream and reality. Man, in so far as he is true to the dream, "goes straight" and has a "fixed" course; but his fall cripples him, bends him, makes him waver or wander. Jim advances "straight at you"—but with "a slight stoop of the shoulders" (p. 3). In his first confrontation of the brutal and unpredictable sea, before his jump from the *Patna*, he is so terrified that he fails to achieve the glory which he feels sure is his destiny. During a week "of which his Scottish captain used to say afterwards, 'Man! It's a pairfect meeracle to me how she lived through it!' " Jim is "disabled by a falling spar" (p. 11). Conrad does not state explicitly that Jim's lameness symbolizes a spiritual defect, but the hints are unmistakable: in the hospital Jim finds himself in the company of other disabled men, one with a broken leg, another "afflicted by some mysterious tropical disease," the majority "like himself, thrown there by some accident" (p. 13). (One remembers Marlow's words to Jim after the jump from the *Patna:* "It is always the unexpected that happens.") The crippled men have one thing in common: "in all they said—in their actions, in their looks, in their persons—could be detected the soft spot, the place of decay, the determination to lounge safely through existence" (p. 13).

Released from the hospital, Jim boards the *Patna* and once again seems secure in a "straight" universe:

> She cleared the Straight, crossed the bay. . . . She held on *straight* for the Red Sea under a serene sky . . . the ship, lonely under a wisp of smoke, held on her *steadfast way.* . . .
>
> The propeller turned without check, as though its beats had been part of the scheme of a safe universe; and on each side of the *Patna* two deep folds of water, *permanent* and sombre on the *unwrinkled* shimmer, enclosed within their *straight* and diverging ridges a few white swirls of foam bursting in a low hiss, a *few ripples, a few*

undulations that, left behind, agitated the surface of the sea for an instant after the passage of the ship. . . . [Pp. 15–17, italics mine]

The dream is straight, is permanent, is still, is flawless; reality is crooked, is impermanent, is a disturbing ripple. "How steady she goes," thinks Jim, marveling at the moral qualities of the dark ship; but moments later the *Patna* strikes something and "the calm sea, the sky without a cloud" appear "formidably insecure in their immobility" (p. 26).

All the men who jump are in one way or another malformed or diseased. One has his arm broken; the engineer with the "drooping white moustache" suffers from d.t.'s and sees the pink toads. The captain "seemed to be swollen to an unnatural size by some awful disease, by the mysterious action of an unknown poison" (p. 46).

The captain's deformity—obesity—is the most obvious token of man's animality, and so it is not surprising to find a number of fat people in the novel. There is Doramin, for example: "His bulk for a Malay was immense, but he did not look merely fat; he looked imposing, monumental. The motionless body, clad in rich stuffs, coloured silks, gold embroideries . . ." (p. 259). There is "nothing of a cripple about him," Marlow observes, but adds quickly that when Doramin walks he "must be supported by two sturdy young fellows" (in "white sarongs and with black caps") (p. 259). There is also the French Lieutenant, a "massive chap" who, "as he sat there, with his thick fingers clasped lightly on his stomach . . . reminded you of one of those snuffy, quiet village priests . . ." (p. 139). Like any good spiritual animal, the lieutenant is worried about two things: wine and honor. Another fat man is Stein's Scottish friend, "who was slightly paralyzed on one side"—a "heavy man with a patriarchal white beard, and of imposing stature" (pp. 205–6); and there is the "queen, a fat wrinkled woman" with whom the Scotsman trades; and Doramin's brown wife, also a queen, also fat.

Equally deforming is starvation, and the betrayer of mankind may be reduced (as we have seen in Brown's case) to that morally dead thing, the skeleton. Thus after the massacre of Dain Waris and his men, a longboat picked up in the Indian Ocean contains "two parched, yellow, glassy-eyed, whispering skeletons" who recognized "the authority of a third, who declared that his name was

Brown" (p. 404). Similarly, the second engineer of the *Patna* is "lean, all hollows," with a head "long and bony like the head of an old horse" (p. 23); he moves "like a skeleton," his walk "mere wandering"—that is, deviation from the straight and narrow. Captain Robinson, the emaciated patriarch, seems "ready to subside passively into a heap of old bones" (p. 166), is "a little deaf," and like Doramin must be supported—"propped" on the handle of his umbrella.

Some miscellaneous instances of malformation and deviation conclude our list. Of Cornelius, Marlow observes: "I suppose he made straight enough for the place where he wanted to go, but his progress with one shoulder carried forward seemed oblique. He was often seen circling slowly amongst the sheds" (p. 285). Stein has "a slight stoop" (p. 203). Brown, before his death, has "fits" and is virtually mad. As for Brown's men, we are told that he addresses them as "dismal cripples" and that each "man of them felt as though he were adrift alone in a boat, haunted by an almost imperceptible suspicion of sighing, muttering ghosts" (p. 399). But Jim, after one experience of being adrift in a lifeboat, returns to his fixed course and remains true to the end: a moment before his death he looks Doramin "straight in the face."

The exploration of these four families does not provide a complete map of the symbolic landscape of *Lord Jim*. We have not looked into a few interesting areas that lie well off the main paths of the symbolism, such as the symbols connected with opiates of various sorts, chiefly tobacco and alcohol, the symbolism of sleep and waking, and that of motion and immobility; or the unexpected glints from the mine of idiom, as when the French Lieutenant employs the slang, "I have rolled my hump (*roulé ma bosse*)." Sufficient ground has been covered, however, to enable us to see clearly the thoroughness of Conrad's vast symbolic system and to appreciate Albert Guerard's remark that Conrad possesses a "highly generalizing imagination." [6]

Lord Jim marks the conclusion of a period in Conrad's writing. As Morton Dauwen Zabel has pointed out, the years between 1902 and 1912 were "a crucial phase in his career." [7] There occurred, as Conrad himself acknowledged, a "change in the fundamental mood" that stole over him "unawares." The change was not (as

Zabel observes) "radically discontinuous with the mood and impetus of certain of his earlier works," but in *Nostromo, The Secret Agent,* and *Under Western Eyes* we witness the abundant exfoliation of the symbolism of disorder, drunkenness, farce, and absurdity, which Conrad had introduced most vividly in *Heart of Darkness.* The satiric spirit gains; irony deepens. The Augustan note—the defense of reason and civilization, of law and order, against "drunkenness and intoxication"—is sounded persistently. If the falsity of the heart and the wildness of the instincts have always engaged Conrad's interest, there occurs now a shift from the interest in the psychology of the irrational (manifested in the study of Willems) to a concentration on the political and social implications of irrationality. Thus disgust and contempt tend to drive out sympathy. Especially in dealing with the Russians—in settling his score with *them*—Conrad expresses an outrage, a bitterness, a loathing nearly unrestrained. *Saeva indignatio.* In *Under Western Eyes* Razumov is like the Marlow of *Heart of Darkness*—struggling to keep irrationality and lawlessness from submerging him. The light of reason and control burns feebly in the Russian immensity, in that sea of darkness, vagueness, shapelessness. And the world is a Dunciad. Even the apparently civilized are savage. The barbarism extends from autocrat to revolutionist and from idealist to peasant:

> Between the two he was done for. Between the drunkenness of the peasant incapable of action and the dream intoxication of the idealist incapable of perceiving the reason of things, and the true character of men. It was a sort of terrible childishness.[8]

And again:

> The true Razumov had his being in the willed, in the determined future—in that future menaced by the lawlessness of autocracy—for autocracy knows no law—and the lawlessness of revolution. [P. 64]

Thus a pattern of ironic deflation is worked into the action, and all the apparently civilized beings are revealed as beasts. Wealthy women dress in "the hairy skin of wild beasts" (p. 32). The revolutionist Peter Ivanovitch, who escapes from a prison to make his way across Siberia, leads a "wild and hunted existence":

It was as though there had been two human beings indissolubly joined in that enterprise. The civilized man, the enthusiast of advanced humanitarian ideals thirsting for the triumph of spiritual love and political liberty; and the stealthy, primeval savage, pitilessly cunning in the preservation of his freedom from day to day, like a tracked wild beast. [P. 103]

Peter Ivanovitch, who has "one of those bearded Russian faces without shape" (p. 101), is a peasant. But the savagery of this peasant, who tells Natalia Heldin, "I want you to be a fanatic" (p. 108), is matched by the madness of the aristocratic Mme de S——, who, in her fixation on revolutionary ideas, shows a "death-like immobility," is like "a galvanized corpse out of some Hoffman's Tale," an "ancient, painted mummy with unfathomable eyes," "a witch in Parisian clothes." All the imagery that Pope employed in *The Dunciad* is required to exhibit the dreamy fixity of such idealists. If Conrad early saw that men live in a dream, he sees now all the dangers of their dreaming—their trance, their abstraction, their fixation. They are all possessed, these idealists, by insane ideas, and their habitations, like the outpost of "An Outpost of Progress" or the Belgian plantations of *Heart of Darkness*, testify to the disorder of mind. The Chateau Borel, for example, with its "green stains of moss on the steps of the terrace," its "hall . . . like a dusty barn of marble and stucco with cobwebs in the corners and faint tracks of mud on the black and white tessellated floor," its "dusty glass skylight" and its "cracked white paint of the panels, the tarnished gilt of the mouldings" suggesting "nothing but dust and emptiness within"—this is a perfect correlative of the disordered, irrational spirit of the revolutionaries (pp. 121, 124, 179). The Manichean vision is, again, extended to all parts of the canvas. On the Boulevard des Philosophes stalks the terrifying Nikita, the fat man with the voice "like the falsetto of a circus clown"—a creature "so grotesque as to set town dogs barking at its mere sight" (pp. 224, 225). Or one observes the antitheses in the portrait of that "true spirit of destructive revolution," Sophia Antonovna:

> A blouse of crimson silk made her noticeable at a distance. With that she wore a short brown skirt and a leather belt. Her complexion was the colour of coffee and milk, but very clear; her eyes black and glittering, her figure erect. A lot of thick hair, nearly white, was

done up loosely under a dusty Tyrolese hat of dark cloth, which
seemed to have lost some of its trimmings. [P. 201]

And the mixture in this description is repeated in the action of the
novel. Lofty ideals, humanitarian sentiments culminate in violence,
disorder, butchery. Freedom becomes "a debauch" and "the Christian virtues themselves appear virtually indecent" (pp. 55–56). As
Kurtz, that pure idealist, wallows in the unspeakable in the Congo,
so the revolutionists and autocrats of *Under Western Eyes* plunge
into the abyss of irrationality.

The Manichean vision is compounded of paradox and contradiction. Nothing is what it seems; all virtue is contradicted by
disclosures so devastating that the very existence of virtue is called
into question. In *Nostromo*, as in *Under Western Eyes* and *The Secret
Agent*, Conrad spares no one. The glorious enterprise to bring
peace, freedom, justice and order to Costaguana becomes, in the
words of the ironist Decoud, "une farce macabre." The project is
foredoomed, accursed. Says Decoud: "There is a curse of futility
upon our character. Don Quixote and Sancho Panza, chivalry and
materialism, high-sounding sentiments and a supine morality, violent efforts for an idea and a sullen acquiescence in every form of
corruption." A conviction is "a particular view of our personal
advantage either practical or emotional" and "no man is a patriot
for nothing." Leaders and followers hope to gain, either practically
or emotionally, from the Ribierist triumph. Charles Gould, master
of the San Tomé mine, may, like Kurtz, have an immense plan, but
the plan is one with the silver mine, the idealism is grounded in
"material interests," and the Gould *imperium in imperio* must fight
for life "with such weapons as could be found in the mire of a
corruption that was so universal as to almost lose its significance."
One is reminded of Hannah Arendt's piercing description of the
phenomena surrounding such men as Adolph Eichmann in the
Nazi era: "the banality of evil." In one way or another the silver,
holding out the promise of opportunities, advantages, possibilities,
corrupts everyone. Even the incorruptible *capataz de cargadores*,
Nostromo, becomes the man of silver—riding the silver-gray mare,
wearing a jacket with enormous silver buttons and trousers with
silver down the seams. Even old Giorgio Viola, the idealistic Re-
publican and Garibaldist, acquiesces to the corruption of the silver,

gratifying his passion for rhetoric and reading his Bible with "a pair of silver-mounted spectacles from Senora Emilia Gould." Even Senora Gould, who lives by devoting herself to others, who is so pure that she resembles a "fairy," is exposed as presiding, like Pope's Belinda, among "vessels of silver and porcelain," and her philanthropy is, precisely, her personal therapy, her emotional advantage. The recognition of all such "secret purposes" culminates accordingly in a skepticism so complete that Decoud, like James's Hyacinth Robinson or Woolf's Rhoda, is driven to suicide—death in "the immense indifference of things."

Decoud is not Conrad, but his vision of the "farce macabre" is not very different from Conrad's, and it is apparent that to present adequately the Manichean vision Conrad needed, in every novel, a complex "register" or "reflector" of events—to use Henry James's terminology. James's solution to the problem of achieving adequate complexity was to employ, at the center of his composition, a mind "subject to fine intensification and wide enlargement." [9] Characteristically, James's central intelligence is a divided soul, and his vision is defined by the "acute perception of alternatives": he sees virtues and vices commingling and is reluctant to take sides. Conrad's solution to this technical problem is similar. Only instead of viewing events from the perspective of the central character, Conrad likes to use the complicated, subtle onlooker, Marlow, to register the full significance, the full ambiguity, of his Manichean vision. The virtue of Marlow is precisely that he is capable of seeing the whole situation: he tries to sympathize, yet his irony and detachment undercut his sympathy: "with Marlow one never could be sure," says the young auditor of the tale of *Chance.* Thus of Flora de Barral we find Marlow saying, "The girl's life had presented itself to me as a tragicomical adventure, the saddest thing on earth, slipping between frank laughter and unabashed tears." [10] And thus he shows "in his eyes that slightly mocking expression with which he habitually covers up his sympathetic impulses of mirth and pity before the unreasonable complications the idealism of mankind puts into the simple but poignant problem of conduct on this earth" (p. 325). He is a fatalist—a believer in Chance; yet for all that, "not exactly a pagan" (p. 447): he believes in "the sacred rage"—the "sovereign power enthroned in a fixed standard of conduct." He wants to believe in Jim—and yet he sees the subtle dishonesty of the man. He likes Captain Anthony of *Chance* and tries to think of him as a knight-errant, "the rescuer of the most forlorn damsel of modern times"; yet he also sees that "not pity alone" motivates Anthony but his fierce will-to-power: "It gave him the feeling that if only he could get hold of her, no woman would belong to him so completely as this woman" (pp. 238, 224). Captain Anthony, Marlow discerns, has tried to act "at the same time like a beast of prey, a pure spirit and the 'most generous of men' " (p. 415). Marlow discovers "the ambiguities" everywhere. No man is good enough; and the truth may be so appalling that the only course open to men who would endure as men is to believe the lie—to follow the dream, to affirm the absolute standard of morality.

The appalling truth—that truth from which James's Maggie Verver averts her eyes, the truth that must be hidden or covered by the gloss of the dream—is, at bottom, as we have seen, that the knitting machine is the sole reality; and "you can't interfere with it." Thus "the attitude of cold unconcern is the only reasonable one." "There is no morality, no knowledge, and no hope: there is only the consciousness of ourselves which drives us about a world that, whether seen in a convex or a concave mirror, is always but a vain and floating appearance" (*Life and Letters*, 1:226). But Marlow cannot repose in the attitude of "cold unconcern." He is not *quite* a pagan, and "the surrender to one's impulses, the fidelity to passing emotions" is "perhaps a nearer approach to truth than any other philosophy of life"—as Conrad writes to Garnett. And because he does not rule out the ideal in life, but sees it as wedded to the material, his symbolism is hardly different in any significant respects from that of Wallace Stevens.

Stevens's idea of poetry as "the interdependence of imagination and reality as equals" is, of course, a general formulation of what is concretely rendered not only in his own poetic world but also in the worlds of all writers whose imaginations trace out the implications of man's paradoxical situation—his living in two opposite camps. Thus Stevens's "reality," his south, his Yucatán or Africa, with its snakes and swine, its stupid grunting animals lolling in the mud, its thick vegetation, is paralleled by Conrad's Congo or by Conrad's lounging seamen who seek only ease and intoxication, or by the innumerable fat men who inhabit his novels and stories: the fat Nikitas, the Verlocs or Mr. Vladimirs or Michaelises of *The Secret Agent*, the German captain of *Lord Jim*, and the other elephants, swine, and carcasses who have ceased to be "men." Stevens's symbolism of "imagination"—the world of form, symmetry, geometry, together with the polarized symbols of raggedness, the slovenly, the wild—is repeated in Conrad's contrast between the reason or discipline that he associated with Roman law and order, and the irrationality, the shapelessness, and disconnectedness that he saw in the Russian, the revolutionist, the autocrat. The color-symbolism of the two writers is also virtually identical, as is the symbolism of heights and depressions, spirituality and animality. It is clear that the symbolizing imagination, searching out the categories best suited to render man's complex experience of the world, returns, again and again, to the old Platonic antitheses. Conrad, like Stevens, creates a world every part of which has been penetrated by his symbolism. The scheme is complete—and so comprehensive that no fact is merely itself. There is not a particle of matter but has its cunning duplicate in mind.

NOTES

1. Conrad, *Joseph Conrad, Life and Letters*, ed. Jean-Aubrey, 2 vols. (London: William Heinemann, 1927), 1:216.
2. Joseph Conrad, *An Outcast of the Islands* (London and Toronto: J. M. Dent and Sons, 1923), p. 70. Subsequent citations are to this edition.
3. Conrad, quoted in the preface to *An Outcast of the Islands* (New York: New American Library, Signet edition, 1964), p. viii.
4. Joseph Conrad, *The Works of Joseph Conrad*, 22 vols. (London: William Heinemann, 1921), 3:1, 195. All subsequent citations are to this edition.
5. Joseph Conrad, *Lord Jim* (New York: Random House, Modern Library, 1931), p. 3. All other citations are to this edition.
6. Albert Guerard, Jr., *Joseph Conrad* (Cambridge, Mass.: Harvard University Press, 1958), p. 63.
7. Morton Zabel, preface to Joseph Conrad, *Under Western Eyes* (New York: Doubleday & Co., Anchor Books, 1963), p. ix.
8. Ibid., p. 25. All other citations are to this edition.
9. James, *The Art of the Novel*, ed. R. P. Blackmur (New York: Charles Scribner's Sons, 1934), p. 67.
10. Joseph Conrad, *Chance* (New York: Doubleday & Co., 1923), p. 310. Subsequent citations are to this edition.

III. "A TERRIBLE MIXTURE
IN THINGS"

The Symbolism of Henry James

HENRY JAMES IS NOT USUALLY REGARDED as a symbolist, even though he expressed admiration for symbolist art, such as that of an Ibsen,[1] and wrote half a dozen novels whose titles are symbolic. He has been classified, more or less officially, as a realist or naturalist, and because realism and naturalism are conventionally opposed to symbolism, it has been presumed that the employment of symbols as a systematic technique was beyond his ambition. Still, he himself sometimes alluded to the symbolism in his work, and in terms suggesting that he had a vision of a symbolic scheme far more comprehensive than many of his critics have guessed. For example, when he writes, in *Notes of a Son and Brother,* that he saw the "inspiringly symbolic" possibilities of the "small dense formal garden" of John La Farge, the "garden of Mérimée,"[2] he alludes clearly to the nature-art (or to what Richard Chase has called the garden-house) antithesis that was to inform almost all of his fiction. And when he speaks of Ida Farrange as "the striking figured symbol,"[3] it is apparent that he means her to stand for an entire society that lives by and for appearances, for show, conspicuous display. A consideration of Ida's symbolic significance leads, indeed, into the very center of the Manichean vision. Ida, with her "huge painted eyes ... like Japanese lanterns swung under festal arches" and her face "like an illuminated garden," this "actress" who is "as distinct and public as a lamp set in a window" and who produces "everywhere a sense of having been seen often, the sense indeed of a kind of abuse of visibility," becomes a sort of pagan goddess presiding with a hideous vitality over the world of appearances, the wasteland of *What Maisie Knew*.[4] As base appearance, she is *not* the *ding an sich;* only a Milly Theale is *that*. But in a world in which men live by and for appearances, the worship of base phenomena rather than the sacred noumena is, alas, "the thing."

Fully to understand James's symbolism, then, we shall have to trace it back to some fundamental categories of Western thought at least as old as Descartes, and finally going back to Plato. But to understand how James's symbolism functions as art we must begin not with philosophical categories but with the basic conflicts and situations with which he is always concerned: the predicament of the "free spirit" in a world that seeks everywhere to deprive people of their freedom, to coerce them into traps or molds or cages, to bully them into doing the world's work for the world's base purposes. Quentin Anderson has shown how deep was the influence upon James of his father's idea of independence from all that "finites" man.[5] Church and state, tribe and marketplace, theater and cave, all the massed conventions and proprieties, all the coercive systems devised by a world whose deepest allegiance is to necessity —these are the great threat to the free spirit. What it wants, this great enslaving world, is to convert men into machines, puppets, things—mere tools to use, mere passivity, helpless to oppose the superior will of matter. In the face of the aggressive assault and effort to seize and entrap, the passive man is helpless, as is the divided spirit who is all vacillation and dispersion: a Hamlet unready to act. James sees the free spirit as hesitant to accept "the responsibility of freedom" and as "tragic, pathetic, ironic, or whatever . . . and successful only through having remained free." [6]

The central symbol in James's work is thus the cage, trap, box, mold, *cadre* in which the free soul is *fixed* or *placed*, compelled to sit motionless, like a still life, a work of art. And the symbolism evolves from the antithesis of freedom and slavery, motion and immobility, life and automatism or mechanism, nature and art. In short, James's symbolism returns, in the last analysis, to the dualism of appearance and reality, and his career shows him working steadily toward a presentation, in all parts of his composition, of "the ambiguities"—that admixture of "bliss or bale," of the ideal and the material, of freedom and necessity, that we have viewed as characteristic of the Manichean vision.

We see James developing these symbolic antitheses even in his

early work, which appears to take over a considerable part of the
symbolic scheme of Hawthorne's *Scarlet Letter* or his *Marble Faun*.
In *The American*, for example, James works extensively with the
contrast between the American as a child of nature, and the European as the stamped-out product of tradition, culture, and art.
Five great symbolic families may be isolated: symbols of expansion
and breadth versus contraction and confinement; freedom and
spontaneity versus mechanism, automatism, slavery; motion versus
fixity; the inner life (the "sacred rage") versus appearances and
externals ("things"); warmth and life versus coldness and death.

The most obvious tokens of the American's romantic commitment to liberty and to possibilities are the many images of expansion and breadth that inform the novel. James begins with a picture
of Newman sitting with "legs outstretched" on a divan in the
Louvre, and thereafter the symbolism of romantic *stretching* recurs
on virtually every page. Newman shows an Emersonian impatience
for confining "circles"; he wants to venture, to experiment, to take
risks. Sharply contrasted with the passivity and stagnation of the
fixed and tradition-bound Old World is the adventurousness and
energy of this "born experimentalist" from the New World with
his "mighty hankering, a desire to stretch out and haul in" (p. 45).[7]
"To expand, without too much ado ... to the full compass of any
such experience as was held to stir men's blood represented his
nearest approach to a high principle" (p. 88). He wants, finally,
everything:

> "I want the biggest kind of entertainment a man can get. People,
> places, art, nature, everything! I want to see the tallest mountains,
> and the bluest lakes, and the finest pictures, and the handsomest
> churches, and the most celebrated men, and the most elegant
> women." [P. 33]

And from this and like passages, a number of antitheses between
him and the Old World Parisians are inevitably engendered. If
Newman is tall—six feet tall—and if he looks at things "from a
height," the Parisians he meets are uniformly small. Valentin is "but
middling high" (p. 129); Mme de Bellegarde, the embodiment of
Old World "conventions and proprieties," is a "little woman" with
"a little pair of lips"; and if Mme de Cintré's "range of expression"
is to Newman "as delightfully vast as the wind-streaked cloud-

flecked distance on a Western prairie," the mother's "respectable countenance, with its formal gaze, and its circumscribed smile, figured a document signed and sealed, a thing of parchment, ink, and ruled lines" (p. 183). The proud Urbain, that elder son who is "the old woman at second-hand," has "small, opaque eyes" (p. 188). The late Count de Cintré "wasn't five feet high" (p. 255). The prince who visits the duchess in chapter 25 is "a short, stout man" (p. 505). The stature of Lord Deepmere, the man chosen by the Bellegardes as a suitable candidate for Claire's hand, is "scant" (p. 266). M. Nioche, the submissive father of the demimonde Noémie, is a "little shrunken bourgeois" (p. 68). And the Unitarian minister Babcock, whom Newman meets on his travels, becomes, by virtue of his closed mind and his conventional attitudes, a "small, spare" man whose digestion is "weak" (p. 90). Indeed, there is in all these contracted little people such oppressive and repressive constraint that Newman, confronting them, frequently wishes "to make some answering manifestation, to stretch himself out at his own length, to sound a note at the uttermost end of *his* scale" (p. 191). So he mocks Babcock's prudery and Puritanism by sending to the minister a statuette of "a gaunt ascetic-looking monk" with a "fat capon" round his waist; and he is prompted several times by the Bellegardes' coldness and snobbery to make them "feel him."

The imagery of expansion and contraction is continued in the descriptions of the residences of the central characters. Newman, of course, likes "to inhabit very large rooms, have a great many of them," and they must be "clear and high and what he called open, and he had once said that he liked rooms in which you should want to keep on your hat" (p. 108). The rooms of the Bellegardes are, on the other hand, even when very large, suggestive of cages, prisons. Thus the Hôtel du Bellegarde, with its "closed windows" and its "dark, dusty, painted portal," is "stoutly guarded" and answers to Newman's "conception of a convent" (pp. 59, 113); and the houses of the Faubourg St. Germain are "as suggestive of the concentration of privacy within as the blank walls of Eastern seraglios" (p. 59). Similarly, the Bellegardes' country house, Fleurières, is "like a Chinese penitentiary" (p. 406) and its gate, with its inevitable "bars," is described as a " 'mean' crevice" (p. 425). Claire de Cintré moves from one prison to another: from the Hôtel du Bellegarde to Fleurières and finally to the high-walled, windowless convent of the Carmelite nuns in the Rue d'Enfer, where Newman, from behind a "large close iron screen," sees her and the other nuns chanting "their dirge over their buried affections and over the vanity of earthly desires" (p. 480). Whether the wall is built by the Old World aristocracy or by Catholicism, or is simply the "wall of polite conversation"—part of the "citadel of the proprieties" (p. 260)—it is always intimidating, always a grave threat to the free man or woman.

Closely linked with the denial of freedom and expansion is the symbolism of mechanisms and *clichés*—the molds or stamps that turn out enslaved "types." The person who has been poured into the mold of Europe or has permitted himself to be used or sold by the Old World system is not really "alive" at all; he is but a thing or machine, a product, like a piece of furniture or a coin; and of course those who live for the world and do the world's work can only regard other people as objects for use, "things," collectors' items. So it is that Mme de Cintré, who has been "sold" to the Count de Cintré (p. 110), is—or may be—but a "great white doll" (as Mr. Tristram observes), and gives Newman "the sense ... of her having been fashioned and made flexible to certain exalted social needs," so that she seems "rare and precious—a very expensive article, as he would have said ..." (p. 165). She becomes—or Newman sees her as—an "object," which he feels he can admire "in all its complexity" while reserving the right to "examine its mechanism afterwards and at leisure" (p. 166). So, too, it occurs that Noémie, the girl who declares that "everything [she has] is for sale," becomes "a very curious and ingenious piece of machinery" that Valentin likes to see "in operation." By the same token, her father, who has surrendered to the way of the Old World, becomes a "smoothly-rounded unit" in Parisian civilization (p. 67). And Urbain becomes "a clock-image in papier-mâché" (308). Even the habitations of the sold and enslaved people give signs of the process of mechanical reproduction on an assembly line: the house of the Tristrams, who have surrendered to Europe, is "one of those chalk-coloured facades which decorate with their pompous sameness the broad avenues distributed by Baron Haussmann all over the neighborhood of the Arc de Triomphe" (p. 35). (In the 1877 edition "manufactured ... in" was used instead of "distributed ... over.")

Since the inhabitants of this closed and rigid society are thus in a sense mere mechanisms or things, James is able further to sharpen our sense of their living death by siezing opportunities to work a pattern of motion and fixity into the novel. Newman, of course, is all restless energy and movement: "He moved through the rooms for some time longer, circulating freely, over-topping most people by his great height . . . and expending generally the surplus of his equanimity" (p. 329). He likes to "set a large group of [people] in motion" (p. 335). When he drives, he "[bids] the driver go fast (he had a particular aversion to slow driving)," and even when he sits he shows such relaxation and "ease" as are contrasted inevitably with the stiffness and fixity of the Old World puppets (pp. 89, 1).

The pattern of immobility and inflexibility is developed very richly. Thus old Mme de Bellegarde is invariably depicted as sitting in one position, and her gaze, like her will, is invariably "fixed" (e.g., pp. 156, 182, 197). Her son Urbain stands "motionless, looking straight in front of him," and becomes a "man of stone" or of "wood" or suggests a "citadel" or "a great facade" (pp. 335, 340, 111). Again, the Italian prince who is received by the duchess wears, we are told, "a fixed and somewhat defiant expression," and his inability to move freely and lightly is suggested by the fact that he's "stout" and seems "to be challenging you to hint that he might be hydrocephalic" (p. 505). The duchess, too, is heavy—"monumentally stout," "a lady of monstrous proportions," and as she sits in her "capacious arm-chair," like some "reverend effigy in some idolatrous shrine," she reminds Newman of "the Fat Lady at a fair." She, too, is of course fixed, and from her entrenched position she "[fixes] her small, unwinking eyes at the new-comers" (pp. 318–19).

Even the Tristrams, after eight years in Paris, have surrendered much of their American lightness and mobility. Mrs. Tristram, who is so devoted to European ways that she "fell back upon the harmonies of dress, which she thoroughly understood, and contented herself with playing in its lock that key to the making of impressions," has not only succumbed to the world of appearances and comfort but has begun to talk of herself "as a languid Oriental" (pp. 37, 42). Her husband is an "idle" and "spiritless" man who, having yielded himself up to pure sensualism and having become "a rather degenerate mortal," is inevitably "corpulent" and has become an authority on "cookery" and champagne (p. 41). And even Valentin, who is in some respects so free—so "intensely alive" with his "agility" and his "quick, light brown eye"—and who is irritated by portraits because of their "great staring eyes and fixed positions"—even he is stout and has "a mortal dread" that his "robustness" will overtake his "agility" (pp. 201, 129).

Equally suggestive of immobility and perfect acceptance of a circumscribed way of life are the recurrent references to the *quietness* of the Europeans. The Hôtel du Bellegarde is "very quiet," says Claire de Cintré, "but that's exactly what we like" (p. 116). Mr. Tristram tells Newman, at the beginning, that he shouldn't take a "fine hotel": "You want something small and quiet and superior . . ." (p. 23). M. Nioche, after he has been compromised by accepting three hundred francs from his daughter, after all his moral indignation has been quelled, is "as quiet as the grave" (p. 295). Claire de Cintré, who has been "sold" once on the marriage-block, is "quiet" at the beginning of the action, then—after meeting Newman—goes off to a dance, and finally returns in the end to the convent of the Carmelite nuns, where "everyone was very quiet" (p. 479). It becomes clear at length that any form of subjugation to the world or to another person's will, any suggestion of surrender or submission, may release the symbolism of quietude and all the associates of that symbolism, such as "sitting," keeping one's hands "folded," being "passive," and so on. Thus it occurs that when Newman sees a chance to convert Valentin into a businessman, when Newman's imagination begins to "glow" with this idea of stamping Valentin out in *his*, Newman's, image, James has his hero say· "There's no reason why you shouldn't have half a million dollars if you'll mind what I tell you—I alone—and not fool round with other parties. . . . *Keep quiet* and I'll find something nice—I'll *fix* you all right" (pp. 345–46; italics mine). And later, when Newman attempts to persuade young Mme de Bellegarde that he wants only to speak to Urbain and the old woman, he says, "I shall not be violent; I am very quiet"—to which Mme de Bellegarde replies, "Yes, you look very quiet!" (p. 484). Then, too, we learn that Mrs. Bread, who has accepted that "a servant [is] but a mysteriously projected machine," has become, by virtue of compromising her liberty and not speaking out against the evil of Mme de Bellegarde, a creature of perfect quietness: "I kept quiet," she tells Newman. "Quiet I call it, but it was a queer enough quietness." And: "I was as still as a stopped clock" (pp. 458–59). There was a time, she indicates, when she was alive—when she wore a "red ribbon" in her cap; but after the old marquise accused her of being a hussy, "I took off my red ribbon and put it in a drawer, where I have kept it to this day. It's faded now, it's very pale pink; but there it lies" (p. 445). Not only the sensual fires, but the flames of liberty have nearly died out in her.

Mention of the red ribbon brings us to another significant lode of symbols that James was to mine extensively throughout his life: symbols of the bright and fetching appearances that conceal the actual darkness and evil—appearances that constitute for the unsuspecting free man a trap, an exquisite bait, a beautiful hook. James is very deliberate in his handling of the motif of the enslaving appearance. At the very beginning of the novel Newman is in the Louvre, in that world of art and appearance, and the note of warning against appearances is sounded by Mr. Tristram:

> "Ah," his friend sagaciously returned, "you can never tell. They imitate, you know, so deucedly well. It's like the jewellers, with their false stones. Go into the Palais Royal there; you see 'Imitation' on half the windows. The law obliges them to stick it on, you know; but you can't tell the things apart." [P. 19]

Newman has in fact *already* been seduced by an appearance. Mlle Noémie, the copyist, the imitator, presents the appearance of a diligent art-student and of a lady; but she is only acting a part.

> As the little copyist proceeded with her task, her attention addressed to her admirer, from time to time, for reciprocity, one of its blankest, though not of its briefest, missives. The working-out of her scheme appeared to call, in her view, for a great deal of vivid by-play, a great standing off with folded arms and head drooping from side to side, stroking of a dimpled chin with a dimpled hand, sighing and frowning and patting of the foot, fumbling in disordered tresses for wandering hairpins. These performances were accompanied by a far-straying glance, which tripped up, occasionally, as it were, on the tall arrested gentleman. [P. 5]

The young copyist has an "aptitude for playing a part at short notice" (p. 6). She appears charming and proper. But that she is in reality but a grasping little materialist (her chief interest is clothes) and a prostitute will be revealed later, when Newman sees her after she has sold herself to a wealthy fifty-year-old man and when James suggests that, for all her apparent youth and vitality, she is as "quiet" and fixed as the others who have delivered themselves up to Old World materialism.

> [Newman] observed the change in her appearance and that she was very elegant, really prettier than before; she looked a year or two older, and it was noticeable that, to the eye, she had only added a sharp accent to her appearance of "propriety," only taken a longer step toward distinction. She was dressed in quiet colors, and wore her expensively unobtrusive gear with a grace that might have come from years of practice. Her presence of mind, her perfect equilibrium, struck Newman as portentous. [P. 291]

But if Noémie, the "perfect Parisienne," knows her appearances and acts a part with facility, there are those even more practiced in the art. Thus when Newman threatens old Mme de Bellegarde and reveals that he possesses the note written by her husband and proving that she tried to kill him, the old woman is superb: " 'What paper is this you speak of?' asked the old lady, with an imitation of tranquility which would have been applauded in a veteran actress" (1877 edition). But of course all of these Europeans may be veteran actors and actresses. At Mme de Cintré's, Newman sits "looking at the entrances and exits" of her guests:

> He felt as if he were at the play, and as if his own speaking would be an interruption; sometimes he wished he had a book, to follow the dialogue; he half expected to see a woman in a white cap and pink ribbons come and offer him one for two francs. . . . [Claire de Cintré] was part of the play that he was seeing acted, quite as much as her companions; but how she filled the stage and she bore watching, not to say studying and throwing bouquets to! . . . it was what she was off the stage, as he might feel, that interested him most of all. [Pp. 144–45]

But as he finds himself in this world of actors, he is himself in danger of losing his spontaneity. After an "extremely solemn" dinner at the Bellegardes, Newman finds himself becoming "for the first time in his life . . . not himself; he measured his motions and counted his words; he had the sense of sitting in a boat that required inordinate trimming and that a wrong movement might cause to overturn" (p. 220). It is as if, momentarily at least, Newman were in the position of an Isabel Archer allowing herself, for the first time in her life, to be "directed" by Gilbert Osmond— directed into the cage of convention and propriety, fixed in the stillness of a portrait.

The imagery of clothes is particularly useful to James since clothes not only cover the naked truth but also are obvious tokens of materialism, the preoccupation with externals and appearances that stamps the slaves of the world. We have seen already that Mrs. Tristram, despite the fact that she has still a spark of the "sacred fire," has fallen back on the harmonies of the toilet and the sacred rites of pride. We see, too, how her husband has permitted himself to be dandified by Europe: when he enters the Louvre he is carrying a "white sun-umbrella, lined with blue silk," and Newman remarks, "So they carry those parasols here—the menfolk?" "Of course they do," replies Mr. Tristram. "They're great things. They understand detail out here" (pp. 17, 19). But in 1877 the word was *comfort*, not *detail*, and James was using the parasol as a token of Old World (or Oriental) epicureanism, along with such symbolic items as ribbons, gloves, furs, and silks. In his presentation of things expensive and sensuous, things appealing above all to "the lust of the eyes," James is already anticipating the dark vision of the later novels: the knowledge that "robes and furr'd gowns hide all," and that robes and furr'd gowns are, for the enslaved devotees of material things, virtually sacred objects. "The 'things' are radiant," says James in his preface to *The Spoils of Poynton*, "shedding afar, with a merciless monotony, all their light, exerting their ravage without remorse (pp. xiv–xv)." It is the mystic radiance that he tries above all to catch, the sacred glow of power and wealth, the charm of conspicuous display. James, almost as vividly as F. Scott Fitzgerald, records the impression of wonder in the presence of opulence that overwhelms and threatens to seduce the unworldly soul; and Fitzgerald was to take a leaf from James's symbolic lexicon when he created the "universe of ineffable gaudiness" of *The Great Gatsby*.

The things are especially prominent in James's descriptions of Old World apartments and rooms. Newman's apartment in Paris is "gilded from floor to ceiling a foot thick, draped in various light shades of satin, and chiefly furnished with mirrors and clocks" (p. 108). Valentin's apartment is a "den" which suggests the cage of Old World appearances as well as the bestial appetites of the "in-

satiable collector": the "ambiguities," the conjunctionings of bright
and dark, refinement and animality, swarm in its presentation.

> Valentin de Bellegarde lived in the basement of an old house in the
> Rue d'Anjou St. Honoré, and his small apartments lay between the
> court of the house and a garden of equal antiquity, which spread
> itself behind—one of those large, sunless, humid gardens into which
> you look unexpectingly in Paris from back windows, wondering
> how among the grudging habitations they find their space ... the
> place was low, dusky, contracted, and crowded with curious bric-à-
> brac. Their proprietor, penniless patrician though he might be, was
> an insatiable collector, and his walls were covered with rusty arms
> and ancient panels and platters, his doorways draped in faded tapes-
> tries, his floors muffled in the skins of beasts. Here and there was one
> of those uncomfortable tributes to elegance in which the French
> upholsterer's art is prolific; a curtained recess with a sheet of look-
> ing-glass as dark as a haunted pool; a divan on which, for its festoons
> and furbelows, you could no more sit than on a dowager's lap; a
> fireplace draped, flounced, frilled, by the same analogy, to the com-
> plete exclusion of fire. The young man's possessions were in pic-
> turesque disorder, and his apartment was pervaded by the odour of
> cigars, mingled, for inhalation, with other dim ghosts of past pres-
> ence. Newman thought it, as a home, damp, gloomy, and perverse,
> and was puzzled by the romantic incoherence of the furniture. [P.
> 140]

Although Valentin lives between the garden and the court of the
house, "nature" seems to have little chance "among the grudging
habitations"; and the rooms bespeak materialism, the contradiction
and debasement of the soul, and the bestiality of acquisitiveness. To
belong to a world like this, an old world charged with possessions,
is thus to become old, to approach death:

> *Old* Madame de Bellegarde was in her place by the fire, talking to
> *an antique gentleman* in a wig and a profuse white neck cloth *of the
> fashion of 1820.* Madame de Cintré was bending a listening head to
> the *historic* confidences of an *old* lady who was presumably the wife
> of this personage, an *old* lady in a red satin dress and an ermine cape,
> whose forehead was adorned with a topaz set in a velvet band. [Pp.
> 227–28; italics mine]

Imagery such as this is worked into the novel with such rigorous
consistency that it takes on, at times, an almost allegorical quality,
as in Hawthorne. James seeks so hard to underscore the meanings

of his symbols that he sometimes forces his characters to speak a sort of "symbolese," as when Claire says to Newman, after Valentin has proposed to show Newman about the house, "Would you not prefer my society here, *by my fire*, to stumbling about *dark passages* after—well, after nothing at all?" (p. 119); or as when Claire, having decided to enter the convent, tells Newman, "I am cold," and he cries out against her submission, " 'That *is* cold; you're right. And what I feel here,' and Newman struck his heart and became more eloquent than he knew, 'is a glowing fire!' " (p. 415). In fact, the symbolism of cold and heat is rather mechanically implanted throughout the action, and one comes to expect that any manifestation of the Old World will be represented as cold (e.g., the corridors and the vestibule in the Hôtel du Bellegarde, Claire's recurrent references to her own coldness, Valentin's damp basement-apartment with its fireplace in which there is no fire, Mme de Bellegarde's need to warm herself at the fire) whereas any reference to life and nature will be symbolized by fire or sunlight, as in *The Marble Faun*. The same observation holds for James's systematic and importunate use of white and black, light and dark.

So much for the basic polarities of James's scheme. It is, one sees, a very simple—though also a highly imaginative—pattern and all parts of the novel are easily accounted for. But there are, as we have noticed, certain ambiguities. Claire de Cintré, like her brother Valentin, is neither "American" nor "European": she is drawn to both worlds—is in fact torn between the two—and hence the imagery used to present her is, quite naturally, mixed. She has, at the beginning of the action, surrendered to the Old World—to her mother and Urbain; she has allowed herself to be "sold once." But she has also fought against her jailors over the question of her husband's property, and when Newman appears she is once again tempted to strike out for independence and "expansion." We see both sides of her nature in James's first description of her:

> She was tall and moulded in long lines; she had thick fair hair and features uneven and harmonious. ... Madame de Cintré was of attenuated substance and might pass for younger than she probably was. In her whole person there was something still young and still passive, still uncertain and that seemed still to expect to depend, and which yet made, in its dignity, a presence withal, and almost represented, in its serenity, an assurance. [Pp. 121–22]

In her "stillness," in her "moulded" passivity, standing serene as "a kind of historical formation," she is the portrait of a lady, the world's victim; but her height, her slenderness, her youth, her "uncertainty" suggest a capacity for free choice and expansion. Again, we learn that

> she was so high and yet so light, so active yet so still, so elegant yet so simple, so present yet so withdrawn! It was this unknown quantity that figured for him as a mystery; it was what she was off the stage, as he might feel, that interested him most of all. [P. 145]

In the 1877 edition James stresses the combination of nature and art in her:

> [Her face] was illuminated with something which, this time at least, Newman need not have been perplexed whether to attribute to habit or to intention, to art or to nature. She had the air of a woman who has stepped across the frontier of friendship and, looking around her, finds the region vast. A certain checked and controlled exaltation seemed mingled with the usual level radiance of her glance. [3rd ed. (Boston: James R. Osgood and Co., 1877), p. 160.]

Even the "exaltation" she feels as she responds to Newman's proposal to make her "perfectly free" is "checked and controlled." And it is a question whether nature and spontaneity or art and control will win out. Finally, of course, Claire simply refuses to choose between her family and Newman; she remains divided, and the tensions within her remain unresolved. She is, to the end, half-American, half-European—that "free spirit" which is unattached, unconsolidated, "uncertain" in a world in which the aggressors of the New World and of the Old go after the things they want with an assurance as bold as it is frightening. She lives in a warlike world in which rival empires compete for dominion. Newman, the "powerful specimen of an American" who "had come out of the war with a brevet of brigadier-general," who looks "like a grenadier on parade" and has a "readiness for aggression or for defense" (pp. 2, 25, 3, 60), is pitted against the fixed, unyielding Bellegardes, maintaining their citadel of propriety against all assaults. All of James's later treatments of life as a war between imperious rivals for the soul of the unattached "free spirit" are anticipated in this early work.

Yet some of the richest symbolic families of the later work have hardly been introduced. There is, for example, almost no thoroughgoing conception of life as an affair of purely financial calculation—no established symbolism of counting, measurement, addition, accumulation, banking—though in revising the novel for the New York edition James was to add a few metaphors of this type. There is only a muted conception of life as a struggle for survival, and very little animal or circus symbolism is introduced. The symbolism of the garden makes an appearance but is not developed. And although James was focusing on the theme of appearance and reality, he had not yet seen the whole of life as exhibiting the sordid concern with "show," and the elaborate play on the words *see, look, notice, show, exhibit,* and *expose,* the sort of recurrent sounding of that leitmotif which all the later novels illustrate, could hardly be predicted from this early book. Not only was the palette of the symbolist less rich than that at his disposal later on; the brushwork was more mechanical, more conservative, more inhibited than that of the major phase. James had not learned in 1877 how to "let himself go."

He was to make a very significant advance in his handling of the symbolism of *Portrait of a Lady.* Indeed, he was to approach, at moments, exactly the sort of rendering of the ambiguities, the admixture of the spontaneous and the artificial, the natural and the ideal, the fair and foul, the light and the dark, that he was to perfect in the novels of the major phase. The "spontaneous young woman from Albany," who is "very natural," whose soul has, as she thinks, a "garden-like quality," becomes the portrait, cold, fixed, finished. The workings of James's imagination, as he develops the symbolism and structure of *The Portrait* are remarkably similar to those of other imaginations that have focused on the nature-art opposition: to Hawthorne's, as we have noted, in *The Scarlet Letter* and *The Marble Faun;* to Wallace Stevens's in virtually all of his poetry; to Joseph Conrad's in half a dozen novels; to Thomas Mann's in *Tonio Kröger, Death in Venice,* and *Doctor Faustus;* to Emily Brontë's in *Wuthering Heights.* In all of these works—and in dozens more that might be named—nature is represented as wild, unrestrained, free; art, or the products of artifice, including social institutions, conventions, forms—civilization itself—is contained, limited, ordered, restrained. Natural creatures are free to move about, to dance and frolic in their sunny green world, the world whose chief symbols are the sun and the garden; in the world of art, of society, all is limitation and fixity, all is enclosed, frozen, fixed, finished. Nature is unguarded, spontaneous, uncouth; art and society impose a thousand precautions, rules, proprieties, conventions, laws—and prisons to enforce the laws. Nature is ever new, ever alive and fresh; art has the stillness of death, and in the old world, the world of great art and great museums, it is the past, it is the old masters, it is the dead, it is Death itself that is worshipped.

Once the symbolizing imagination goes to work on equations such as these, the proliferations run in surprisingly similar channels. But the ingenious development of a symbolism is of course never sufficient to give power and beauty to a work of fiction. The symbolism must function in the artistic whole, and it must function both as meaning and as an element in the dynamics of the action. It must deepen our sense of what is at stake in the action, everywhere enhancing the expressiveness of the work at as many points as possible; and it must participate in the *movement* of the whole, must generate the proper expectations or proper apprehensions, or sharpen ironic reversals, and everywhere must underscore, define, reinforce the major effects that the artist seeks. James's success in this, in *The Portrait*, let us say straight out, is indisputable. It is a remarkable book. And if it was to seem a bit ghostly and Victorian to the James who in 1896 remarked that he had "bloodier things en tête," it was, as he saw in his preface to the New York edition, a splendid piece of architecture, a solid and square edifice, built brick by brick. Not the least impressive aspect of this solid structure is the perfect employment of the symbolism as meaning and as an element in the action. Lacking its informing symbolism, *The Portrait of a Lady* would be neither as comprehensively intelligent nor as moving an image of life as it is.

The central question on which the action hangs is, stated simply, whether Isabel Archer will act in a manner commensurate with all the high hopes and expectations she arouses in intelligent people of good will, or whether she will be injured, trapped, forced into a base and servile condition. James gives his heroine every opportunity: he makes her one of the freest natural spirits in the Western world, a woman not attached or held either by an American or a European provincialism, and, moreover, blessed by wealth, able to taste all the possibilities of life: to venture as far as the human spirit endowed with almost every conceivable blessing *can* venture. And then James reveals, horribly, her enslavement to the base material earth, the world of mere appearances. Seeking expansion and unlimited vistas, Isabel gets a cold cell in Osmond's prison, the Palazzo Roccanera. Seeking brilliant achievement and "greatness," she gets darkness and pettiness. Seeking freedom—seeking to fly high above the cages of a sordid American or European materialism—sordid arrangements, sordid forms, a sordid and sterile worldliness of fallen and cynical creatures—she finds herself condemned to live *for* the world, for the invidious, for convention and propriety and all the appearances. Seeking everything, Isabel gets "nothing, nothing, nothing."

The intensity of the novel's effect—the dread or horror peculiar to it—is overwhelmingly the result of these reversals. And it is largely through his symbolism and through action which has symbolic structure that James is able to deepen and sharpen our sense of the appalling distortion and perversion of Isabel's "natural mission."

The novel begins in a very leisurely way: the evil that occurs later will be the more intense because we first find ourselves in a world so easy, so charming, so genial, that malignancy seems impossible in it. Gardencourt is serene, and the gentlemen gathered on the lawn are good-humored and easy. But James is already building his symbolic edifice: the garden and the court, nature and art commingle. We see an "English picture," a house with a "rich red front" and a "smooth, dense turf" which "seemed but an extension of a luxurious interior."[8]

> The great still oaks and beeches flung down a shade as dense as that of velvet curtains; and the place was furnished, like a room, with cushioned seats, with rich-coloured rugs, with the books and papers that lay upon the grass. [3:3–4]

The mingling of art and nature is ambiguous, and the ambiguity stirs the faintest doubt. *Is* there a ghost at Gardencourt? Is all natural and easy, or is all dense shade and artifice?

When Isabel appears on the scene, she, too, exhibits this double aspect. She sits with "*white* hands . . . folded upon her *black* dress" (3:21). Though her "*flexible* figure [turns] itself easily this way and that," her smile is "a clear, *still* smile" (3:21). She is like "a free greyhound," is "willowy," and we see her "rustling, quickly moving" (3:39, 61); she is "fond of [her] liberty," and as a small girl has protested against the "laws" of the primary school (3:24, 29). Yet the "elation of liberty" has been coupled with the "pain of exclusion" from a school in which childish voices are heard "repeating the multiplication table" (3:29–30); and for all her adventurousness, she "had never opened the bolted door" of the "office" in which, as a child, she secludes herself, that "chamber of disgrace for old pieces of furniture" (3:29–30). What is it that she wants, then? Liberty or laws, originality or repetitions and copying, motion and quickness or a bolted prison full of mouldering furniture? Is she, as Ralph Touchett affirms, "very natural," or is she (as Ralph also observes) a "Titian" (3:58, 86)? She herself hopes to bridge the gulf between appearance and reality, artifice and nature: "Her life should always be in harmony with the most pleasing impression she should produce; she would be what she appeared, and she would appear what she was." But in James's most deliberate summation of her character, it is the "mixture" and the "combination" in her that is stressed:

> Altogether, with her meagre knowledge, her inflated ideals, her confidence at once innocent and dogmatic, her temper at once exacting and indulgent, her mixture of curiosity and fastidiousness, of vivacity and indifference, her desire to look very well and to be if possible even better, her determination to see, to try, to know, her combination of the delicate, desultory, flame-like spirit and the eager and personal creature of conditions: she would be an easy victim of scientific criticism if she were not intended to awaken on the reader's part an impulse more tender and more purely expectant. [3:69]

The spirit is "desultory" as well as "flame-like"; and her "infinite hope that she should never do anything wrong" (3:68) may be a noble desire for perfection; but it may also be the social animal's fear of the *faux pas*, the trepidation of the timorous "creature of conditions," the creature determined to "look very well." Isabel, like all of James's free spirits, is divided. A part of her is indisputably American; yet to Americans she appears "foreign."

Very delicate are the intimations of evil in the Old World in which Isabel finds herself. Smooth and harmonious appearances mask the Old World cynicism and enslaving conventions. To Isabel, Gardencourt is part of a dream, a fairy tale: "a picture made real" (3:73). It is, to the reader alert to James's symbolism, but the token of the world, the heavy, enslaving world of darkness and "property":

> Her uncle's house seemed a picture made real; no refinement of the agreeable was lost upon Isabel; the rich perfection of Gardencourt *at once revealed a world and gratified a need.* The large, *low* rooms, with *brown* ceilings and *dusky* corners, the deep embrasures and curious casements, the *quiet* light on dark, polished panels, the deep greenness outside, that seemed always peeping in, the sense of well-ordered privacy in the centre of a "property"—a place where sounds were felicitiously accidental, where the tread was muffled by *the earth itself* and in thick mild air all friction dropped out of contact and all shrillness out of talk—these things were much to the taste of our young lady, whose taste played a considerable part in her emotions. [3:73; italics mine]

Her taste plays, indeed, too considerable a part in her emotions, and she is attracted here to what is low, dark, still, exclusive: a materialism so intense that the "earth itself" is inevitably suggested. It is a world of invidious distinctions, of wealth and property and position. It is a world of the conventional, in which "They've got everything pretty well fixed," as Mr. Touchett says. "It's all settled beforehand . . ." (3:78). No freedom, no spontaneity, no soaring; all is stamped out, copied, repeated, passed on, and one has only to accept, surrender. Like Adam Verver, Mr. Touchett, with his ivory-smooth head and his folded hands, presides passive and godlike over this estate, perpetually sitting, a strange combination himself of the New World and the Old, a man who speaks with an "aged, innocent voice," and who has surrendered himself to comfort and "conditions."

Apprehension is raised as a number of people, struck by Isabel's remarkable spirit, ask what she is going to "do with herself" (3:87). Isabel's chief dread is that she will appear "narrow-minded" (3:83). Her "fine free nature" cannot tolerate limitations, and desires "free expansion" (3:87). And it is for this reason, of course, that she must refuse both Lord Warburton and Caspar Goodwood. She may be attracted to the type of the Englishman or of the American. In her largeness, she may like them both, just as she likes those opposites Henrietta Stackpole and the Misses Molyneaux. But all these types are, or seem to be, *mere* types, copies, and all represent, for Isabel, an intolerable limitation, confinement within an established and rigid system: encagement.

Warburton, this "specimen of an English gentleman" (3:90), may be a reformer and a radical, "a condemner of ancient ways" (3:95), but he is still cut to a pattern—is a "nobleman of the newest pattern." For all his virtue, he is still the world's creature, "knowing almost everything in the world" (3:97). Isabel cannot decide whether she's on the side of the old or the new—she's both revolutionist and loyalist (3:100)—but she sees that Warburton, whatever he is, has a fixed "position" to maintain (3:98, 102). His old house, Lockleigh, brings to mind, again, the locks and bolts of her little office—the office which she escapes when she ventures abroad; and, like Gardencourt, Lockleigh is "a noble picture" (3:108). Again, Isabel may admire Warburton's sisters, but they too are cut to the pattern, "since there were fifty thousand young women in England who exactly resembled them" (3:104). Indeed, they are the round world's round smooth prisoners, "round, quiet and contented, and their figures, also of a generous roundness, were encased in sealskin jackets" (3:104). Isabel thinks it is "lovely to be so quiet and reasonable and satisfied" (3:105), but she also fears the "world of hereditary quiet" (3:180), and fears the "peace . . . the possessions, a deep secularity and a great exclusion" (3:189). She senses that England, "this minute island," is too small for her (3:178); indeed, the world "comes to strike one as rather small" (3:227). And she comes to see Warburton's admiration as "an aggression almost to the degree of an affront" (3:143):

> He appeared to demand of her something that no one else, as it were, had presumed to do. What she felt was that a territorial, a political, a social magnate had conceived the design of drawing her into the system in which he rather invidiously lived and moved. A certain instinct, not imperious, but persuasive, told her to resist—murmured to her that virtually she had a system and an orbit of her own. [3:144]

In fact, though she is "lost in admiration of her opportunity," she sees his proposal as drawing her into "a vast cage" (3:153); and James's references to Warburton's boots and hunting crop, together with the buried allusion to aggression in the lord's name, reinforce the idea of a coercive and enslaving warrior: an anticipation, in truth, of such later aggressors as Owen Gereth, Paul Muniment, Colonel Assingham, or a dozen military gentlemen whom James introduces as much for their symbolic value as for their interest as part of the human comedy.

After rejecting Warburton, Isabel has, in London, "a feeling of freedom . . . as she wandered through the great city" (3:200). Yet there are limitations everywhere. Ralph's place in Winchester Square is a "limited enclosure" (a bit like the "court" of Gardencourt), a place where no *"fête-champêtre"* could occur (3:200–201). Isabel and Ralph sit in "the enclosure"—there are "rusty rails" surrounding them—and the scene is "perfectly still" and "limited" (3:204–5). There is no light, and the shutters and blinds of the windows in the houses are "closed" (3:204–5). Yet Isabel does not precisely dislike this perfect quietude. As always, she is *drawn* to the fatal passivity, the fatal quietude of merely looking and accepting. "I'm not in the least an adventurous spirit," she tells Ralph; and he remarks that she wants to "see, but not to feel" (3:214, 213).

Caspar Goodwood, when he arrives in London, constitutes, like Warburton, a threat to her freedom. It is the American cage into which he would put her, and he is "plated and steeled, armed essentially for aggression" (3:220). All the imagery James uses to depict him suggests hardness, stiffness, rigidity. He is the man of wood, the man of "infallible mould" (3:139); the "different fitted parts of him" are like plates of steel (3:165). His eyes are of "remarkable fixedness" and his jaw is of "somewhat angular mould" (3:47). And not only is he at home in the world of aggression and appearances, but like Henrietta Stackpole he invariably fixes people with his eyes. He sits "with his eyes fixed" on Isabel (3:217), eyes that "seemed to shine through the vizard of a helmet" (3:218). He tells her, "I hate to lose sight of you!" (3:222) and refers to his project of "keeping [her] in sight" (3:223). Isabel remonstrates, "It's . . . being out of your sight—that I like"; and: "I should feel you were watching me, and I don't like that—I like my liberty too much" (3:227–28). She will not surrender to this second aggressor; yet she is attracted, once more, to the cage, the coffin of peace; Goodwood sometimes seems to her "a clear and quiet harbour enclosed by a brave granite breakwater" (3:323). But her encounter with him in London ends with her symbolic flight into a dark apartment where she can make out "the masses of furniture, the dim shining of the mirror and the looming of the big four-posted bed" (3:231). Once again—the point must be stressed, for it anticipates a major element in James's psychology—James suggests that it is perfect quietude she wants, the quietude of a nun, of a convent or prison, or a return to the "office" of her childhood where the furniture is stored: the quietude, in short, of a collector's world, a world of motionless things, of art, of peace, of death, a world in which there are no freedoms and no risks. James is very clear about this. Isabel wishes to be like a piece of furniture, perhaps like the holland-covered furniture at Mr. Touchett's place in Winchester Square: she would "case herself again in brown holland" (3:232), thus escaping the world of light and action, the world in which the aggressors move and seek their prey. In this, Isabel anticipates Fleda Vetch, whose fear of Owen Gereth compels her again and again to run away from him. Unlike Henrietta Stackpole, who has no difficulty whatever functioning in the world of action and aggression—who, on the contrary, is constantly on the offensive, fixing people with her remarkable eyes, getting "hold of" people, putting them in her pocket (3:116–17)—Isabel trembles at the "exercise of her power" and is afraid of "freedom" (3:232, 320).

Once she has rejected Warburton and Goodwood, those two "images of energy" (3:322), Isabel is absolutely free of narrow, provincial threats. She can expand, she can soar, there are no limits. But James beautifully drops one warning after another, and the novel now begins to move with quickened suspense and apprehension. Henrietta Stackpole sows a seed of doubt: "You're drifting to some great mistake," she tells Isabel (3:235); but of course we hardly take seriously her warning. In chapter 18, however, when Isabel meets Madame Merle, submerged warnings flash dimly in the imagery. Images associated with the Molyneaux sisters return: Madame Merle is a "smooth woman; everything in her person was round and replete" (3:249). She is "round" and "ample" and her smile is "world-wide" because she is the "great round world itself" (3:248, 362); she lives for the world, for convention and propriety, for the greater glory of matter. She takes "the worldly view" (3:289) and she *knows* the world: "I think I know my Europe," she says (3:276), and Mrs. Touchett agrees, "She knows absolutely everything *on earth* there is to know" (3:277; italics mine). She may have "quick and free motions," but her manner expresses "repose," and her talents are "enclosed" (3:249–50). Isabel, we are told, "wandered, as by the wrong side of the wall of a private garden, round the enclosed talents, accomplishments, aptitudes of Madame Merle" (3:270). The imagery hints that Isabel, in wishing to be like Madame Merle, will not expand but will enter a prison, another place of *exclusion*. And James reinforces the fear of entrapment when he says, a page later, "I may not count over all the links in the chain which led Isabel to think of Madame Merle's situation as aristocratic" (3:271).

The fear connected with Madame Merle's association with Isabel is augmented significantly as the contrasts between nature and art, the new and the old, light and dark, flying and crawling, expansion and contraction, life and death are worked into the symbolism of the next several chapters. The danger of artifice and appearance is everywhere. Madame Merle is "not natural," is "too perfectly the social animal" who has "rid herself of every remnant of ... tonic wildness" (3:274); she is a "charming surface" and, as she says to Isabel, "A woman ... has to remain on the surface and, more or less, to crawl" (3:280). Equally ominous, to the reader alert to the developing symbolic equations, is her remark that she is "old and stale and faded," that she was "born before the French Revolution" and belongs to "the old, old world" (3:279). But Isabel, ironically, sees such remarks as testifying to a larger, a more complete spirit than that which she possesses. Nor does Isabel grasp the implications of Madame Merle's view that the self is indistinguishable from the "shell," the "whole envelope of circumstances," the *things* that surround one. Good Emersonian, Isabel affirms the primacy of the spirit: "Nothing that belongs to me is any measure of me; everything's on the contrary a limit, a barrier, and a perfectly arbitrary one" (3:287–88); but it does not occur to her that Madame Merle could be leagued with the limiting forces of the material earth, and Isabel's love of freedom is all "theoretic."

When Mr. Touchett dies and Isabel is given the seventy thousand pounds, the danger to her mounts rapidly and is subtly suggested in an offhand remark of Mrs. Touchett's: "She has a look as solemn, these three days, as a Cimabue Madonna" (3:300). She will in fact *become* such a portrait, become such a "madonna" to Pansy, and James, in marrying her to a "sterile dilettante," may be suggesting that she remains, somehow, like the madonna, virginal.

She journeys to Paris, there to meet various creatures who have surrendered to the Old World. There are the Luces, for example, who (like the Tristrams in *The American*) keep to the "well-cushioned corner" (the "dusky corners" of Gardencourt and Isabel's "office," those havens of perfect quietude and security, keep reappearing throughout the novel) and who prefer the Empire and are, as they say, of 1830 (3:304). There is Edward Rosier, whom Isabel knew as an obedient "neat little male child" with a "bonne all his own," a child who (like young Henry James) "never went to the edge of the lake" (3:306). Rosier, like poor Pansy, has never known freedom or spontaneity. He is the world's humble servant, a conservative, a collector with "old Spanish altarlace" in his apartment, a gentleman who "knows" Paris as Madame Merle knows her Europe and who is, as Henrietta sees him, "most unnatural" (3:309). Rosier will seek to add Pansy to his collection as Osmond adds Isabel to *his*. But observe: even Henrietta is now becoming ensnared by the Old World and is in danger of "drifting toward those abysses of sophistication" (3:313). Indeed, Henrietta now "knows" Versailles (3:314); and she has attracted that other inveterate worldling, that "perfect man of the world," Mr. Bantling (3:313), a gentleman who is "made ... for her use" and who has a "remarkable knowledge of Paris" (3:312, 311). And is not Bantling, too, of the warlike earth—a former colonel and thus, like Caspar Goodwood or Warburton, equipped for aggression? The geniality of this novel is deceptive.

As Isabel moves toward her encounter with Gilbert Osmond, the reader, assimilating all these evidences of Americans seduced by the Old World, foresees a similar doom for Isabel—supplies the middle term, "Isabel, too, is an American exposed to these seductions." Will she, too, have to "crawl"? Mrs. Touchett asks her to "understand how much [she is] at liberty" (3:315); Ralph tells her, "Spread your wings; rise above the ground" (3:319). And it is at this point that she meets that *homme du monde,* Osmond, the man who lives for the base world at which he sneers.

Osmond's house, with its "cross-barred" windows, its furniture, and its *objets d'art,* is the cage in which she will be trapped. It is the cold house of art, "composing well" (3:325), owned by the man who is "artistic through and through," whose face is "modelled and composed" or "overdrawn, retouched," or is like a "fine gold coin" (3:352, 376). There is not an ounce of freedom or nature in him; he has been stamped out by the world, by convention and propriety. Yet ironically he seems original: "he suggested, fine gold coin as he was, no stamp nor emblem of the common mintage that provides for general circulation; he was the elegant complicated medal struck off for a special occasion" (3:329). But of course he is a copy of all the other materialists; he can only copy; that is why we see him later copying the portrait engraved on an antique coin.

He is, as several critics have pointed out, very much like George Eliot's Grandcourt; and there is an additional element in him that reminds one of Hawthorne's Chillingsworth: he blights whatever he touches, he is "malignant." Thus a significant part of our fear for Isabel issues from our sense of what Osmond has done to his daughter, Pansy. Her face "painted with a fixed intensely sweet smile," Pansy is the Portrait of a *Jeune Fille*, a collector's joy, appealing to the man who regards her as a "consummate piece" and a "Dresden-china doll"—Edward Rosier (4:90). Imprisoned from birth, "formed and finished for her tiny place in the world," indeed "made for the world" and "impregnated with the idea of submission" (3:401, 333, 337–38), Pansy is not really alive, not really free at all, but appears with "a kind of finish," with her "hands locked before her" or "folded together" (3:367, 387). She has been made into nothing: "like a sheet of blank paper" (3:401). If Osmond has made his daughter into a blank, what will he do to Isabel?

James plays ironically with the motifs of blankness, smallness, and nothingness. The blank Pansy is "diminutive" and has small hands: her place in the world is to be "tiny." Osmond does "little" watercolors (3:347) or composes a little sonnet. He finds Saint Peter's "too large" and he is, he says, "content with little" (3:427, 382). This man, whom Isabel supposes to know "everything" and to understand "everything," who seems not at all provincial (3:377) but somehow larger than Warburton or a Goodwood, is in fact nothing. His house has a blank look. Madame Merle, when she first mentions him to Isabel, says that he is "not anything," is "very indolent," and quotes Osmond, " 'Oh, I do nothing; I'm too deadly lazy' " (3:281). Archetype of a long line of absolutely passive leeches who infest the Jamesian world, Osmond is repeatedly described in this manner. The Countess Gemini sounds the note clearly: there is "nothing, nothing, nothing" of any distinction or significance in Osmond's past (3:391). "He is nothing at all," says Ralph; and Osmond himself admits that he is "nobody" (3:427). Again, when Caspar Goodwood asks who Osmond is, Isabel is driven to say that he is "nobody and nothing but a very good and very honourable man" and that he has done "nothing at all" and is a "perfect nonentity" (4:46–47). Later Mrs. Touchett warns Isabel, "There's nothing *of* him" (4:57). The word *nothing* recurs like a refrain in a novel by Hemingway, and poor Isabel, whenever she hears it, interprets it to mean *everything!*

The process by which she is trapped and enslaved is attended by a very deep dread. We see her enslavement coming, its progress is subtle but unmistakable—and horribly inevitable. At her first meeting with Osmond, there is a hint of the immobility she will come to assume when she has been finished as a work of art: she sits quietly, "as if she had been at the play," attending to Osmond and Madame Merle; and she is so restrained, so guiltless of any tonic wildness, that Madame Merle congratulates her: "You were just as one would have wished you" (3:357). Later, at Osmond's house, she is afraid to "put herself forward" (3:368), she is "very careful" (3:379), and her natural desire for perfection is now converted into the social animal's fear of bad taste and the *faux pas.* Most ominous of all is the information that "she waited, with a certain unuttered contentedness, to have her movements directed" (3:374). Thoroughly intimidated by Osmond's gospel of taste and propriety—that perversion of his "natural mission" (3:376)—Isabel lets him direct her steps into the garden. For the first time in her life she submits to another person's direction—and she is to Osmond as he is to those powerful rulers of the earth who permit least freedom to their subjects, the pope, the emperor of Russia, and the sultan of Turkey: a blinded devotee.

The warnings multiply. Countess Gemini likens Osmond and Madame Merle to Machiavelli and Vittoria Colonna; "You're capable of anything, you and Osmond," she says to Madame Merle. And she warns Isabel against her brother. Again, the imagery of a fall, of crawling, is reinstated when Madame Merle tells Osmond, "I'm frightened at the abyss into which I shall have cast her"

(3:411). And the ambiguities connected with Osmond's contemplation of Isabel suggest a terrifying violation of her soul and body by this sterile dilettante. She will "figure in his collection of choice objects," like "handled ivory to the palm" (4:9, 11). A refrain in the novel, introduced very early when Ralph Touchett first talks to his mother about Isabel, is the question: What do you want to do with her? Now, horrifyingly, it becomes clear that Osmond fully intends to make her into the frozen portrait. When he declares his love, in chapter 29, the image of the prison door reappears: "The tears came into her eyes: this time they obeyed the sharpness of the pang that suggested to her somehow the slipping of a fine bolt— backward, forward, she couldn't have said which" (4:18). And in chapter 30 Isabel's "pilgrimage in solitude" to see Pansy reinforces the fear that Osmond will do to Isabel what he has done to his daughter: will convert her into a creature with "no will, no power to resist, no sense of her own importance" (4:27).

Yet for a time Isabel continues to enjoy her sense of freedom. In chapter 31, after the visit of her sister, Mrs. Ludlow—a visit which has confined Isabel's movements "to a narrow circle" (4:32) —we learn that Isabel "had never had a keener sense of freedom, of the absolute boldness and wantonness of liberty" (4:35); "the world lay before her—she could do whatever she chose" (4:36). And so she travels "rapidly and recklessly" over the world (4:38). Yet again a fear is stirred when she perceives, on her journey, that Madame Merle's "freshness" is "slightly mechanical, carried about in its case like the fiddle of the virtuoso, or blanketed and bridled like the 'favourite' of the jockey" (4:39). And when, returning to Florence, she accepts Osmond's proposal, fear rises as she persistently ignores the warnings of her friends. Ralph is very explicit: "You're going to be put into a cage," he tells her (4:65), and he entreats her to soar and sail "in the bright light," not to "come down so easily" and "drop to the ground" (4:69–70). When he leaves Isabel, having failed to make her see that Osmond is "small" and "a sterile dilettante" (4:71), he feels "the lurking chill of the high-walled court" of the Palazzo Crescentini (4:76).

Particularly frightening are the reflections and the remarks of Osmond in chapter 35. Immensely "pleased with his young lady," he reflects that "the softness" of her will "be all for one's self," and

he regards her intelligence as "a silver plate . . . that he might heap
up with ripe fruits. . . . He could tap her imagination with his
knuckle and make it ring" (4:79). The presentiment that he will
inflict some unspeakable cruelty upon her is again raised in his
remark that he "used to have morbid, sterile, hateful fits of hunger,
of desire" (4:81); and presently we learn that he has already produced an alteration in Isabel: "The desire for unlimited expansion
had been succeeded in [Isabel's] soul by the sense that life was
vacant without some private duty that might gather one's energies
to a point" (4:82). A very small point indeed! And equally ominous
are Pansy's observation that Isabel and Osmond are "both so quiet
and so serious" (4:82) and the Countess Gemini's condemnation of
her brother and her warning that the marriage will be a "steel
trap."

In handling the effect of the marriage upon Isabel, James works
beautifully with understatement, ambiguity, and incremental
glimpses of the appalling truth of what has occurred, to create a
maximum impression of horror. He *builds* horror, and, like Hemingway, shows us only the frightening tip of the iceberg. The *full*
horror of what has happened between Isabel and Osmond—of
what he has done to her—is largely submerged, a matter of conjec-
ture. We feel it to be immense, and our sense of the extent of the
injury mounts almost in proportion as we are obliged to infer what
has occurred—in proportion as Isabel refuses to speak of her mi-
sery, maintains her "mask," and—most horribly of all—works for
a time as Osmond's instrument in the ugly business of marrying
Pansy. Her own life blasted, Isabel joins in the blasting of another
life!

With respect to the basic theme of the novel, what occurs in the
second half raises in a fresh way the question of whether Isabel can
achieve maximum freedom: it *tests*, once again, her capacity for
"rising" and "soaring." In the face of Osmond's cold ceaseless pressure—a pressure to which she at first yields—she must, once again,
assert her independence: must act not as Osmond's agent and manipulator, not as the world's slave, but as the spontaneous, autonomous spirit she aspires to be. Yet before she can act, she must
realize that she has indeed become a victim, the base servant of
darkness, materialism, and convention.

We discover the full truth very slowly. When Rosier goes to see

Madame Merle (in chapter 36), we learn that there is a conflict between Isabel and Osmond. Then we see the palace in which the Osmonds live—"the house of darkness, the house of dumbness, the house of suffocation"—the Palazzo Roccanera, which is "a dungeon to poor Rosier's apprehensive mind" (4:196, 100). And we wait apprehensively for a glimpse of Isabel. When she appears she is dressed in "black velvet" and is "framed in the gilded doorway ... the picture of a gracious lady" (4:106). Her face is a "mask." Her smile is "fixed and mechanical," serenity is "painted" on her face (4:142). She tells Warburton that she "can never propose anything" but accepts "what others propose" (4:131). And again: "She appeared now to think there was nothing worth people's either differing about or agreeing upon" (4:143). This, after James's early depictions of her intellectual volatility, her spontaneity, her fervent aspiration to know the truth that makes men free, is frightening in itself. Terrible must have been the experience that could so alter her. But when she begins to work for Osmond, when, like the other base slaves of the world, she proceeds to "arrange" and "manage," to bully and coerce, the perversion of her soul from its "natural mission" reaches an intensity of ugliness. Osmond presses her to bring about Pansy's marriage to Warburton, and Isabel reflects, in a "strangely cynical" way, that the matter can "be arranged" (4:175–76). Osmond tells her that she can "manage" the affair (4:185), and Isabel, utterly surrendering her independence, sets about the sordid work of fettering Pansy to a man she does not love, of handling the girl like an object, "as you would put a letter in the post-office" (4:205).

The symbolism strongly reinforces our sense of the perversion of Isabel's soul. Symbols of darkness, heaviness, and constriction are everywhere. "Her light step drew a mass of drapery behind it" (4:143). The "infinite vista of a multiplied life" has become "a dark, narrow alley with a dead wall at the end," and she has gone "downward and earthward, into realms of restriction and depression where the sound of other lives, easier and freer, was heard as from above, and where it seemed to deepen the feeling of failure" (4:189). The "dusk" has "steadily deepened" (4:190). A "rigid system" has closed about her, and she, who "had pleaded the cause of freedom," is now "shut up with an odour of mould and decay" (4:199). The "circle" of her life is "blasted" (4:203). In chapter 45, we see her "smoothing her gloves," and the notion of freedom appears in a sense strangely twisted: they are "long, loose gloves on which she could *freely expend herself*" (4:249). For Pansy, the "martyr decked out for sacrifice," Isabel has become, at this point, "the Madonna" (4:254, 256).

But it is in this chapter that Isabel's plunge toward the heart of darkness comes to a halt. When, "bitter and angry," she works for Osmond to persuade Pansy to reject Rosier, when she tells the girl that her having so little money is "a reason for looking for more," Isabel feels so acutely her dishonesty and insincerity that she is "grateful for the dimness of the room" (4:257). She can go no further: Osmond has done his utmost, and a counteraction is inevitable. In chapter 46, then, Isabel confronts Osmond, and it is clear that all respect for him has vanished. "He was going down—down; the vision of such a fall made her almost giddy: that was the only pain. He was too strange, too different; he didn't touch her" (4:275). She will remain with him, accepting the consequences of her solemn vows, even after she realizes that he has married her for her money. But she will work for him no longer. She will work instead, James implies, for freedom. When she sees Pansy in the convent, that "well-appointed prison," she promises that she will not desert the girl (4:374). She believes, we know, in keeping her promises. She will not abandon Pansy to Osmond, will preside neither at Pansy's "surrender of a personality" to the church nor at her surrender to a rich nobleman of Osmond's choosing. She will not, although the vision of death is appealing—death like "a cool bath in a marble tank, in a darkened chamber, in a hot land" (4:391)—will not hide from her responsibility. The moments when "she sat in her corner, so motionless, so passive, simply with the sense of her being carried, so detached from hope and regret, that she recalled to herself one of those Etruscan figures couched upon the receptacle of their ashes" (4:391)—these will vanish, and she will "live."

After Caspar Goodwood's final effort to win her away from Osmond, after that encounter with "each thing in his hard manhood that had displeased her, each aggressive fact of his face, his figure, his presence," she is again "free" (4:436). She escapes this enslaver once again. The image of "the world" as a "mighty sea" in which she might sink (4:435) fuses with the idea of Goodwood's attempted "act of possession," and when Isabel finds that she has not been drowned by the world, by Goodwood, she is ready once again to act independently. Will she ever be submerged by the world? She returns to Osmond's prison, but she returns not to obey but to redeem her promise to Pansy: perhaps to strike a few blows for Pansy's freedom.

And yet the division in her nature that we have seen from the beginning can scarcely be forgotten. She *does* return to a prison— to a counterpart of the "office," another dark corner, a place of quiet and peace. A part of her still craves that peace, that stillness, that utter passivity. If she has taken one great step in leaving Osmond against his wish, she cannot take the second step. To the end she remains, for all her admirable freedom, a creature who harbors a wish to retreat from the battle of life; who can envy the "security of valuable 'pieces' which change by no hair's breadth, only grow in value, while their owners lose inch by inch youth, happiness, beauty" (4:403). For all her love of liberty, the spontaneous young lady from Albany has all along been half in love with easeful death. And her final decision testifies to the division in her nature that James has insisted upon from the beginning.

The method by which James leads Isabel to discovery of the truth about her marriage—that method which Joseph Warren Beach has described so admirably in his *The Method of Henry James* —is essentially incremental, a method of hinting, of implying through images or symbols, of piercing the bright, genial surface of human intercourse with point after point of dark intimation, until the accumulated impressions come together in a single revelation of the utter darkness below, behind, within, and the last illusion dies.

The world of *Portrait* is thus ambiguous—a maze of deceptions. The ambiguities are indeed so dense, so "bristling"—as James might have said—that the novel clearly anticipates a plunge into the total ambiguity of James's last great works. Now the fact is that James's handling of "the ambiguities" was already pervasive in *The Princess Casamassima* (1886), where, as John L. Kimmey has pointed out,[9] Hyacinth Robinson's "bewilderment" issues from his discovery of a world aswarm with contradictions; and any of the novels of the nineties might be taken to illustrate the preoccupation with the admixture of "bliss or bale." But we pass over these works in order to contemplate the luxuriant symbolism of "the major phase." The novels of that phase are, of course, gigantic symphonies, the orchestration of the chief motifs is complete. Everywhere the glittering appearance and the foul reality commingle. James's vocabulary is altered, and every word participates in the symbolism. Great new families are born, or the old families are extended in ingenious ways. Everywhere there are glints and gleams of irony. The sublimest virtue is depicted in metaphors of finance or of predation or mechanism. Love, honor, fidelity, kindness—all ironically appear in conjunction with shillings and pounds, masses and quantities, springs and wheels and levers. Nothing may be what it seems: what is high may be low; what is bright, dark; what is alive, dead; what is free, encaged. And even James's heroes and heroines are not spared the ironic dissection of the doubling symbols.

We can see how complete and how pervasively ironic is James's symbolism in the later novels if we look carefully at what is, for many mature readers, the most charming of the three—*The Ambassadors*. It is a book whose total "meaning" criticism has been slow to appreciate. The received interpretation of the novel has it that the remarkable transformation of James's hero consists in his emancipation from the narrowness of Woollett, Massachusetts, and his moral and emotional blossoming in the rather heady air of Paris, a Paris which Strether discovers to be finer, more charming, and far more ennobling than Woollett, darkly suspicious, can possibly imagine.[10] Strether's close relationships with Maria Gostrey and with Mme de Vionnet are, according to this interpretation, evidence of his growth in awareness and freedom, and the two women come to represent, for him and for the reader, a social and moral sensitivity that, in its richness and depth, cannot but be salutary. This conclusion, based chiefly upon the severest possible repudiation of Woollett, squares nicely with *some* of the evidence in the novel; but what many otherwise astute readers have not seen in *The Ambassadors* is that James's distrust of Paris is at least as violent as his distrust of Woollett, and that his view of Maria Gostrey and of Mme de Vionnet is by no means as sympathetic as it is usually made out to be. A close study of the novel's imagery and symbolism discloses a pervasive irony that deeply undercuts even the most extravagant praise of Paris and of its chief jewel, Mme de Vionnet. In truth, if we would describe the premises from

which the imagery and symbolism spring, we must, instead of
praising Paris at the expense of Woollett, recognize that both cities
represent, for Strether and for James, attitudes and meanings
which are both valuable and dangerous to the free soul. Woollett
is "the sacred rage," all beautiful devotion to duty, principle, morality; Paris is the beautiful capacity to enjoy, to feel, to respond, to
enlarge one's nature by opening one's eyes to the glorious richness
and variety of the external world. Woollett is all spirit and conscience; Paris is all worldliness, all eye—is light itself, the brilliance
of surfaces and things. Yet both cities, Strether comes to realize,
are, for all their strong claims upon the soul, but molds into which
"the jelly of consciousness" may be poured to harden and and, harden-
ing, to die. Thus Woollett, whatever its virtues, is also narrowness,
pride, lack of imagination and sympathy—it is all "fine cold
thought," all repudiation and denial of life; and Paris, despite its
great charm, is but the "vain Appearance," acquisitiveness, a surrender to conventional arrangements and conditions of an old and
cynical world. None of the people attached to either city are
capable of free choice, of spontaneity, of revising received attitudes and values: attachment to either city is therefore moral slavery. It is for this reason that the most important symbols in the
novel are (again) various prisons, traps, cages, molds. But since the
prison of Paris *appears* to offer (in a sense it does offer) freedom to
Strether's soul, the symbols are everywhere employed ironically,
and the discrepancy between the pleasant appearance and the appalling reality informs every page of the book. Strether's new
freedom may be his enslavement; the brilliance and charm of Paris
conceal an abyss. For the light of the city is "becoming, yet treacherous," it is "alternately dazzling and dusky." [11] White is, and is
not, black; fair is, and is not, foul. In a world in which it is so easy
for one to be deceived—a world in which rival empires vie with
each other for the possession of souls, each seeking to trap and hold
one within its own narrow system and way of life—the man who
would save himself must be nimble. In James, as in Wallace Stevens, "The Good Man Has No Shape," and in the most marvelous
irony of all the evasive Strether, the fifty-five-year-old man who
has all along been "had," used, imprisoned, throws off his chains,
enslaves the enslavers and, newborn, toddles off to live his own life,
the freest and youngest person in the book.

The novel begins with Strether's arrival in Europe with "such a consciousness of personal freedom as he had n't known for years" (21:4). Released from what he calls the "prison-house" of Woollett, he feels himself inclined to form new—and possibly dangerous—friendships; and he at once takes up with Maria Gostrey, though not without first casting "a rueful glance" at the hotel receptionist, "the lady in the glass cage" (21:7). James observes: "It was as if this personage had seen herself instantly superceded" (21:7). Strether escapes the lady in the glass cage but finds himself, a moment later, in the hands of Maria Gostrey. Her eyes "had taken hold of him straightway, measuring him up and down as if they knew how; as if he were human material they had already in some sort handled. Their possessor was in truth . . . the mistress of a hundred cases or categories, receptacles of the mind, subdivisions for convenience, in which, from a full experience, she pigeon-holed her fellow mortals with a hand as free as a compositor handling type. She was as equipped in this particular as Strether was the reverse . . . " (21:10–11). Strether acknowledges that he has fallen "utterly into [Maria's] hands" and indeed it is not long before the charming woman has backed him, literally, against a wall. In a thoroughly symbolic Chester, the description of which introduces such symbols of restraint and enslavement as the girdle, the cathedral, and the fixed masses of painting, Strether stands against the rampart of the "tortuous wall—girdle, long since snapped, of the little swollen city, *held half in place by careful civic hands*" (21:15; italics mine)—stands looking up at "the high red-brown mass" of the cathedral, a mass which has been "retouched and restored"; and under the spell of this Old World scene, "charming to his long-sealed eyes" (21:17), he very nearly, surrenders to Maria, who has asked him, "*Will* you give yourself up?" Besieged at the ramparts, Strether cannot quite go so far as to surrender; but he appeals to Maria, "Then get me out!" (21:19). Maria will get him out of the prison of Woollett—out of the feeling that he ought not to enjoy—but the danger is that she may only lure him into another prison—another glass cage, as it were.

Strether is indeed, good humoredly, "afraid" of her. He is aware that, from Waymarsh's rigid point of view, Maria must appear as

> a Jesuit in petticoats, a representative of the recruiting interests of the Catholic Church. The Catholic Church, for Waymarsh—that

was to say the enemy, the monster of bulging eyes and far-reaching, quivering groping tentacles—was exactly society, exactly the multiplication of shibboleths, exactly the discrimination of types and tones, exactly the wicked old Rows of Chester, rank with feudalism; exactly in short Europe. [21:41]

Strether's view of Waymarsh's fears is amused, but the passage must be noted with especial care, for it contains imagery which is to grow in importance as the novel proceeds. The most striking image, once again, is that of imprisonment, seizure: the octopus of Roman Catholicism and of Old World institutions threatens to take hold of Strether and to deprive him of his freedom. But the reference to the octopus's "bulging eyes" calls attention once again to the world of mere forms and appearances—the eye's world— as distinct from the world of inner light and the sacred rage. Strether, in his search for moral freedom and spontaneity, will frequently have to beware of being enslaved by the eye—by all brilliant appearances.

Imagery of light and darkness, implicit in the references to the bulging eyes, is quickly developed in the scene in which Strether, Maria, and Waymarsh go strolling in Chester. Waymarsh suddenly leaves his companions, dashes across the street, and is "engulfed in the establishment of a jeweller, behind whose glittering front he was lost to view" (21:42). Maria asks, "What's the matter with him?" and Strether, after studying the "close-hung dangling gewgaws" in the shop, answers that Waymarsh "has struck for freedom" (21:43) —a remark which, in the context, means that Waymarsh has found the burden of culture, the effort of appreciating, too strenuous, and has wished to be released from the evil and worldly clutches of Strether and Maria. "It's the sacred rage," Strether later explains, and the phrase is associated in his mind with the "periodical necessities" of the American to assert his freedom in the teeth of an ominous and enslaving Europe.

Yet the action and the imagery of the scene are unquestionably ironic. Waymarsh's peculiar way of asserting his freedom consists in his succumbing to a glittering appearance, the "glittering front" of the jeweller's shop—succumbing exactly as Strether succumbs, for a time, to Paris, which, as we are told in book 2, "hung before him this morning, the vast bright Babylon, like some huge iridescent object, a jewel brilliant and hard, in which parts were not to be discriminated nor differences comfortably marked. It twinkled and trembled and melted together, and *what seemed all surface one moment seemed all depth the next*" (21:89; italics mine). The surface, the front, is brilliant—supremely attractive. Yet Waymarsh is "engulfed in the establishment," "lost to view"—apparently seduced by the "close-hung dangling gewgaws." The danger for him is suggested in the delicate observation that the "Row" in which the jeweller's shop appears is "particularly crooked and huddled" (21:42). Has he, then, been "had"? We shall not discover the truth until much later, in book 10, when Waymarsh appears to inform Strether that Sarah wishes to speak to him. The Waymarsh whom Strether sees on this occasion is no longer the inflexible proponent of the sacred rage; he has been subtly corrupted by Europe, by, for example, Miss Barrace, the woman of the tortoise-shell glass and the "convex Parisian eyes." He is a "genial new pressing coaxing Waymarsh; a Waymarsh conscious with a different consciousness from any he had yet betrayed, and actually rendered by it almost insinuating" (22:187). Waymarsh, in truth, is no longer his own man; even his dress—the rose he wears in his buttonhole and the panama hat—have been chosen by Sarah. The sacred rage has become "too mixed with another consciousness—it was too smothered, as might be said, in flowers" (22:190). Moreover, the "right to the sacred rage . . . he Waymarsh also seemed in a manner, and at Mrs. Pocock's elbow, to have forfeited. . . . Waymarsh was having a good time—that was the truth that was embarrassing for him, and he was having it then and there, he was having it in Europe, he was having it under the very protection of circumstances of which he did n't in the least approve; all of which placed him in a false position, with no issue possible—none, at least, by the grand manner" (22:190). He is now "small." He has learned to tell fibs. Thoroughly compromised, he is thoroughly enchained. Unable to act from within, he permits himself to be guided now by Europe in the form of Miss Barrace, now by America in the form of Mrs. Newsome, whom Waymarsh, in his trepidation, has cabled. "[Mrs. Newsome's intention] had reached Waymarsh from Sarah, but it has reached Sarah from her mother, and *there was no break in the chain* by which it had reached *him* [Strether]" (22:189; italics mine except for the word *him*).

Waymarsh, then, is to lose his freedom. He will be softened, led astray, he will stick in the marsh that his name suggests. And ironically he will exchange positions with Strether: the free Waymarsh becomes the slave of Mrs. Newsome; the "kept" Strether becomes the free man.

The imagery of freedom and slavery is of course continued into book 2 of the novel, where the true ignominy of Strether's position is revealed for the first time. Not only has he permitted himself, in Woollett, to be "got hold of"; he has also consented to join in the sordid business of "getting hold of" others: he will "get hold of" Chad. But in rescuing the young man from "the wicked woman" who has presumably "got hold of" him, Strether cannot help feeling uneasy. "I'm acting with a sense, for him, of other things too," he tells Maria Gostrey. "Consideration and comfort and security—the general safety of *being anchored by a strong chain.* He wants, as I see him, to be protected. Protected I mean from life" (21:71; italics mine). But for a man who has made the terrible mistake of allowing himself to be "protected from life" and who is seeking unconsciously to make amends for the "opportunity lost" in the rearing of his deceased son, the notion of enchaining —of protecting from life—the young man who represents his own youth and is surrogate for his dead son is not only egregiously immoral; it is also psychologically intolerable, as we shall presently see.

Arriving in Paris, Strether is again assailed by a consciousness of freedom and begins to detect "the dregs of youth" in his cup. It occurs to him that he is there "on some chance of feeling the brush of the wing of the stray spirit of youth" (21:94); and it is not long afterward that, looking up, he beholds Little Bilham on the "perched privacy" of Chad's balcony: "There was youth in that, there was youth in the surrender to the balcony, there was youth for Strether at this moment in everything but his own business. ... The balcony, the distinguished front testified suddenly, for Strether's fancy, to something that was up and up ... on a level that he found himself at the end of another moment rejoicing to think that he might reach" (21:97–98). It is as if Strether might suddenly grow wings and fly up to the balcony, escaping thus the prison of his hotel, which "affected him somehow as all in-door chill, glass-roofed court and slippery staircase" (21:98)—quite as cold and slippery as Mme de Vionnet's apartment. But the bird who takes such a flight may of course be caged, and it must be

noted that the imagery is ambiguous. The balcony is elevated,
splendid, distinguished; on it stands a handsome young man, "light,
bright and alert." But it may be no more than a front—the bright
appearance which takes the eye and causes one to "surrender."
Indeed, all of Paris may be only that—"all surface one moment"
and "all depth the next." If Strether observes "the light flit, over
the garden-floor, of bare-headed girls"—if there is this natural
charm and spontaneity—he cannot fail to notice that these girls
appear "with the *buckled strap of oblong boxes*" (21:79; italics mine).
Indeed, he watches "little brisk figures, figures whose movement
was as the tick of the great Paris clock, take their smooth diagonal
from point to point; the air had a taste as of something mixed with
art, something that presented nature as a white-capped master-
chef" (21:79). The white cap conceals an unspeakable darkness of
slavery and automatism in the temporal world, the world of the
"great Paris clock."

    In book 3 the dangers multiply. Maria, who earlier has been
likened to Mary Stuart, now listens, as good Jesuit priestess, to
Strether's "confession." It will be some time before Strether sees
her with entire clarity—recognizes that she is not entirely honest
with him and is disturbed by her implied cynicism that freedom
and virtue cannot coexist. But even in these early chapters James
hints at darkness and duplicity and establishes an ominous association between the religious imagery introduced at Chester and the
imagery of worldliness and vain appearances. In Maria's "compact
and crowded little chambers, almost dusky as they first struck
him," Strether feels that "the lust of the eyes and the pride of life
had indeed thus their temple. It was the innermost nook of the
shrine—as brown as a pirate's cave. In the brownness were glints
of gold; patches of purple were in the gloom; objects all that
caught, through the muslin, with their high rarity, the light of the
low windows. Nothing was clear about them but that they were
precious . . ." (21:119–20). Maria—that she is named, like her good
friend Mme de Vionnet, after the virgin is scarcely accidental—is
a citizen of the empire of the eye, a worshipper of appearances and
things. And the chiaroscuro of her chambers, the duskiness, the
glints, the gloom, the light of the low windows, symbolize the
ironic and ambiguous admixture of beauty and corruption, appearance and reality. Strether, in fact, becomes increasingly aware of

the irony that there is a money-changer in the temple: "The sense
of how she was, in advance, always paying for something was
equalled, on Strether's part, only by the sense of how she was
always being paid; all of which made for his consciousness, in the
larger air, of a lively, bustling traffic, the exchange of such values
as were not for him to handle" (21:128–29). Maria's life is "more
charged with possessions even than Chad's or than Miss Barrace's"
(21:119). The relationship between materialism and "the lust of the
eyes" is strongly emphasized in the passage in which the vision of
Mrs. Newsome's gold, as James observes, "held for a little Miss
Gostrey's eyes, and she looked as if she heard the bright dollars
shovelled in" (21:66). And James stresses several times that Maria
is "dear," "expensive." Indeed, should Strether "surrender" to her
as she wants him to, he would have to pay the enormous price of
his freedom—freedom from worldliness.

The danger to Strether is further emphasized in the adroit handling of the imagery of theater and acting. The evil of the theater
has already been suggested in the scene at Chester in which
Strether observes that on the stage "a series of strong stamps had
been applied, as it were, from without; stamps that his observation
played with as, before a glass case on a table, it might have passed
from medal to medal and from copper to gold" (21:53). There is
no life, no spontaneity, no freedom in the performance of a role,
the reading of a script written by someone else. Even Strether, as
Mrs. Newsome's ambassador, cannot help feeling that he has "acted
his part" (21:149). But if in these early chapters he is one of the
actors, how much more is he acted upon! What he takes for a
spontaneous meeting with Little Bilham has, Maria tells him, been
"arranged." Maria, who "knew her theater," warns Strether that
Little Bilham "was acting—he is still—on his daily instructions"
(21:133). And it is, appropriately, in a box at the theater that Chad
makes his first appearance. He appears to be "smooth," a gentleman, but he may in fact be a brute, an animal, a pagan. He appears
to be young, yet in his submission to Paris—or is it to Woollett?
—he may be old. To some extent, the mixed light and dark of his
portrait remind one of Maria Gostrey's apartment: "In gleams, in
glances, the past did perhaps peep out of it [Strether's picture of
Chad]; but such lights were faint and instantly submerged. Chad
was brown and thick and strong, and, of old, Chad had been

rough" (21:152). Like the red-brown cathedral at Chester, the portrait has been worked over—"retouched." If his smile has been encouraged to "more play," "his other motions" have been encouraged to "less." Indeed, whatever Chad is, he is anything but free: he is but a work of art, a medal or coin, a thing of value in the world: "It was as if, in short, he had really, copious perhaps, but shapeless, been put into a firm mould and turned successfully out" (21:152). Strether, in his freedom from theories and preconceptions, is of course loathe to judge by the appearance. He must proceed cautiously, look further: there are "too many clues" that he still lacks, there is "more in it than meets the eye" (21:161). He will revolve for several days the question of whether Chad is "free" of attachment to a wicked woman or, if not free, virtuously "attached." He will disagree with Maria Gostrey on the question of whether freedom and virtue may coexist. But not until much later will he discover that Chad is neither free nor virtuous.

It is in book 5 that the most striking and brilliant development of the ironic symbolism occurs—together with the most explicit statement of the novel's basic premises. The visit to the "queer old garden" of the sculptor Gloriani is a trip into the center of Paris, the heart of light—or is it the heart of darkness?—the citadel of the past, of feudalism, of Roman Catholicism, of art, of appearance. Ironic in the extreme is Strether's rejoicing in the "liberty" of the guests "to be as they were" (21:195). For everything in the setting suggests not liberty but total submission to the past. It is a place that, as Little Bilham observes, "puts us all back—into the last century" (21:201). The small pavilion is "on the edge of a cluster of gardens *attached to old noble houses*" (21:195; italics mine). There are "high party-walls" surrounding the garden and, as we learn, "the open air was in such conditions all a chamber of state. Strether had presently the sense of a great convent, a convent of missions, famous for he scarce knew what, a nursery of young priests, of scattered shade, of straight alleys and chapel-bells, that spread its mass in one quarter ..." (21:195–96). Presiding over this party is Gloriani, "a dazzling prodigy" who "with a personal lustre almost violent ... shone in a constellation: all of which was more than enough to crown him, for his guest, with the light, with the romance, of glory" (21:196). The sun-king of this Paris, with its "dear

old light," the city in which men have "so much visual sense" that
they seem to have no other, is the artist, the man of the eye. And
yet James suggests that for all the dazzling beauty of the court, it
has grave dangers. The king, Gloriani, despite his luster, has a
"medal-like Italian face, in which every line was an artist's own"
(21:197). Although there is a "terrible life" behind the charming
smile, and Strether is moved by his vision of the artist to regret his
own waste of life, yet when he sees the duchess and Gloriani
together, he notes "there was something in the great world co-
vertly tigerish which came to him, across the lawn, in the charming
air, as a waft from the jungle" (21:219). One may admire Gloriani,
"the glossy male tiger, magnificently marked," but one cannot help
observing that beneath the elegance of the court lies the jungle of
predation, of acquisitiveness, the appetite of the eyes for things.
The traps are everywhere. Bilham warns Strether, "There are lots
of people ... with collections. You'll be secured!" Maria is one
collector; Mme de Vionnet is another—"almost celebrated"
(21:202). Indeed, as Bilham observes a few moments later, the canni-
bals, the savages, may not merely convert one; they may devour
one: "I'm but the bleached bones of a Christian" (21:205).

When Strether is introduced to Mme de Vionnet, he thus feels
himself "handed over and delivered; absolutely, as he would have
said made a present of, given away"(21:209). Again the ambiguities
swarm. Mme de Vionnet, we are told, "was dressed in black, but
in black that struck him as light and transparent; she was exceedingly fair. ... Her smile was natural and dim; her hat not extravagant; he had only perhaps a sense of the clink beneath her fine
black sleeves, of more gold bracelets and bangles than he had ever
seen a lady wear" (21:210). The lightness and naturalness are of
course, once again, deceptive. Mme de Vionnet, as *femme du monde*,
worshipping at the shrine of the vain appearance, is anything but
free or natural. Everything about her is fixed and formed. When
Strether visits her later, her hands are "clasped in her lap" and there
is "no movement in all her person, but the fine, prompt play of her
deep young face" (21:247). The clasp of her hands remains "un-
broken" and her expression has the look of "being most natural
when her eyes [are] most fixed" (21:249). She "was not to shift her
posture by an inch" (21:247). As for her house in the symbolic Rue

de Bellechasse (she is, of course, the *belle chasseresse,* and perhaps James wants us to think of *chasse* in the sense of a punch or nail driver or in the sense of a reliquary or shrine), it is, like the woman herself, equivocal. Despite its "large and open" court, Strether feels "the ancient Paris" in "the immemorial polish of the wide waxed staircase and in the fine *boiseries,* the medallions, mouldings, mirrors, great clear spaces, of the grayish-white salon" (21:243). Again, light and dark commingle, and all is impressed with the stamp, the pattern, of the past. There is in it "some dim lustre of the great legend" of the Empire. The postrevolutionary period has "left its stamp of harps and urns and torches, a stamp impressed on sundry small objects, ornaments and relics" (21:244). Unlike Maria Gostrey's "little museum of bargains," this house is "founded much more on old accumulations . . . than on any contemporary method of acquisition or form of curiosity. Chad and Miss Gostrey had rummaged and purchased . . . whereas the mistress of the scene before him, beautifully passive under the spell of transmission— transmission from her father's line, he quite made up his mind— had only received, accepted and been quiet" (21:244–45). For all her fineness and distinction, Mme de Vionnet remains a prisoner of an old, invidious way of life; of feudalism, the Catholic church, and Old World "arrangements." Formed, not free herself, she will not hesitate to form her daughter—to put Jeanne into a mould as inflexible as the one employed by Gilbert Osmond for the turning out of his Pansy. Small wonder that Jeanne, like her mother, appears with her "hands clasped together as if in some small learnt prayer" (21:222) and that, like Chad, she resembles "a picture"— "the portrait of a small old-time princess of whom nothing was known but that she had died young" (21:259). She has, in truth, in her submission to the past, never lived—never been free.

Strether does not judge Mme de Vionnet. Tolerant, sympathetic, aware of his own enslavement to another way of life, he can only, at this point, remark fatalistically, with his eye on both Paris and Woollett, the "fluted and embossed" or the "smooth and dreadfully plain" mold,

> "The affair—I mean the affair of life—could n't no doubt have been different for me; for it's, at the best, a tin mould, either fluted and embossed, with ornamental excrescences, or else smooth and dread-

fully plain, into which a helpless jelly, one's consciousness, is poured
—so that one 'takes' the form, as the great cook says, and is more
or less compactly held by it: one lives, in fine, as one can. Still, one
has the illusion of freedom." [21:218]

But in advising Little Bilham to live, Strether is in truth preparing
for his own emancipation. He has not yet begun to act for himself,
but it will not be long before his freedom, his self-assertion, will
become actual. Later on, when he chooses Little Bilham as his heir
and arranges to marry the little artist-man to Mamie Pocock, his
choice will of course fall upon the one person in the novel who,
like himself, is free. For Little Bilham, like Strether, is able to
assimilate both America and Europe without surrendering to either. He is the one young American in Paris who manages not to
be spoiled—who holds onto the precious American "state of faith"
(21:131). While he discerns all the beauty and charm of Paris, he
has not succumbed to the Old World materialism: he is no collector and his apartment, instead of being stuffed with things, is a
"rather cold and blank little studio." He is both old and new: "He
lived at the end of an alley that went out of an old short cobbled
street, a street that went, in turn, out of a new long smooth avenue"
(21:127). If, in his studio, Strether delights in the "delicate daubs"
of conversation, he is also pleased by the "free discriminations."
Bilham's studio is, in short, the one place in Paris "to which our
hero unreservedly surrendered" (21:127). Bilham, as artist-man, yet
with his share of the sacred rage, is the only logical heir for
Strether. Chad, the brown pirate, the "social animal," the brute and
pagan, will be disinherited by his surrogate father.

    It will be some time, however, before Strether is able to make
so free and happy a decision. In Gloriani's garden, where the
shadows have become "long," it is as if "something had happened
that 'nailed'" Strether's impressions (21:227). Strether, consenting
to see Mme de Vionnet, concludes his agreement with Chad: "if I
surrender myself to Mme. de Vionnet, you'll surrender yourself to
me" (21:237). It crosses his mind that he is being used, that his
service is "highly agreeable to those who profited by it" (21:256),
yet when he sees Mme de Vionnet for a second time, at Chad's
home, he is so struck by her beauty that he ignores the many
evidences of her enslavement. That he is deceived is hardly surpris-

ing, for the intimations of her attachment to the past are delicate indeed. Her bare shoulders and arms are "white and beautiful," yet her dress is "of a silvery gray" that suggests the silver coin, the stamp of profit and of art as well as the admixture of white and black, the dazzling and dusky (21:270). Her enslavement is further suggested by the "collar" she wears round her neck, and one is reminded that her friend and confidante, Maria Gostrey, wore, at Chester, "round her throat a broad red velvet band with an antique jewel." The two Marys have been collared by Europe, yet the colors of their chains are, ironically, suggestive of life and freedom. Mme de Vionnet's collar is of "large old emeralds, the green note of which was more dimly repeated at other points of her apparel" (21:270). The green suggests nature, the garden, life, artlessness, as Maria Gostrey's red collar suggests sensuality, blood, life, and, especially, the lust of the eyes—for James speaks later (22:173) of the "rose of observation, constantly stronger for [Strether], as he felt, in scent and colour, and in which he could bury his nose even to wantonness." But the appearance of life and nature is deceptive: Mme de Vionnet's head is like "a notion of the antique, on an old, precious metal, some silver coin of the Renaissance" (21:270). Her house is cold "even in summer." Yet, again ambiguously, she shows a "slim lightness and brightness." She is perhaps a Cleopatra, perhaps "a goddess." Like the light of Paris she is alternately "dazzling and dusky": "She was an obscure person, a muffled person one day; and a showy person, an uncovered person the next" (21:271). Strether, unable to distinguish between art and nature—indeed, as we learn later, art *is* nature, the appearance *is* the reality in this disturbing woman ("It's how you see me," she will say to him, "and it's as I am, and as I must take myself" [22:285])—allows himself to be nailed. The "little golden nail" is driven in. He is chained, perhaps by Mme de Vionnet's "linked hands." Indeed, he is so deeply impressed by this *femme du monde* and her daughter that he not only decides to work for the mother but also, in an access of vision, foresees a marriage between Jeanne and Little Bilham and asks Jeanne's mother to allow the girl to choose freely: "She's the most charming girl I've ever seen," he says to Mme de Vionnet. "Therefore don't touch her" (21:276). It will be her breaking of her promise not to "touch" her daughter that will later so deeply disturb Strether and force him to revise his impressions.

In book 7 Strether discovers Mme de Vionnet in Notre Dame —in an encounter that has perhaps been anticipated by Maria Gostrey's remark that Mme de Vionnet would turn out to be one of those "minds with doors as numerous as the many-tongued cluster of confessionals at St. Peter's" (21:230). Strether, having deposited his "copper piece" to enter the cathedral, finds himself in the darkness of the enslaving past. Yet once again the imagery is ambiguous: it is a "great dim church," but Strether observes "the brightness of the many altars." Indeed, Notre Dame is in many respects indistinguishable from Maria Gostrey's apartment: all is glitter and gloom, spiritual brightness or base payment. Mme de Vionnet, praying "in the shade of one of the chapels," is again "strangely fixed, and her prolonged immobility showed her . . . as wholly given up to the need, whatever it was, that had brought her there" (22:6). But has Mme de Vionnet *arranged* to meet Strether at the church? James hints delicately that the appearance is not the reality: the lovely woman resembles "some fine, firm, concentrated heroine of an old story, something he had heard, read, something that, had he a hand for drama, he might himself have written . . ." (22:6–7). A few moments later, "he next perceived that the lady was Mme. de Vionnet, *who appeared to have recognized him* as she passed near him on her way to the door" (22:8; italics mine). She is wearing black and a "slightly thicker veil"; yet once again the red of passion and of observation shows: "a dull wine-colour seemed to gleam faintly through black" (22:9). Her hands are, of course, "folded," and her gloves are, appropriately, "gray." Strether's "surrender" is "made good"—over an *"omelette aux tomates"* and a "bottle of straw-colored Chablis" (22:13), the vivid colors of which bring to mind, as F. O. Matthiessen has noted, a painting, and are perhaps also meant to suggest the glitter of a court, of a chamber of state. One is reminded, in any case, of the seventy volumes of Victor Hugo in "red-and-gold" that Strether has recently purchased, as well as of the "crimson-and-gold elegance" of Sarah Pocock's hotel room (22:149). It is hardly surprising to discover such conjunctions of the rose of observation and the gold of acquisitiveness.

Even as he surrenders to Mme de Vionnet, Strether is, however, ironically liberated. He has by now changed places with Chad: it is Chad who wishes to return to America, Strether who forces him to remain in Paris. In the giddiness of his new freedom, Strether declares, "I should n't be at all surprised if I were mad" (22:40). He has dared to act, not as ambassador, but as free agent. He, who has been reluctant to seize people with his eyes and whom James has described earlier as passively keeping his hands in his pockets (21:11, 15, 110), now actively takes hold of Chad: "he [Chad] was amazed to find the hand I had laid on him to pull him over suddenly converted into an engine for keeping him still" (22:41). Moreover, Strether is becoming younger: "you *are*, at this time of day, youth" (22:50), Maria Gostrey tells him. He is indeed but newborn —he has learned to "toddle."

Betrayed by Waymarsh, who, a spirit "strapped down," "cabined and confined" (22:57), has, in his slavery, written Woollett asking that Strether be saved from himself, Strether awaits the arrival of the Pococks, prepared to pay the price of his emancipation. The arrival of the new contingent of ambassadors in book 8 is of course a grave threat to Strether. It is now the Protestant queen, Queen Elizabeth, not Mary Stuart, with whom he must deal —or, rather, it is Sarah, steaming up in the "becoming, yet treacherous" light of Paris (22:76)—it is all the "bridling brightness" of Woollett. "Yes," Strether reflects, "they would bridle and be bright" (22:80). But the agile Strether is not slow to discern all the dangers of their bridles. Has he not before him the example of Jim Pocock, enslaved, reduced to silence on "the moral side" by the American "society of women" (22:83)? The danger is emphasized in an adroit continuation of the imagery of the jungle and of painting. If Gloriani and the other social animals of Paris suggest to Strether a jungle of acquisitiveness, the American woman is equally rapacious in her cage: " 'They don't lash about and shake the cage,' said Jim . . . ' and it's at feeding-time that they're quietest' " (22:87). Strether is aware that they "don't show [their] claws," and he will presently perceive that it is he, not Chad, whom they have come to get hold of. He will realize, too, that Mrs. Newsome "has n't budged an inch" and that she, no less than Mme de Vionnet, may most aptly be described not as a living creature but as a painting, fixed, composed, finished: if Mme de Vionnet is so perfect that "another touch will spoil her—so she ought n't to *be* touched" (22:153), so Mrs. Newsome "won't be touched. I see it now as I've never done; and she hangs together with a perfection of her own . . . that does suggest a kind of wrong in *any* change in her composition. It was ... the woman herself, as you call her, the whole moral and intellectual being or block, that Sarah brought me over to take or leave" (22:239). Moral enslavement amounts, in the end, to a kind of bestiality—or to the deathlike fixity of the work of art.

The Pococks, in their pride, commence their assault on Mme de Vionnet, who, as we learn in chapter 3 of book 8, is "already on the field" and strikes Strether "as dressed, as arranged, as prepared" (22:90, 92)—though it is a preparation "infinitely to conciliate" (22:92). The scene of the battle is once again a salon both charming and treacherous: there is nature and art, the open and the closed, the bright and the dark, the civilized and the animal:

> The glazed and gilded room, all red damask, ormolu, mirrors, clocks, looked south, and the shutters were bowed upon the summer morning; but the Tuileries garden and what was beyond it ... were things visible through gaps; so that the far-spreading presence of Paris came up in coolness, dimness and invitation, in the twinkle of gilt-tipped palings, the crunch of gravel, the click of hoofs, the crack of whips, things that suggested some parade of the circus. [22:97]

Inevitably, James returns to the imagery of the theater: "It was indeed as if they [Mrs. Pocock and Waymarsh] were arranged, gathered for a performance, the performance of 'Europe' by his [Strether's] confederate and himself" (22:105). Mme de Vionnet, despite her apparent wish to conciliate, remains as fixed, as unbudging as Sarah. At the beginning of the scene she extends her hand "without moving from her place" and at the end she declares: "We shall sit, my child and I, and wait and wait and wait for you" (22:92, 108). Only Strether, endlessly pacing, keeps on the move. Woollett may try to get hold of him, but he will "wriggle out" (22:113).

In book 9 Strether, by now accepting fully his role as Mme de Vionnet's confederate and no longer restrained by his scruple that he ought not to visit the countess, is suddenly drawn up short. Standing in Mme de Vionnet's house—in the antechamber which is "a little cold and slippery even in summer" (22:126)—he learns that Jeanne is to be married off by an arrangement "founded on a *vieille sagesse*" (22:130). He senses at once that he has fallen into a trap: it is "as if he had even himself been concerned in something

deep and dim. He had allowed for depths, but these were greater
..." (22:129). Despite its "high and square" appearance, the antechamber is, after all, but the "hole" in which, as Mme de Vionnet
remarked earlier, she lives (21:190). High is low and light is dark,
and Strether, shocked, perceives acutely "the refined, disguised,
suppressed passion" of Mme de Vionnet's face. Small wonder that
the apartment, for all its coldness, reveals "pale shades of pink and
green" (22:125)!

With the discovery that Jeanne is to marry M. Montbron (James
arrives at the name, one suspects, by combining the notion of
nobility—*Mont*— with that of spiritual darkness: the *brown* of
Maria Gostrey's apartment, her pirate's "cave of treasures"),
Strether is driven to make new plans for Little Bilham. He will
marry the little artist-man to Mamie Pocock. The choice is of
course perfection. For not only does it coincide with the free
wishes of Mamie and Bilham, it also represents Strether's recognition that these two are beautifully suited to each other. Mamie may
be a Pocock, but she has "bloomed ... freely" (22:147), and if
Woollett has caused her to age ("she was dressed ... less as a young
lady than as an old one ... the complexities of hair missed moreover also the looseness of youth; and she had a mature manner of
bending a little ... while she held together in front of her a pair
of strikingly polished hands " [22:149–50]), she is also "light of
touch" and her appearance on the symbolic balcony of youth,
where she stands looking for Little Bilham, reveals that she is still
morally alive. Chad may have given her a copy of Fromentin's
'*Maitres d'Autrefois*' (22:143), but Little Bilham will prevent her
from becoming enslaved by the past or by America. Strether, in
arranging the marriage, at last finds a measure of expiation for the
sin of false worship: "I've been sacrificing so to strange gods," he
says to Little Bilham (22:157–68), "that I feel I want to put on
record, somehow, my fidelity—fundamentally unchanged, after all
—to our own. I feel as if my hands were embrued with the blood
of monstrous alien altars—of another faith altogether." In the context the alien altars are presumably those of Europe, for which
Strether, like Maria Gostrey, has been working. But another interpretation is also implied: the alien altars include, surely, Woollett's
as well. It is at last only at freedom's altar that Strether will worship.

The battle between Mrs. Newsome and Mme de Vionnet continues in part 10, where Chad, in his attempt to get hold of Sarah, invites her to his crowded apartment and seats her in such a way as to immobilize her: she is "packed so tight she can't move." Miss Barrace, with her incessant tortoise-shell glass that symbolizes "the lust of the eyes" and looking, as ever, like "the old French print, the historic portrait" (22:174), focuses Strether "with her clink of chains" (22:177) and remarks of Sarah: "She's bricked up, she's buried alive." But Strether perceives that Sarah, despite the fact that she sits there like a work of art, as "the motive of [Chad's] composition and dressed in a splendor of crimson which affected Strether as a fall through a skylight" (22:163–64), is still alive—alive, that is, with all the fierce energy of the sacred rage. The corrupted Waymarsh may be "too smothered ... in flowers," but Sarah "can breathe"—the cold air of righteous indignation (22:176). When, in chapter 3 of book 10, Strether is summoned to appear before her as she sits "there in her state," in her "court," with her tall "parasol-stick upright and at arm's length, quite as if she had struck the place to plant her flag" (22:196), he is forced to choose between independence and "submission." And of course he refuses to submit.

Appropriately, after this magnificent assertion of his freedom, Strether, in book 11, takes "possession" of Chad's balcony (22:210); for, in a beautiful irony, James makes it clear that it is not Mrs. Newsome and Mme de Vionnet, those two great rivals for empire, who colonize most, but rather the mild Strether, who, as Maria remarks (22:227), "reduces people to subjection" and plants his flag now upon the balcony of youth and of "moral elevation." In the severest terms he can summon up, Strether accuses Chad of lacking imagination, of failing to see the immensity of his debt to Mme de Vionnet. Moreover, to ensure that Chad will not desert the lady, Strether decides to remain in Paris a time longer; and at this point James prepares beautifully for the famous recognition scene on the river by having Strether observe that "the summer here must be amusing in a wild—if it is n't a tame—way of its own: the place at no time more picturesque" (22:235). Strether will at last come face to face with the wildness of the reality—the jungle of lust and of possessiveness.

Chapter 3 of book 11, in which Strether discovers Mme de

Vionnet and Chad in the boat on the river, deserves its reputation
as a piece of masterful writing. The sources of the scene's power
are various, but one of the most important is that every item in the
discovery episode is thoroughly symbolic. Strether has gone into
nature, the world of "French ruralism, with its cool special green"
(22:245), yet nature here is, of course, all art and artifice, a beautifully baited trap. The scene reminds him of a painting he coveted
in his youth, a little Lambinet that he had seen in "the maroon-
colored, sky-lighted inner shrine of Tremont Street" (22:246). The
artless countryside exhibits all the symbolic motifs introduced in
the scene at Chester. Seen from the train, it is enclosed in an
"oblong gilt frame"; it "fell into a composition" (22:247). The ambiguities, the conjunctionings of good and evil, are everywhere.
Strether presently finds himself in a "village that affected him as a
thing of whiteness, blueness, and crookedness set in coppery green"
(22:252). There is a "small old church, all steep of roof and dim
slate-color without and all whitewash and paper flowers within"
(22:252). Darkness and brightness continue to mingle equivocally,
and the *Wahrheit* is all *Dichtung*. There is nothing in the scene that
"was n't somehow a syllable of the text" (22:254).

A few moments later the "pink parasol" appears, and Mme de
Vionnet's suppressed passion can no longer be concealed. Strether,
Mme de Vionnet, and Chad will continue to play their parts, but
the drama will go dead. In "the darkening summer night" Strether
is forced to "make believe more than he liked." The whole episode
is "as queer as fiction." Chad and Mme de Vionnet have, Strether
realizes, "something to put a face upon, to carry off and make the
best of" (22:261). "Fiction and fable *were,* inevitably, in the air"
(22:262), and Mme de Vionnet's manner "had been a performance,"
one that "faltered toward the end, as through her ceasing to believe
in it" (22:263). She is at last stripped of her concealing clothes—
"with not so much as a shawl to wrap her round" (22:264).

In book 12, when Strether meets her for the last time in her
house, the ironic symbolism is handled with the greatest delicacy
and care. The house is still, as much as ever, all appearance—like
"a gallery" in which Strether moves "from clever canvas to clever
canvas" (22:273). The light is "dim." The candles glimmer "like the
tall tapers of an altar" (22:274). Strether again feels the dim past,
the smell of revolution—"or perhaps simply the smell of blood"

(22:274). It is, in truth, the lair of the beast, the social animal. In one of his most exquisite strokes James presents Mme de Vionnet for the first time as dressed not in black but in "simplest, coolest white." It is as if Strether has now come full circle: if, at the beginning, the exterior had been black and the soul bright, now the exterior is white, the soul black. (By the same token, the old church in the preceding chapter has a dim exterior and a bright interior —exactly the reverse of what Strether has encountered all along in Paris.) Mme de Vionnet is not young but "old, old, old." She realizes now that she has only taken, selfishly, and that, unlike Strether, she has been unable to give. She has "betrayed" her higher "possibilities" (22:286). Her hands, so free to handle and touch, are "unholy." Her final shame is that in her allegiance to the past, in her lack of spontaneity, she has ceased, morally, to interest Strether. "We bore you," she recognizes (22:288). Her sin is, in the last analysis, pure, vulgar greed: her last words are: "You see how, as I say, I want everything. I've wanted you too" (22:289). And Strether replies, ambiguously, "Ah, but you've had me!" (22:289). For she has had all his sympathy and appreciation; and she has nailed him to an appearance.

There remain, for Strether, two important meetings: with Chad and with Maria Gostrey. In the meeting with Chad, the imagery returns once again to the theme of the jungle. Chad will be "a brute," says Strether, if he forsakes Mme de Vionnet. But that Chad will foresake her is of course made evident by the young man's lack of imagination. Not fairness or principle is on Chad's mind but advertising and profit. He will, in truth, become a "beast"; he will return to America and "take hold." As he cynically observes of the profession whose art so intrigues him, "With the right man to work it *c'est un monde*" (22:316). Chad, never out of the world, will take the world's immense "bribe."

In the meeting with Maria Gostrey, James reveals that Strether, because it is his scruple that he must not gain by his mission abroad, will not marry his confidante. Yet the deeper reason for his not marrying her has already been suggested: Maria, like the other Mary, Mme de Vionnet, is the victim of the "empire of things"; is "drearily, dreadfully old" (22:52). She has not, in her allegiance to that world and to Mme de Vionnet, dealt honestly with Strether. Indeed, her behavior has inclined him to a "revulsion in favor of

the principle of Woollett" (22:296). Little Bilham's lie, Strether
finely discerns, has been "technical"; Maria's has been more than
that. The real difference between her and Strether is that she, like
Chad, is thoroughly at home in the world. There is nothing she
"would n't do" for Strether—"nothing ... in all the world"
(22:326). But the one thing Strether requires is emancipation from
the world:

> "I'm not," he explained, leaning back in his chair, but with his eyes
> on a small ripe round melon—"in real harmony with what sur-
> rounds me. You *are*. I take it too hard. You *don't*. It makes—that's
> what it comes to in the end—a fool of me." [22:320]

Strether cannot remove his eyes from the melon that, in its roundness, suggests the ball of the world, but he is not finally at home
on this planet. The beautiful lemon color of the melon—the lemon
of Strether's books, lemon that reminds one so much of spring and
youth but that may turn easily, in a slight shift of light, to copper
or gold—is not to be repudiated entirely. Yet Strether's truest
home is not earth, and he must finally be "up and up."

Ironically, the man who has lost the world has gained it: in the
last incident in the novel Strether receives the surrender of Maria,
who, assenting to the bright logic of his free man's morality, says:
"I can't indeed resist you."

In a letter written in 1889 to the Deerfield Summer School,
James pointed out that neither "materializing tendencies" nor
"spiritualizing" or "etherealizing" tendencies are meaningful to the
novelist: "There are no tendencies worth anything but to see the
actual or the imaginative, which is just as visible, and to paint it.
I have only two little words for the matter remotely approaching
to rule or doctrine; one is life and the other freedom." [12] His
repudiation of excessive emphasis upon either a materialistic or a
spiritual presentation of life is coupled with his rejection both of
the excessive optimism of English novels (particularly novels written by women) and of the excessive pessimism of French natural-
ists. The artist who would master the art of *complete* representation
(and James makes clear in "The Art of Fiction" that the only duty
of the novelist is to be complete) must reject all single-minded,
exclusivist versions of reality. And for this reason James prefers, to

the limited vision of tragedy and the limited vision of comedy, a complex fusion that renders the diversity of life.

Ellen Leyburn's excellent study *Strange Alloy* calls our attention to the "mingled tragedy and comedy of life" in James's work and argues persuasively that James's career is marked by an effort to do away with comedy and tragedy as "separable" elements in his composition. In the early work comedy remains "separable"; in the later novels the comedy becomes inseparable from "tragic" experience. She also finds in James's employment of fools who are often pathetic, of partly tragic minor characters, and of "free spirits," an attempt to render the mingled tragedy and comedy of life. And she might have carried her argument further, I believe. For while it is roughly true that Strether (for example) is "tragically involved" and also "comically detached enough to see the incongruity [of his situation] as comic," it is perhaps even more to the point that Strether is viewed both sympathetically and ironically by James. Strether is a hero, to be sure, but with his bright nippers bestriding his nose, his timid gaze, and his inveterate "Do I dare?" he is second cousin to J. Alfred Prufrock. And, as we have seen, he is in his own way capable of aggression—of forcing others to do what *he* wants them to do. James was, in fact, determined to resist the easy moralism which divides mankind into two camps, the good and the wicked. If romance thrives on the convention of the "rank vegetation of the 'power' of bad people that good get into," [13] in James's art, although its melodramatic structure often leads readers to see a simple division of the good and the bad, there are really no good people and no bad. Or, if there are "bad" people, they are creatures like Charlotte Stant and Kate Croy, creatures whose "evil" turns out to be their "necessity," their daily worldliness, normal acquisitiveness and normal appetition. Nor are there any heroes in James's work who are seen without irony and without a view of their motives that is often, in the last analysis, devastating. Maggie Verver is a saint, but she's also a cunning little manipulator, a dismal nun, and a bore. Fleda Vetch is a high priestess at the altar of the ideal—and a leech, an avid little profit-seeker with an eye on the spoils. Even the resplendent Isabel Archer is, as we have seen, a combination of the flamelike spirit and the creature of conditions.

Thus when James says, in the often quoted passage in his preface to *The Spoils of Poynton,* that the tormented "free spirit" in his composition is "heroic, ironic, pathetic, or whatever," he means, in fact, that the free spirit is all of these in combination, is hero and antihero in one, is in short a real human being. Or as he observed, when asked by Henry Harper to write a story on American snobbishness abroad, "But the only way that's at all luminous to look at it is to see what there may be in it of most eloquent, most illustrative and most human—most characteristic and essential: what is its real, innermost, dramatic, tragic, comic, pathetic, ironic *note.*" [14] The evidence is indeed overwhelming that James was very deliberately, throughout his career, both in constructing his characters and in plotting their fortunes, seeking to achieve a sort of "balance and reconciliation of discordant qualities," and the passage from which Leyburn takes the title of her study is only one of many eloquent passages that might be cited to show that James's determination was to "reflect for us, out of the confusion of life, the close connexion of bliss and bale, of the things that help with the things that hurt, so dangling before us for ever the bright hard medal, of so strange an alloy, one face of which is somebody's right and ease and the other somebody's pain and wrong." [15]

It is not surprising, then, that James's highest praise goes to those artists who represent the "terrible mixture" in things. The greatness of Balzac, for example, consists to a very great extent in "the mixture of sun and shade suffused through the *Comédie Humaine*— a mixture richer and thicker and representing an absolutely greater quantity of 'atmosphere,' than we shall find prevailing within the compass of any other suspended frame." [16] The same sovereign mixture is found in Daudet, in Turgenev, in Maupassant, and even in Tintoretto, in whose work "the eternal problem of the conflict between idealism and realism dies the most natural of deaths. In his genius the problem is practically solved; the alternatives are so harmoniously interfused that I defy the keenest critic to say where one begins and the other ends. The homeliest prose melts into the most ethereal poetry—the literal and the imaginative fairly confound their identity." [17]

The synthesis, the admixture, the fusion is the great thing. The greatness of the novels of the major phase is very largely due to the fact that they are the perfect application of James's idea that such a synthesis—such an assimilation of the whole of reality—is, for the lover of the image of life, the most precious issue of his freedom to partake of the whole of life. Looking over James's entire development as a writer, we see him in the stories of the eighties already beginning to present characters and action in such a way as to capture the synthesis of the ironic and the tender, the poetic and the prosaic, the ideal and the material; but in the early work the story tends to rule the artist, and James has not found a way to render sensitively and copiously his sense of life as Manichean. In *The Princess Casamassima* there is a considerable advance toward his goal: Hyacinth Robinson discovers contradictions everywhere, and neither those who breathe the "upper air" nor those condemned to penury are what they seem. Power-seeking and black egotism lie behind even the fairest appearances. But James had not in 1886 developed a vocabulary perfectly expressive of the "terrible mixture" in things, and some of his most expressive achievements had to wait upon the steady addition to his word-hoard of terms to render, in every sentence, the double aspect of reality. By the time he came to write "The Aspern Papers," the vocabulary of predation and commercialism was generally mixed with a vocabulary expressive of an exquisite sensibility and fine moral appreciation. In a story like "The Marriages," written in 1891, James is able to present a heroine who is both "priestess" and power-seeker in one. In *The Spoils of Poynton* (1897) the later style flourishes, and there are a hundred valuable additions to the Jamesian symbolism. He is able, at last, to write the novel in which virtually every sentence reveals the strange admixture in life. Religious imagery fuses beautifully with imagery of rapacity, and the result is a novel of such rare balance that critics are still trying to decide whether Fleda Vetch is a beautiful "free spirit" or a pathetic and self-deluded slave of materialism. And then the novels of the major phase: James at last truly lets himself go. The mannered style is perfectly symbolic: is mannered *because* it is symbolic. Everywhere the sun and shade coexist, the light and the dark, the spiritual and the bestial, the expansive and contractive, the high and low, freedom and slavery; all of these opposites inform the action of the novels, and not a single word is employed without James's full awareness of its place in his comprehensive scheme. It is in this development of a style and a symbolic diction that James realizes the perfection of his realistic art—achieves maximum grasp of reality at every instant, at every point of presentation. And it is in his effort to escape all partial views of reality, in his refusal to surrender to the idols of tribe and cave, market place and theater, in his struggle to achieve perfect detachment, perfect freedom, that his art acquires such importance and such rare beauty as even the slaves of time and the world cannot fail to appreciate.

NOTES

1. Leon Edel, *Henry James: The Treacherous Years, 1895–1901* (Philadelphia: J. B. Lippincott Co., 1969), p. 29. Extensive treatments of James's imagery are Alexander Holder-Barrell's *The Development of Imagery and Its Functional Significance in Henry James's Novels*, Cooper Monographs, No. 3 (Bern: Francke Verlag, 1959) and Robert L. Gale's *The Caught Image: Figurative Language in the Fiction of Henry James* (Chapel Hill: University of North Carolina Press, 1964). It is perhaps a weakness of both of these studies that image-categories are considered apart from the central conflicts that give rise to the imagery and symbolism; but there are many helpful observations for students interested in the habits of James's imagination.

2. Henry James, *Notes of a Son and Brother* (New York: Charles Scribner's Sons, 1914), p. 92.

3. Henry James, preface to *What Maisie Knew* (New York: Charles Scribner's Sons, 1909), p. xii.

4. Ibid., pp. 143, 211, 8, 218.

5. Quentin Anderson, *The American Henry James* (New Brunswick, N.J.: Rutgers University Press, 1957).

6. James, Preface, *The Novels and Tales of Henry James*, 26 vols. (New York: Charles Scribner's Sons, 1907–17), 10:xv.

7. James, *Novels and Tales*, vol. 2. All subsequent citations are to this edition.

8. James, *Novels and Tales*, vol. 3. All subsequent citations are to this edition.

9. John L. Kimmey's "*The Princess Casamassima* and the Quality of Bewilderment, *Nineteenth-Century Fiction*, June 1967, pp. 47–62, seems to me the best study of that novel. Kimmey's definition of the central problem stresses the "intricate pattern of contradictions working from both within and without Hyacinth" (p. 48).

10. Of the many studies of James's work in which the influence of Paris and of Mme de Vionnet upon Strether is regarded as a virtually unmixed blessing, one may mention as illustrative F. O. Matthiessen's *Henry James: The Major Phase* (New York: Oxford University Press, 1944), pp. 19–41; Christof Wegelin's *The Image of Europe in Henry James* (Dallas: Southern Methodist University Press, 1958), pp. 86–105; F. W. Dupee's *Henry James* (New York: William Sloane Associates, 1951), pp. 242–45; and

Henry Seidel Canby's *Turn West, Turn East: Mark Twain and Henry James* (Boston: Houghton Mifflin Co., 1951), pp. 270–72, 277. What is almost invariably stressed in studies of the novel is that, as Matthiessen says, Mme de Vionnet is "an exquisite product of tradition" and that Strether learns in Paris how to "live" in the sense of feeling abundantly. (Matthiessen writes: "both Strether and James could have subscribed to much of Pater's famous exhortations for fullness of life. . . .") But such an interpretation is entirely misleading if the critic fails to point out the great moral danger of being "an exquisite product of tradition" and if he fails to discern the inadequacy of the Paterian exhortations. Quentin Anderson has pointed out that Strether's advice to Little Bilham—the exhortation to "live"— "offers no principle to guide his young friend" (*The American Henry James*, p. 212); and that of course is perfectly true if *living* means only sensuous indulgence. But, as I hope to make clear, James obviously meant *living* in the sense of achieving freedom—of not allowing one's self to be fixed in the molds of Paris or Woollett. In *The Novels of Henry James* (New York: Macmillan Co., 1961), Oscar Cargill has observed a connection between Strether's advice and that of Louis Leverett in "A Bundle of Letters." Inspired by Paris, Leverett writes to his friend in Boston: "The great thing is to *live*, you know—to feel, to be conscious of one's possibilities; not to pass through life mechanically or insensibly, even as a letter through the post office. . . ." The stress here, as in *The Ambassadors*, is upon "possibilities" as opposed to fixation, mechanistic behavior, automatism. Anderson's argument that Strether is "inclined to be a determinist," that Strether makes the error of conceiving "the bowl of selfhood to be unbreakable," and that in the end he "falls back on the formula of righteousness; . . . He is self-righteous; he has denied life, not affirmed it" (pp. 215, 216, 221), fails to discern that Strether changes in the course of the action; that he does in fact break "the bowl of selfhood" (as the self has been made by Woollett); and that, in refusing to take anything for himself at the end, he is affirming his moral freedom. Anderson's reading would in effect make Strether contemptible; such an interpretation clearly substitutes an external philosophy for the novel itself.

    11. James, *Novels and Tales*, 22:249. All subsequent citations are to this edition, vols. 21 and 22.

    12. Henry James, *Selected Letters of Henry James*, ed. Leon Edel (London: Rupert Hart-Davis, 1956), pp. 122–23.

    13. James, *The Art of the Novel*, ed. Blackmur (New York: Charles Scribner's Sons, 1934), p. 37.

    14. James, *The Notebooks of Henry James*, ed. Matthiessen and Murdock (New York: Oxford University Press, 1947), p. 176.

    15. James, *The Art of the Novel*, p. 143.

    16. James, *The House of Fiction*, ed. Leon Edel (London: R. Hart-Davis, 1957), p. 73.

    17. James, *Italian Hours* (New York: Grove Press, Evergreen Books, 1959), p. 58.

IV. "ORTS, SCRAPS, FRAGMENTS" AND THE CIRCLE OF WHOLENESS

The Symbolism of Virginia Woolf

PERENNIAL IN LITERATURE is the theme of the quest for certainty in a world in which all things pass away; but when a writer's sense of the precarious condition of life before the onslaughts of time and change is as acute, when it is as enlarged and sensitive as it is in the fiction of Virginia Woolf, that old vision of human fate acquires a singular potency. The search for a rock of ages assumes psychological as well as philosophical significance. Time and mutability mean, psychologically, the terrible necessity to adapt, to adjust; but the insecure soul apprehensively questions: "Will I be able to adapt? Will I be equal to the challenge?" The fear that one may fail to be ready, that one is not strong or agile enough for the great dislocations and disjunctions in life, grows as the neurotic feels his incapacity for spontaneous and independent action. He would cling to what is known; but the world is never "known," never safe. It is one great threat, and engulfment may come from anywhere. "It is always the unexpected that happens," says Conrad's Marlow. Pitiful, then, is the clinging to an apparent permanence, and delusive. How urgent, how pathetic, is the quest for the sheltering home, the mother, the rock of ages! And—to shift the perspective—how amusing! Irony and pity commingle in the apprehension of this spirit caged in an alien world, poor slave of matter and time.

Virginia Woolf's lyricism was, essentially, the expression of a poet whose dominant sense of life issued always from "the acute perception of alternatives." Her wit was (to follow T. S. Eliot's phrasing) the recognition, in a given experience, that other kinds of experience are possible. Life might be round and whole; instead, it is fragmented, cut into bits and pieces. Personality might be a crystal globe; but the globe shatters, one is split up into a thousand shards. Only in a vision, in an artifice of eternity, is there completeness. The vision obsesses and torments. The sea of time casts up images of the perfections we crave; but the swimmer drowns in the great flux, the machine of ocean, before he can seize and hold a single one. Woolf's sense of life is all Sophoclean; but she is, like Wallace Stevens, a connoisseur of chaos, and her vision, shaped by the struggle between art and time, is essentially Manichean and ironic.

Even in her early work we see her in possession of the central categories of art-nature, essence-existence, and working to make every corner of her canvas exhibit the simultaneous participation in both worlds. In *Jacob's Room* there are scores of tragicomic passages in which the Platonic essences are contrasted with the mutability of things in the flux.

> Such is the fabric through which the light must shine, if shine it can —the light of all these languages, Chinese and Russian, Persian and Arabic, of symbols and figures, of history, of things that are known and things that are about to be known. So that if at night, far out at sea over the tumbling waves, one saw a haze on the waters, a city illuminated, a whiteness even in the sky, such as that now over the Hall of Trinity where they're still dining, or washing up plates, that would be the light burning there—the light of Cambridge.[1]
>
> > "Rock of Ages, cleft for me,
> > Let me hide myself in thee,"
>
> Jacob sang. . . . Infinite millions of miles away powdered stars twinkled; but the waves slapped the boat, and crashed, with regular and appalling solemnity, against the rocks. [P. 52]
>
> The British Museum stood in one solid immense mound, very pale, very sleek in the rain, not a quarter of a mile from him. The vast mind was sheeted with stone; and each compartment in the depths of it was safe and dry. The night-watchmen, flashing their lanterns over the backs of Plato and Shakespeare, saw that on the twenty-second of February neither flame, rat, nor burglar was going to violate these treasures—poor, highly respectable men, with wives and families at Kentish Town, do their best for twenty years to protect Plato and Shakespeare, and then are buried at Highgate. [P. 109]

Like Yeats, Woolf might say: "Man is in love, and loves what vanishes." Everywhere she is obsessed by the torments of the flux, the wind and the waves and the presence of death:

> As for the beauty of women, it is like the light on the sea, never constant to a single wave. They all have it; they all lose it. . . . Thus if you talk of a beautiful woman you mean only something flying fast which for a second uses the eyes, lips, or cheeks of Fanny Elmer, for example, to glow through. [P. 115]

The tree falls on a windless night; the wicker armchair creaks; the skeleton is wrapped in flesh (pp. 23, 39, 162). Jacob, the first time we observe him, sees a man and woman making love, and then the skull of a ram. His mother thinks of the dead Seabrook—and of the living Captain Barfoot (p. 7). Thinking of Seabrook, she hears her son's voice, which, "sounding at the same moment as the bell [for service or a funeral] . . . mixed life and death inextricably, exhilaratingly" (p. 16). The vision of this strange admixture of life and death is everywhere, and is of a piece with the admixture of beneficence and malevolence, comedy and tragedy, in the universe:

> Now it was clouding over.
> Back came the sun, dazzlingly.
>
> [P. 24]

Jacob's tale ends with a depiction of confusion in the flux: in his room, left "just as it was," there is "nothing arranged" (p. 176). " 'Such confusion everywhere! ' exclaimed Betty Flanders, bursting open the bedroom door." Jacob's past lives on in the disarray of the present: life and death commingle in his room—the rose and the ram's skull (cf. p. 70). But Woolf has of course no salvation, no release from the torments of confusion. There are only the moments of beauty, poetry, light. We have them; we lose them. Like Wallace Stevens, she knows that the only emperor is the emperor of ice cream.

Her effort to reach a whole and steady view of life was intense. Like Keats she wished to avoid mere self-assertion; she felt that the complete artist should be androgynous, with the sensibility of a woman and the intellect of a man. Transcending sexual and temperamental limitations, he must penetrate all perspectives and attitudes. Thus her ideal artist is identical with Henry James's:

avoiding the extremes of pessimism or optimism, he seeks to capture the strange irregular rhythms of life—to capture that rounder, more balanced, though uncertain, vision that we have described as Manichean. The magnificent final soliloquy of *The Waves* presents this complex vision:

> Life is pleasant. Life is good. The mere process of life is satisfactory. Take the ordinary man in good health. He likes eating and sleeping. He likes the snuff of fresh air and walking at a brisk pace down the strand. Or in the country there's a cock crowing on a gate; there's a foal galloping round a field. Something always has to be done next. Tuesday follows Monday; Wednesday Tuesday. Each spreads the same ripple of well-being. . . .
> Lord, how pleasant! Lord, how good! [P. 358]

> Lord, how unutterably disgusting life is! What dirty tricks it plays us, one moment free; the next, this. Here we are among the breadcrumbs and the stained napkins again. That knife is already congealing with grease. Disorder, sordidity and corruption surround us. We have been taking into our mouths the bodies of dead birds. It is with these greasy crumbs, slobbered over napkins, and little corpses that we have to build. Always it begins again; always there is the enemy; eyes meeting ours; fingers twitching ours; the effort of waiting. Call the waiter. Pay the bill. We must pull ourselves up out of our chairs. We must find our coats. We must go. Must, must, must—detestable word. Once more, I who had thought myself immune, who had said, "Now I am rid of all that," find that the wave has tumbled me over, head over heels, scattering my possessions, leaving me to collect, to assemble, to heap together, summon my forces, rise and confront the enemy. [P. 380]

In apprehending the nature of reality, the admixture of life and death, comedy and tragedy, the beneficent and maleficent, the poet must "let the atoms fall upon the mind in the order in which they fall." He must write not to please, but to grasp the truth of things —of Monday or Tuesday. And because his concern is undoctored reality, "things as they are," "veracious page on page, exact," he must eschew plot, the simplifications of characterization, all the ordinary apparatus and contrivance of fiction. Woolf's Manichean vision brings her, at last, to plotlessness—to integration by means of symbolism rather than by unified action.

The representation of her Manichean vision is most perfectly realized in the early *Night and Day,* in *The Years,* and in *Between the Acts. Night and Day* is so comprehensive in its development that it anticipates everything else in Woolf. It is not a particularly good novel: it lacks tension; the problems confronted by Woolf's characters are never adequately dramatized; and the theme is so dominant that the people seem not to breathe—they have no life independent of the informing ideas. But if character is thus subordinated to idea, the idea, at least, is splendidly articulated. The Manichean oppositions inform every aspect of life. The world is split into light and dark: on the one hand the objective world of facts, the impersonal world of science, reason, and law, the masculine world of time, work, and business; on the other hand the night world of dream, sleep, and poetry, of love and feeling, the world of the mother, of faith and vision and eternity. The Gemini character of the soul, the oscillations between night and day, dream and reality, are very explicitly stated in Katherine Hilberry's choral reflection:

> Why, she reflected, should there be this perpetual disparity between the thought and the action, between the life of solitude and the life of society, this astonishing precipice on one side of which the soul was active and in broad daylight, on the other side of which it was contemplative and dark as night? Was it not possible to step from one to the other, erect, and without essential change?[2]

And these great symbolic oppositions are complemented by others: by the split between country and city, the river and the strand, the poor and the rich, family life and solitude. The plot, which deals with the trials and tribulations of people who don't know their own minds (Katherine Hilberry thinks she loves William Rodney and agrees to marry him; then she realizes that she loves Ralph Denham and becomes engaged to *him;* Rodney thinks he loves Katherine, then falls in love with Katherine's cousin, Cassandra, and decides to marry *her;* Denham for a time falls in love with the working woman, Mary Datchet, or thinks he does; then reverses himself; etc., etc.)—this plot reinforces the theme of "oscillations" and becomes an elaborate demonstration of the conclusion of Wallace Stevens's Crispin: "Can one man think one thing and think it long?" The tone is tragicomic, and the novel is wound up, more or less conventionally, with Katherine Hilberry's attainment of such qualified happiness as may exist in a world of contradictions. To be sure, Woolf *glances at* the abyss: there are moments when she is driven toward a vision, such as one finds in Conrad's darkest stories, of "the dark, flying wilderness of the world"; or a vision such as Wallace Stevens discovers when the illusions are stripped away: "the mist departed, a skeleton world and blankness alone remained—a terrible prospect for the eyes of the living to behold." Katherine confronts such a world as that from which Maggie Verver must avert her eyes, the world in which "there's nothing —nothing, nothing left at all" (pp. 418, 437, 163). But having confronted the Medusa-face of naked reality, the "jungle in itself," as Stevens calls it, Katherine turns back to a more comforting sense of life, and in the end her happiness seems assured.

But the great weakness of *Night and Day*, from Woolf's own point of view, is that, while pressing toward perfect plotlessness, it remains more or less conventional in its structure: a sort of *Emma*, lacking Jane Austen's sense of a reality solid to the touch. Woolf could not long remain contented with such plot-structure, and it is in *The Years* that she achieves the perfect freedom to render the dense reality of life that she was groping for in *Night and Day*. Discarding plot altogether, she contents herself, in *The Years*, with a pure image of life's raggedness; the formlessness of "things" replaces schematic form, and the only means left for insuring integration and coherence in the novel are symbolic. Yet it is precisely because Woolf has here eschewed all other means of integrating her work that she has been criticized—even by those inclined to grant her the freedom to do away with plot. Thus David Daiches, though impressed by certain aspects of the novel, finds it to be "repetitious" and "to have an unnecessary expansion": "The pleasure in reading *The Years*," he writes, "derives more from a recognition of virtuosity, let us say, than from our complete domination by the novel as an integrated work of art." [3] Joan Bennett argues, similarly, that "with so large a canvas and so many background and foreground characters, the reader's attention is insufficiently centered ... the book, even after several readings, does not give the reader the sense of a single, organized whole." [4] Charles G. Hoffman, after agreeing with Bennett's observation, goes on to say, "The farther the novel moves in time from the enclosed circle of the Victorian family the more diffuse it becomes"; moreover, Woolf's handling of the central vision is uncertain: she fails to achieve a proper "balance between fact and vision"—between the facts of history and Eleanor's "tentative and indefinite" vision of these facts.[5] E. M. Forster dismisses the novel laconically in a sentence: "As in *Night and Day*, she deserts poetry, and again she fails." [6]

The dissatisfaction is of course understandable, particularly if one is looking for the sort of focus and integration normally provided by plotted fiction. But if one accepts—as in fact Woolf's critics *have tried* to accept—that the purpose of the novelist is to convey the erratic, uncertain, unplotted character of life and that it is sufficient for the novelist to provide poetic integrations of his material, musical or symbolic integrations, then—whatever the failure of *The Years* to "interest" us—it can scarcely be argued that the novel is not well integrated. On the contrary, it is, I believe, so very well integrated that there is not a single detail in it that does not arise from Woolf's central vision. But to appreciate the novel's extraordinary integration, we must expand our understanding of the central vision and principle of selection. Once we recognize the Manichean vision as central in the novel, we discover there is nothing accidental, nothing casual or gratuitous, in the entire action. But fully to grasp what Woolf is doing, we would do well to glance first at a novel whose theme and whose developmental patterns are so profoundly similar to those of *The Years* that it seems impossible Woolf could not have been strongly influenced by this work as she traced the development of the Partiger chronicle. I refer to E. M. Forster's *Howards End*.

The theme of Forster's novel, as we know, is *connection*: overcoming the disjunctions and fragmentations of personality and of society, reconciling the contraries in life. The basic connection is the marriage of two houses, the house of the German idealist Schlegel and that of the English businessman and utilitarian Wilcox. Idealism must be connected with materialism; spirit with flesh; subjectivity—the *personal*, the *I*—with objectivity and things. Dreams must be connected with facts, with the outer world of "telegrams and anger." And females (the Schlegel house is dominated by women) must connect with men (the Wilcox house is predominantly male).

But as Forster works out his central vision, he touches on a great many more disconnections than these. The social and economic division of mankind is underscored: poor and rich must be united.

(Thus the rich Helen Schlegel wishes to unite with the poor Leonard Bast, and Helen bears Bast's child.) There is the disconnection of the young and the old, of the past and the present, the dead and the living. There are national divisions: Germany and England are sundered. There is increasingly, as the populace is urbanized, the disconnection from nature: the landlord has "split the precious distillation of the years," and the "binding force" of the earth is being steadily lost. Only, perhaps, at a Howards End, at such English farms, can one "see life steadily and see it whole, grasp in one vision its transitoriness and its eternal youth, connect—connect without bitterness until all men are brothers." [7] "Proportion" is Forster's ideal, but it is achieved only by "continuous *excursions*" into the opposite worlds of spirit and matter, mystic and businessman, monk and beast. Or it is achieved only, perhaps, by a miracle, by the miraculous curative powers of the pig's teeth in the wych-elm at Howards End—only, that is, by the healing and reconciling touch of a Mrs. Wilcox.

Forster makes it clear that connecting is fearfully difficult. To connect, men must overcome their instinctive clannishness and their fear of those different from themselves; they must overcome "panic and emptiness"—the terror arising from suspicion and cynicism. They must conquer an instinctive tendency to withdraw from others (as Tibby, the scholar, withdraws into his Chinese studies, eschewing all responsibility). They must struggle against ignorance and "imaginative poverty," against misunderstandings and misinterpretations. And even chance may add to our difficulties, as when a casual remark about the Porphyrion Insurance Company sets in motion a series of events that lead to Leonard Bast's impoverishment. There is, indeed, in Forster's fictional universe, a propensity toward chaos, toward *dis*connection: life has a Punch-and-Judy aspect.[8] Again and again, in *Howards End*, things move quickly out of control; irrational concatenations of events produce upheavals, disaster: a woman suddenly dies; a cat is run over by a motorcar; tempers flare; families feud. (In like manner nations may declare war.) And because connection is so exceedingly difficult in such a world, the ending of Forster's novel has a miraculous quality about it. Life and joy emerge unexpectedly. Bast dies; his baby is born. As death and life are linked early in the novel (after Mrs. Wilcox's funeral the man who pollards the churchyard elms and who, we learn, is "mating," takes from the grave a chrysanthemum, which he presents to his sweetheart before a "night of joy"), so they are linked again; the "transitoriness" and the "eternal youth" of life are connected, and one has a sense of perfect transmission, perfect continuity.

Howards End is so good a novel that it is hard to imagine the sensitive reader who would not be impressed by it. But its appeal to Virginia Woolf must have been extraordinary. For the novel reflects that special state of mind, that intellectual, emotional, and moral ambience which we designate by the term *Bloomsbury,* and Forster's rendering of the Punch-and-Judy aspect of life is precisely the sort of thing that Virginia Woolf, with her enormously, her almost neurotically enlarged sense of the erratic and uncertain nature of life, would have noted with especial interest. Furthermore the idea of escaping the torments of confusion by marrying the opposites, by effecting a *rapprochement* of the warring social classes, by realizing the liberal dream of a New World in which emancipated and equal men and women may live happily and variously, all the old shackles of convention thrown off, all the old lies exposed, all the rich human possibilities given freedom to unfold—that dream of wholeness was, as we know, very precious to Woolf throughout her life.

The quest to achieve wholeness, integration, connection is the central concern of *The Years.* Woolf's ideal, like Forster's, is an integrated personality in a congenial world, a world based on freedom and justice. And like Forster, Woolf sees everywhere profound obstacles to wholeness. Life destroys all integrations. As Eleanor Partiger reflects, "Directly something got together, it broke. ... And then you have to pick up the pieces, and make something new, something different. . . ." [9] The self is fractured by its opposed desires: the desire for solitude, the desire for society; the desire for action, the desire for rest and sleep. The world is fractured by injustice, by the division of mankind into classes. The family is fractured by disagreement or infidelity. Wholeness fails, and the novel works extensively with a vocabulary of fragmentation: *break off, cuts, gaps, splinters, bits,* and *parts* are recurrent terms. Further, a motif of *deformity* is worked richly into the novel after the introduction in the first scene of the image of Colonel Partiger's mutilated hand that "resembled the claw of some aged bird"

(p. 13). No one is whole; all are deformed.[10] But divisions are found, too, in the alternation of seasons; of day and night; of rain and sunshine; fire and water; earth and air. "Roaring and cursing" are followed by "beauty and joy" (p. 189), and life is no more than these oscillations, this inconstancy. Yet isn't there a pattern behind the flux of separate moments? And can't one, like Forster's Mrs. Wilcox, reconcile the antagonistic parts, connect and live wholly, a whole person in a whole world? Eleanor Partiger is Woolf's Mrs. Wilcox.[11] It is Eleanor who, more ardently than the others, seeks the blessed integration and has a vision of the new whole life in which living men and women are happy together, all differences resolved. She is the healer and reconciler, the sanguine "soother, the maker-up of quarrels" (p. 14). But all of the sensitive characters in the novel hanker for this wholeness of being and so Eleanor is in a sense absolutely typical. The novel does not affirm her faith. It does not "affirm" at all. It presents the tragicomic spectacle of life, the patterns of recurrence, the endless and incessant fragmentations, and *the endless search*, in the face of fragmentation, for the perfect integration of self and of the self and the world.

The novel begins with *deformity* and *division*, reflected in a thousand tiny and apparently unsymbolic details. In the opening paragraph, for example, after sounding the note of tension in the first sentence—"it was an uncertain spring"—Woolf proceeds to call our attention to farmers in the country, shoppers in the city; to the sounds of street musicians and the "echoes" or "parodies" of the sparrows, thrushes, pigeons; to the princess and "ladies in many-coloured dresses," and to servant girls "in the basements of the long avenues of the residential quarters"; to the "million little gaslights" and to "broad stretches of darkness"; to the admixture of the artificial and the natural—"the mixed lights of the lamps and the setting sun"; to a moon that shines "with serenity, with severity, or perhaps with complete indifference." Thus the old Manichean vision of symbolists from Hawthorne and Melville through James and Conrad and up to the present day is asserted: life may be "serene" or "severe," or it may of course be no more than mechanical process, indifferent to us. For everywhere there are, along with the buoyant hopes for freedom and justice, intimations of a darker, a frighteningly enslaved reality: automatic collocations of matter, of cause and effect, "caravans perpetually marching" (p. 3) as the years go "slowly wheeling" and pass "one after another across the sky."

The terrifying aspect of this world is clearly suggested in the 1880 section of the novel. Colonel Partiger, whose wife, Rose, lies dying, pays a visit to his mistress, Mira, in a sordid street under the huge bulk of the abbey. He gives the woman two sovereigns. The scene ends as he caresses her with his mutilated hand, "the hand that had lost two fingers" (p. 9). His rapacity—clearly betokened in the image of the claw—is the deformity that shatters any vision of an integrated family life or of a just society. The rich use the poor; family life is a lie. The motif of the social lie—the contradiction issuing from dishonesty, hypocrisy, injustice, bullying—is thus announced. And the motif is developed richly in the subsequent scenes of the chapter. A happy family life? But Delia, who yearns for a new life ("Somewhere there's beauty, Delia thought, somewhere there's freedom" [p. 12]), sees the dishonesty in her father and wants her mother to die (p. 22). She thinks of Parnell, of "Liberty" and "Justice," but she encounters only a "hopeless situation." Freedom to develop without deformity? But Rose is, from the beginning, formed in the image of "Colonel Partiger of Partiger's Horse" (pp. 27, 157, 416); she will from beginning to end "clap spurs to her horse and gallop" (pp. 27, 157, 169). Formed by nature as the militant feminist, is she ever free to be something more, to achieve "wholeness"? Moreover, her encounter with a sexual pervert who exposes himself to her permanently affects her personality. (See pp. 166–67.) The deformity of the pervert is part of the nightmare that will torment her, and society, for the years to come. The pervert's "horrid face; white, peeled, pockmarked" (p. 28) is but one of the recurrent physical horrors that betoken the failures of Victorian society to achieve "wholeness."

Eleanor is already, in 1880, brooding on such failures as these. She has been visiting the poor, and, as the family joke has it, "Look out. Eleanor's broody. It's her Grove day" (p. 31). She is conscious too that her sisters have been "cooped up" too much (the image of the coop or cage or prison recurs throughout the novel, symbolic of the failure to break free and achieve wholeness), and know nothing of the outside world—of the poor, for example (p. 32). Disturbed, she takes up a poker and strikes the coals, "and a shower of gold-eyed sparks" goes "volleying up the chimney" (p. 32).

Eleanor's cousin, Margaret, will do the same thing in 1917 (p. 294) —such minor recurrences are of course everywhere—and the significance of the act will become apparent then. Eleanor, in that scene, has asked, "When will this New World come? When shall we be free? When shall we live adventurously, wholly, not like cripples in a cave?" And then, watching Maggie strike the wood and send the sparks volleying up the chimney—those sparks that her cousin Sarah has described as "the soul flying upwards"— Eleanor reflects, "We shall be free, we shall be free . . ." (p. 297).

In Abercorn Terrace in 1880, however, Eleanor discerns no freedom or wholeness of being. Nor is she able, being young, to discern the pattern of recurrence in life—the endless repetitions of the same words and phrases and acts. Milly frays the wick of the lamp (p. 10); Eleanor will repeat that act in 1908. Colonel Partiger pinches Rose by the ear and calls her a "grubby little ruffian" (p. 12); he will say the same words to his niece Maggie in 1891 (p. 126). A cab stops "two doors lower down" (p. 18); in the "Present Day" section, a taxi will repeat that event (p. 434). Rose Partiger's hair is "white, save that there were queer yellow patches in it, as if some locks had been dipped in the yolk of an egg" (p. 21); Eleanor's hair will look the same (p. 376). Frightened and bewildered, Rose Partiger awakes, exclaiming, "Where am I?" (p. 23); Eleanor asks herself the same question (p. 43). The pattern endures, but it has an ambiguous character. It may prove beneficent—may reflect the eternal youth present in the transitoriness of life; it may thus suggest wholeness. But it suggests also a terrifying automatism, an inexorable bondage to habit and conditioning—in short, a humanity caged by heredity and environment and incapable of removing deformity and fragmentation from life. From start to finish, Woolf's vision is Manichean.

In Oxford, too, we discover deep obstacles to the longed-for integration. Edward Partiger, we learn, is so deeply divided that he is fond both of Gibbs, the "huge young man" whose chief interest is hunting (Gibbs's hand is "a great red paw," "like a piece of raw meat"), and of Ashley, scholarly, quiet, delicate, "the very opposite of Gibbs" (pp. 52–53). Again, Edward is in love with Kitty Malone, whom he thinks of as an Antigone; but he is in love, also, with scholarship. And here too we discover a lie, a contradiction: Edward pretends to "despise examinations," but such behavior is only "pretense." And, as Woolf suggests delicately, there may be still another division in his nature: the heterosexual at odds with the homosexual.

Kitty Malone finds the problem of integration equally taxing. Formed, or bullied, to live "in Oxford, in the midst of everything" (p. 82), she craves most deeply nature and solitude. That is why she is attracted by the flowers "stuck into a cushion of wet green moss" that she sees at the home of her tutor, Miss Craddock (p. 65); that is why she is attracted to young Robson, the young man with wood-shavings in his hair, and to the Robson family, plain, simple, associated with "the north" and nature. Not society and action, but the cooing of pigeons takes her heart; yet she will marry, not "Chingachgook," but the stuffy Lord Lasswade. Contradiction, division, falsehood are everywhere.

Even the funeral of Rose Partiger seems false. "What a lie!" Delia cries to herself, hearing the parson's words. But she has, for a moment, a sense of something "far more deeply interfused": "she was possessed by a sense of something everlasting; of life mixing with death, of death becoming life" (p. 87). As Forster makes us aware of that beautiful and blessed commingling, upon the death of Ruth Wilcox, so Woolf here; the integration occurs that Bergson speaks of as issuing, never from mere intellection, but from intuition. The "myth of isolation" is done away with. All things come together as one, and there occurs that blessed vision of the unity of being, precious to symbolists and mystics alike.

In the years that follow 1880 the search for wholeness continues, though we encounter an inexorable proliferation of divisions and fragmentations. The 1891 section has everywhere a Manichean aspect. It is October, and everywhere there are leaf-fires, bonfires. The fires of destruction, of hell, or those of creation, of the life-giving sun? October, Woolf reminds us, is "the birth of the year"; but it is also the season of death; and life and death mingle, even as the red and yellow of the autumnal leaves mingle with the red and yellow festoons in London ballrooms.

Eleanor, ever cheerful, hopes of course to see creative flames. She has become a landlady, and her symbol is the sunflower:

> She gave one look at the sunflower on the terra-cotta plaque. That symbol of her girlish sentiment amused her grimly. She had meant

it to signify flowers, *fields in the heart of London;* but now it was cracked. [P. 191; italics mine]

Her effort to fuse the opposites fails; the circle, symbol of eternity, is severed by the crack. Her London life is a series of separate encounters, and she herself is fragmented, partly the bullying manageress, partly the obedient daughter and surrogate wife, partly the committee member . . . but the list is endless. The sunflower also signifies the soul, the "I," that center "from which spokes radiated" (pp. 91, 367), but even the self is cracked: "She did not exist; she was not anybody at all" (p. 95). Her life is without a center:

> What did you spin things round on? . . . a pivot? The scene had changed so often that morning; and every scene required a different adjustment; bringing this to the front; sinking that to the depths. And now she felt nothing; hungry merely; merely a chicken-eater; blank. [P. 104]

The fire that her father applies to his cigar, the fire that Martin strikes from a match to save himself from a frightening night in India, the bonfire that Eugénie Partiger burns for Maggie's birthday—the fire of life and joy, leaping high, "clear gold, bright red" (so that life-affirming Eugénie cries out, "Make it blaze! Make it blaze!" [p. 124])—is also the destructive fire: is the soul burning, is the soul flying like sparks volleying up a chimney. Parnell dies in 1891, and Delia's dream of liberty and justice—does that, too, go up in smoke? The flames of the bonfire sink, and as the year ends old Abel Partiger, "depressed and disappointed" because he has not seen Eugénie, reflects, "After all . . . it was his own affair; it didn't matter to anybody else. One must burn one's own smoke . . ." (pp. 127–28). He is alone and old; the integration *he* had hoped for is impossible, and he envies his brother Digby.

In 1907 the atmosphere is pure romance: summer, a moon, a dance—the perfect setting for a midsummer night's dream. And Sarah reads a book in which the author states that "the world is thought." But the old divisions and fragmentations are inescapable. "The lights—the sunlight and the artificial light—were strangely mixed" (p. 131). Thought and matter, country and city, nature and art commingle in the oddest ways. Vegetables, fruit, and flowers are brought from the country into London, "the eternally burning city" (p. 129); we see "a woman iridescent with green beetles' wings in her hair" (p. 130). (The woman, we learn later, is the divided Kitty, condemned to London, always hankering for the north.) Sarah reads Edward's translation of *Antigone*—the dream of freedom and justice rises again—but in the play, as in life, there are vultures that gather (p. 136), and Antigone dies.

Maggie enters Sarah's room, and the two sisters discuss broken hearts. Thus, subtly again, the motif of fragmentation is repeated. We sense its presence in the assertion that the world is nothing but thought; the sisters cannot accept *that* fragment of the whole truth. Sarah puzzles: "Am I that, or am I this? Are we one, or are we separate . . . ?" (p. 140) Physically deformed (one of her shoulders is higher than the other), she cannot discover wholeness anywhere, and sees only the separate parts of herself: "legs, body, hands," never "the whole of her" (p. 133).

Eugénie enters, and the girls ask her to show them how she used to dance. And here Woolf introduces a major integrating symbol. The dance, the symbol of pattern in the flux, of being in becoming, is employed, as in Yeats's "Among School Children," to suggest the only integration that temporal creatures can know. Eugénie dances in circles, symbols of eternity, while the "eternal waltz" plays on:

> . . . she twirled round and round in the space which Maggie had cleared. She moved with extraordinary stateliness. All her limbs seemed to bend and flow in the lilt and the curve of the music; which became louder and clearer as she danced to it. She circled in and out among the chairs and tables and then, as the music stopped, "There!" she exclaimed. Her body seemed to fold and *close itself together* as she sighed "There!" and sank *all in one movement* on the edge of the bed. [P. 143; italics mine]

The symbol of a beautiful integration and completion.[12] "Wonderful!" exclaims Margaret. Yet Eugénie calls attention to the shattering flux: "Nonsense . . . I'm much too old to dance now; but when I was young; when I was your age—" (p. 143). Has the integration been mere illusion? The limbs "*seemed* to bend and flow"; the body "*seemed* to fold and close" (italics mine). And ironically, the old mother dances while her daughter reads the book declaring that all is thought. At the end of this section, then, the door flapping to

and fro downstairs—symbol of the inexorable mutability of things
—recalls us to the necessity for endless new integrations. Eugénie
has forgotten to have the door attended to. How ragged life is! If
memory and imagination fail, life's incoherence overwhelms us.

In 1908 it is the March wind that Woolf uses as token of the
destructive flux. "With one blast it blew out colour—even a Rem-
brandt in the National Gallery, even a solid ruby in a Bond Street
window: one blast and they were gone" (p. 146). Digby and Eugénie are dead. Martin has returned from India (as North will return
later from Africa). He and Eleanor reminisce. They are now beginning to look back, and are trying to gather up the past to make
a seamless whole of their lives. (Eleanor's reading of Renan is a
token of this desire to retrace the past—back to the origins of
Christianity.) Yet the passage of the years causes confusion. Eleanor has fallen a week behind, and thinks it's the eleventh of March
when it's the eighteenth. And she reflects that old age is terrible:
the faculties decay, and one is left with "a game of chess, a drive
in the park, and a visit from old General Arbuthnot in the evening": fragments (p. 152). Fragmentation is evident, too, in an ineluctable subjectivity: Digby's obituary, she reflects, is not
accurate: the man was "not like that in the least" (p. 154); but then
"it was odd how different the same person seemed to different
people" (p. 154). The whole person is repeatedly dismembered, and,
meanwhile, the wind does its vicious work. As the section ends,
there is "another gust and the sound of glass crashing" (p. 159). The
glass of Miss Pym's conservatory, symbol of the Platonic abstractions, of the fixed transparency of art, is shattered. All the lovely
integrations collapse.

By 1910 Sarah and Maggie have fallen into poverty: poverty
contrasted with Kitty's wealth. The social and economic divisions
are more strongly felt than ever before. Kitty goes to the opera,
hears *Siegfried*. She pushes through glass doors, enters an artificial
world: daylight is "extinguished," and the air glows "yellow and
crimson"; the smell of "oranges and bananas" is replaced by "another smell—a subtle mixture of clothes and gloves and flowers
that affected her pleasantly" (p. 181). Yet as the dwarf in the opera
hammers, she recalls the young man with shavings in his hair, and
a farmer leading a bull with a ring through its nose. Longing for
nature, she is condemned to artifice.

But the "hammer, hammer, hammer" of the dwarf is repeated later, an ironic leitmotif, when a neighbor of Sarah and Maggie returns home drunk and hammers on the door to be let in (p. 190). Sarah and Maggie live in a tiny apartment overlooking a sordid street: "a little cave of mind and dung," as Sarah calls it—a sort of prison, a contradiction of the dream of wholeness, freedom and justice. And if the spring night is full of "beauty and joy" for some, it is also full of "roaring and cursing; of violence and unrest." Sarah stands looking down at a drunkard thrown out of a public house. For Woolf never allows us to forget the lie, the contradiction. If the queen has "a face like a flower petal, and always wore her pink carnation" (p. 160), what is one to make of the peddlers crying "any old iron" (p. 172) or the "elderly man, battered and red-nosed," selling violets? Freedom? Justice? Or utter enslavement and injustice?

As before, the novel is suffused with the sense that no one escapes the wheel of time, the bondage to temperament and to conditioning. Dismal indeed are Sarah's predictions:

> "Rose is coming," she said, "and this is where she'll sit." She placed the chair at the table facing the window. "And she'll take off her gloves; and she'll say, 'I've never been in this part of London before.' "
> "And then?" said Maggie, looking at the table.
> "You'll say, 'It's so convenient for the theatres.' "
> "And then?" said Maggie.
> "And then she'll say rather wistfully, smiling, putting her head on one side, 'D'you often go to the theatre, Maggie?' " [P. 164]

None of Sarah's predictions are borne out, but there are stale repetitions enough. Twice Rose asks, "Don't you find it very noisy here?" (pp. 167, 165). Kitty asserts, "Force is always wrong—don't you agree with me?—always wrong!" (p. 179) and she will repeat these words twenty-five years later (p. 420). Like the birds that rise or settle automatically (p. 181), they all seem condemned to be what they are—their sweating selves. "But must you get out?" Kitty asks Eleanor, who has accompanied her in her "magnificent car" to the tube-station. "I must, I must," says Eleanor (p. 180). And the motif of necessity is developed so copiously that the creation of a new self in a new world would seem a pathetic delusion.

In 1911 Eleanor, now fifty-five, takes a holiday in August. She has already, in her quest for wholeness of being, begun her globe-trotting; she has been to Spain. Yet she likes this return to England. Her father has died; Abercorn Terrace has been shut up; and she wonders whether she ought to live in a village. We learn later, from Nicholas, "The soul—the whole being ... wishes to expand; to adventure; to form—new combinations?" (p. 296). But the soul has also an opposite hankering: to contract itself; to hold itself close; to rest and to have perfect solitude and peace: "Everything looked very settled; very still; very pure ..." (p. 205). But is the quiet country, *that* part of the whole, enough? After her visiting, after the chatter with Celia and Morris, North and Peggy, Eleanor retreats to her room—to encounter books that underscore again the problem of division and fragmentation. One of the books, *Ruff's Tour*, or *The Diary of a Nobody*, calls to mind the inability to be a single unchanging self. The other, a copy of the *Divine Comedy*, reinforces the sense of the difficulty of fusing the self and others, the self and the world:

> chè per quanti si dice più lì nostro
> tanto possiede più di ben ciascuno.

What did that mean? She read the English translation

> For by so many more there are who say 'ours'
> So much the more of good doth each possess.
>   [P. 212]

The motif of the lie, the ineradicable distortion at the bottom of personal and social life, continues in the 1913 and 1914 sections. In 1913 Abercorn Terrace is sold. For the nanny Crosby the sale is "the end of everything"; but Martin, who has discovered his father's infidelity, condemns family life as "abominable" and reflects that at Abercorn Terrace people had lived "boxed up together, telling lies" (p. 223). Thus the image of the birdlike claw of Colonel Partiger reappears again and again. In 1914 the birds are everywhere. But the symbol is complex, like the moon that is both "serene" and "severe"—or simply indifferent to us. The birds may make "a sweet chirping in the branches" (p. 242); or they may be rapacious, like the screaming gulls (p. 244) or like the owl whose talons have seized a mouse (p. 204). Or their behavior may suggest

mere automatism, as when their mechanical rise and fall is analogized to the human scene of London: "The pigeons were swirling
up and then settling down again. The doors were opening and
shutting . . ." (227). Whatever the particular meanings of the birds,
however, the tragicomic fragmentations and divisions are as abundant as ever. Early in this section Martin observes organ-grinders
and beggars along with lighthearted women who cluster around
the plate-glass windows—the cheerful people who seem "to have
money to spend." Meeting Sarah on the steps of Saint Paul's, Martin observes her "queer little shuffle as if she were a bird, a somewhat dishevelled fowl. . . ." But again there is the "odd mixture" in
things: this bird has been to service in Saint Paul's and carries a
prayer book.

Martin's search for integration in this section is everywhere
frustrated. He has wanted to be an architect, but has been sent into
the army. Now he is in business and successful, but the old love
of architecture has sent him to Saint Paul's. Again, in the restaurant
with Sarah, the sought-for integration cannot occur because "conversation in a restaurant was impossible; it was broken into little
fragments" (p. 230). Then a waiter attempts to cheat him, and he
is confronted by the social split that makes rapacity inevitable. The
restaurant, he decides, is "a beastly hole" (p. 233); he is glad to get
outside and breathe fresh air. This little oscillation between the
closed and open worlds (both of which he desires) is attended by
still another confrontation of deformity in society: they pass a
woman selling violets—a woman who has no nose and whose face
is "seamed with white patches" (p. 235). The woman wears "an old
straw hat with a purple ribbon round it" (p. 235). Shortly afterwards he encounters "a lady, fashionably dressed with a purple
feather dipping down on one side of her hat," a lady who sits
"sipping an ice" (p. 241). Thus it is no accident that he and Sarah
pass, in the park, orators speaking of "Joostice and liberty," nor is
it an accident that they see an old lady "saying something about
sparrows."

Other contradictions and divisions flourish as well. After the
furious rush of the London season, there is rest: Sarah sleeps in the
park. Sarah is devout, but Renny, Margaret's husband, believes that
"science is the religion of the future" (p. 238). In this immense

confusion of opposites, Martin seeks an integration that allows for
freedom. He explains to Maggie that there is a lady who wants "to
keep him" and that he wants to be "free" (p. 246). He denounces
selfishness and possessiveness: "Possessiveness is the devil" (p. 245).
Thus, like Dante, he would have people say "ours," not "mine." But
he is himself a member of the selfish upper classes, one of those
who cross the street to avoid contact with a noseless peddler of
violets. And if his freedom is prevented by the possessive lady,
Maggie is bound too—by her baby, who is "a tie" (p. 245).

Martin goes on to Kitty's party, his thoughts, as he approaches
the Marble Arch, duplicating exactly those of his Aunt Eugénie
seven years earlier (pp. 248, 131). At Kitty's magnificent London
house, he encounters the "man in gold lace," who circulates
throughout the novel (pp. 139, 169, 250), the epitome of the glittering London scene—that fragment of life. But in this artificial world
of paintings and black-and-white paved halls, Kitty is again seen
chafing. She sees the women as "gulls settling on fish. . . . There was
a rising and a fluttering" (p. 260). " 'Damn these women!' " she
exclaims to herself (p. 259). Her situation is the more painful because wealth has cut her off from her family—her "poor relations"
have "dropped" her (p. 263). And she must escape. She leaves her
dressing room (like Pope's Belinda's, with its "silver pots, powder
puffs, combs and brushes" [p. 266]); she hurries to the train station.
The train leaves London, the "fiery circle": "the train rushed with
a roar through a tunnel. *It seemed to perform an act of amputation:*
now she was *cut off* from that circle of light" (p. 270; italics mine).
The "amputation," recalling Colonel Partiger's deformed hand or
the street-peddler's noseless face or, in the "Present Day" section,
the reference to a man who hacks off his toes with a hatchet, is
accomplished. London is shut out; the country, and then sleep,
claim Kitty. And in the north, the world in which "the green light
dazzled her," the secret principle of her being that has operated
from the beginning is again asserted: the "blue flowers and white
flowers, trembling on cushions of green moss" that she sees in the
woods near her castle (p. 277) are duplicates of those she had seen
at Miss Craddock's thirty-four years earlier. She has fled a world
of endless repetitions, a world of people whose clothes and whose
lives are "the same" (p. 271); she has sought liberation from the

fiery circle of London. Yet the very act of flight, here, reminds us of her sad bondage to her psychic economy. Is she free to be anything but "deformed" in her own way?

With the advent of the war, the fragmentation of the lives of the Partigers and their enslavement to the patterns established in the past are felt more intensely than ever. Integration, freedom, justice—never have they seemed further away. Instead, we see the Partigers living near the Abbey (like old Partiger's mistress, Mira, at number thirty) in the old "cave of mud and dung" (p. 293; cf. p. 189). They speak of a New World and a new soul (pp. 292, 296), of freedom, of living "wholly, not like cripples in a cave" (p. 297). Yet they seem helpless. They do not know themselves, Nicholas argues, "and if we do not know ourselves, how then can we make religions, laws, that—" "That fit—that fit," Eleanor supplies the word that underscores the motif of harmony and integration (p. 281). They are helpless, too, because they all keep thinking and doing "the same things" (p. 282). Sarah, again, gets tipsy on wine (as in 1914); Maggie sends sparks volleying up the chimney (as Eleanor had done in 1880). And they are helpless because each "is his own little cubicle; each with his own cross or holy books; each with his fire, his wife . . ." (p. 296). How to break out of the circles —the circle of London and of the country, of spirit and of flesh? How to unite all the fragments? They all sit "round in a circle" as the Germans bomb London. Nicholas's image of the soul is, in fact, a circle or sphere: " 'The soul—the whole being,' he explained. He hollowed his hands as if to enclose a circle. 'It wishes to expand. . . .' " But are they condemned to isolation, to say "I" and never "we"? Eleanor, for example, senses that she should have married—she'd have liked to marry Nicholas; yet the "happy marriage"—both with another person and with the world—has not occurred, and the chapter ends with a chilling encounter in a London omnibus. An old man, catching her staring at him, asks, "Like to see what I've got for supper, lady?" and holds out "for her inspection a hunk of bread on which was laid a slice of cold meat or sausage" (p. 301). A happy marriage with a world in which old men eat such suppers on London buses?

The magnificent "Present Day" chapter brings together all the images and motifs of the novel. Woolf's principle of composition here, as everywhere, is basically simple: everything must seem casual, accidental; everything must be meaningful—must refer to the central theme. All the polarities of human life must be caught: the parts, the bits and pieces, must be assembled; and that is why the main action is the dance given by Delia, who takes "pride in promiscuity" (p. 404) and whose aim has been "to mix people; to do away with the absurd conventions of English life." There are "nobles and commoners; people dressed and people not dressed; people drinking out of mugs, and people waiting with their soup getting cold ..." (p. 398). There are, in addition, as dominant observers or "reflectors" of the action, the young and the old: the cold, scientific, misanthropic Peggy; the man of letters, her brother North; and Eleanor, whose hopeful search for integration culminates in one deeply affecting passage in which life and death, past and present, eternity and time, oneness and multeity, are all brought together in a superb allusion to Eugénie Partiger's circular waltz.

The sun is setting as the chapter begins. Young North has returned from "the wilds of Africa." Like Martin, who earlier went off to India; like Eleanor, who fled to the village; like Kitty, who sought out the north; he has gratified *one* part of his nature. But now London attracts him. Or rather, he is, like all men, divided: "He felt repelled and attracted, attracted and repelled" (p. 414). If he had hoped for an integration of his personality in London, he has found, in ten days, that his mind is "a jumble of odds and ends" (p. 309). He sees hideous contradictions everywhere: "—they all romanticized solitude and savagery ... the lady with the ear-rings gushed about the beauties of Nature" (p. 309). The talk, in fact, touches on these opposites: " 'Was solitude good; was society bad?' " And later he will recite a part (never the whole!) of Marvell's "The Garden":

> Society is all but rude—
> To this delicious solitude.
>
> [P. 339]

The theme of divisions and contradictions is carried out in a hundred ways. Sarah, who is poor, remembers the time she lived "on the other side of the river" and rode in a Rolls Royce (p. 322). She protests she loves Nicholas, but when he phones she cries out, "I'm not here! ... Not here! Not here! Not here!" Eleanor observes that "one thing seemed good to one generation, another to another" (p. 326). Eleanor herself, we discover, is a composite of opposites: spirit and animal, tragic and comic: "a fine old prophetess, a queer old bird, venerable and funny at one and the same time" (p. 328). Similarly, Renny, the man of science, is also the man who weeps over a bad play (p. 347).

The search for the ideal integration, on conditions of freedom and justice, also continues—as part of the endless recurrences. The motif is sounded early in the chapter when Eleanor, seeing in the evening paper the photograph of a fat man gesticulating—perhaps Mussolini—denounces him as a damned bully (p. 330), and explains to Peggy, "You see ... it means the end of everything we cared for. ... Freedom and justice" (p. 332). But we cannot forget that Eleanor, forty years earlier, bullied the repairman Duffus; and Peggy, although she feels Eleanor's appeal—the appeal of a "generation of believers"—does not believe. "I'll never be as young as you are!" she says to Eleanor (p. 335); for Eleanor's insatiable interest in life, her extensive traveling, her search for "something different," her delight in new fashions—all these signs of a hopeful, affirmative spirit—are counterpointed, throughout the chapter, by Peggy's powerful nay-saying, by North's assorted revulsions.

The sense of fatality is what most deeply undercuts Eleanor's optimism. Everywhere North sees a hideous automatism, hideous repetitions: "Door after door, window after window, repeated the same pattern" (p. 310). There are no intimations of the new soul, the new world. "They all had lines cut; phrases ready-made" (p. 310). When Sarah greets him (he remembers her in fragments: "she came back in sections; first the voice; then the attitude"), "You've not changed," he observes (p. 313). Nor, apparently, had Nicholas changed, who repeats to North the same ideas he had voiced in 1917 (p. 315). Nor has Eleanor, who repeats, "Don't people wear pretty clothes nowadays?" (pp. 335, 336). Nor Rose, who twice says, "D'you think you can get a rise out of me at this time o' the day?" (pp. 358, 420). Unutterably sad are these repetitions, and one has Hopkins's sense of unregenerate humanity, the generations that "have trod, have trod, have trod," unaware of God's grandeur. As Peggy reflects, "Each person had a certain line laid down in their minds ... and along it came the same old sayings. One's mind must be criss-crossed like the palm of one's hand ..." (pp. 358–59).

This sense of the irreversible is reinforced in the scene in which Sarah and North converse (pp. 338–43). Here we again meet the fear of society, the reluctance to join with the *we:* Sarah would rather retreat to "a rocky island in the middle of the sea" (p. 346). But the motif of necessity appears when North tells her, "You must [go to the party]," and thereafter the word *must* recurs a score of times. "I must, must I?" says Sarah; and later, referring to the "bowler-hatted, servile innumerable army of workers": "Must I join your conspiracy ... and sign on, and serve a master ... ?" (p. 341). Sarah sees only horrors: " 'Polluted city, unbelieving city, city of dead fish and worn-out frying pans' "—sees corruption and her own dismal poverty and, once again tipsy on wine, tells North a bitter, ironic story about how "pull" got her a job (pp. 341–42). The way of the world endlessly repeated? Can any change, any progress toward wholeness be made in such a world? When Maggie and Renny arrive, Maggie sits observing the room:

> She ran her eye from thing to thing. In and out it went, collecting, gathering, summing up into one whole, when, just as she was about to complete the pattern, Renny exclaimed:
> "We must—we must!" [P. 349]

As they pass out of the room Maggie observes "an odd combination" that is difficult to form into a whole: "it was an odd combination—the round and the tapering, the rosy and the yellow" (p. 350). And when she switches off the light, a phantom world arises—a world of appearances severed from the world of material objects. Once again, just as she is about to achieve an integration, as her eyes grow used to the darkness and as color and substance begin "returning," the voice of necessity prevents the consummation:

> Then a voice shouted:
> "Maggie! Maggie! "
> "I'm coming! " she cried, and followed them down the stairs. [P. 350]

At the party, Peggy girds herself and joins the conspiracy. She reflects that "pleasure is increased by sharing it," yet people do not really listen, so that " 'sharing' is a bit of a farce" (pp. 352–353). Divided, she too seeks wholeness: "But what makes up a person—(she hollowed her hand), the circumference ..." (p. 353). Drawn to

others, she senses the need for a larger integration—not "I" but
Dante's "ours"; not her bitter isolation and misanthropy but a fusion, herself and the world together. Nevertheless, like her patients,
she also seeks to escape from society, seeks

> rest. How to deaden; how to cease to feel . . . to rest, to cease to be.
> In the Middle Ages, she thought, it was the cell; the monastery; now
> it's the laboratory; the professions; not to live; not to feel; to make
> money. . . . [P. 355]

And Peggy's life-repudiation reaches an intensity of disgust when
she is forced to endure the conversation of a young poet who
keeps saying "I, I, I" and who cannot "free himself . . . detach
himself" but is "bound on the wheel with tight iron hoops" (p. 361).
    The dance begins, for young people "must dance" (p. 365). The
dance of necessity, then? But after all, says Delia, "Dance or not
—just as you like" (p. 365). Eleanor, watching the dancers, watching that symbol of harmony and integration, reflects again on her
sunflower with the crack in it. She decides, again, that the *I* is
nothing, is dissolved into the *we:* "My life's been other people's
lives, Eleanor thought—my father's; Morris's; my friends' lives;
Nicholas's . . ." (p. 367). And, since events recur, she finds "a pattern; a theme, recurring, like music; half remembered, half foreseen? . . . a gigantic pattern, momentarily perceptible?" (p. 369). She
wishes Nicholas would "finish her thoughts": "She wanted him to
finish it . . . to make it whole, beautiful, entire" (p. 369).
    The dancers keep circling, tracing the symbol of the integration
that she seeks. But when Milly arrives, with her husband Gibbs,
animal noises, "half-inarticulate munchings" are heard. In North's
mind not a vision of integration but one of terrifying physical
fragmentation and proliferation arises: "the women broke off into
innumerable babies. And those babies had other babies; and the
other babies had—adenoids. The word recurred; but it now suggested nothing. He was sinking; he was falling under their weight.
. . . Could nothing be done about it? he asked himself. Nothing
short of revolution, he thought" (p. 375). All's "poppycock," he
thinks, picking up a word Sarah had used during the war. The
animals are one by one growing sleepy: first Sarah, then North,
then Eleanor. When Maggie approaches, North feels a strong impulse to warn her: "The long white tentacles that amorphous bod-

ies leave floating so that they can catch their food, would suck her in. Yes, they saw her: she was lost" (p. 377). They are so brutish, these animals, that they can say only "I" and "my":

> *My boy—my* girl . . . they were saying. But they're not interested in other people's children, he observed. Only in their own; their own property; their own flesh and blood, which they would protect with the unsheathed claws of the primeval swamp, he thought, looking at Milly's fat little paws, even Maggie, even she. For she too was talking about my boy, my girl. How then can we be civilized, he asked himself? [P. 378]

All men, then, are deformed: "we cannot help each other, he thought, we are all deformed" (p. 380). But Eleanor, after sleeping, wakes "extraordinarily happy" and feeling an "unreasonable exaltation": "It seemed to her that they were all young, with the future before them. Nothing was fixed; nothing was known; life was open and free before them" (p. 382). Although the dance, continuing, resembles, for Peggy, "some animal . . . dying in a slow but exquisite anguish," although "the tune seemed to repeat over and over again," and although Peggy sees only death—"on every placard at every street corner was Death; or worse—tyranny; brutality; torture; the fall of civilization; the end of freedom" (pp. 384, 385, 388) —the yea-saying Eleanor affirms that men are happier, freer. Her vision is clarified, and to Renny, who has accused her of talking of "the other world," she explains:

> "But I meant this world! . . . I meant, happy in this world, happy with living people." She waved her hand as if to embrace the miscellaneous company, the young, the old, the dancers, the talkers. . . . [P. 387]

And the idea of the parts' uniting to form a whole is picked up ironically in the composite picture that the group draws:

> Each of them had drawn a different part of a picture. On top there was a woman's head like Queen Alexandra, with a fuzz of little curls; then a bird's neck; the body of a tiger; and stout elephant's legs dressed in child's drawers completed the picture. [P. 389]

Peggy, hearing the laughter provoked by the cartoon, is, for a time, affected by Eleanor's vision of reality—"a state of being, in which there was real laughter, real happiness, and this fractured world was whole: whole, vast, free" (p. 390). But when she sets out to explain, she can "[break] off only a little fragment of what she meant to say" (p. 391) and she falls into a denunciation of an unregenerate mankind that cannot change—can only have babies and make money. Again, she longs to leave the company: to "rest, to lean, to dream" (p. 391).

Even speech, then, is fragmentary—does not represent the whole of thought or of reality. As North reflects, "Something's wrong ... there's a gap, a dislocation, between the word and the reality" (p. 405). And even the act of perceiving may provide no more than fragments, parts of a whole, as when Peggy sees Renny approach: "She saw his thin cheek; his big nose; his nails, she noticed, were very close cut" (p. 386).

As we might expect, the talk at the dinner table turns obliquely on the theme of freedom and wholeness. "You don't enjoy your freedom [in Ireland]?" Kitty asks old Patrick; and he responds, "It seems to me that our new freedom is a good deal worse than our old slavery" (p. 399). Kitty's own bondage is alluded to when, to North's remark that he had enough of farming in Africa, she answers, "And I'd have given anything to be a farmer!" Again the motif bubbles up when Patrick complains about his tight shoes, and Kitty tells him, "Kick 'em off" (p. 402); and again Delia tells the company, "Do just what you like—just what you like" (p. 403).

Edward's bondage to the life of the don is another evidence of the gulf between the word and reality that North has observed. Orators cry "Justice! Liberty!" but Edward is "like a horse champing a bit ... an old horse, a blue-eyed horse whose bit no longer irked him" (p. 405). He has "the air of being stamped" (p. 406) and his attitude, the attitude of the professor, is "fixed on him." Why can't he flow?" North muses. "Why's it all locked up, refrigerated?" And like Peggy, like Eleanor, North too imagines "a different life" —a world in which, as in a glass of claret, there are "the bubble and the stream, the stream and the bubble—myself and the world together" (p. 410). Like Dante, North is "in the middle of a dark forest" (p. 413) and needs to cut his way "towards the light"; he must "break through the briar-bush of human bodies, human wills and voices, that bent over him, binding him, blinding him ..." (p. 411). Fear, he sees, separates people (p. 414). Edward is too afraid to translate the Greek of Antigone—a line alluding to Edward's failure to free himself and to find love in his life.[13]

Nicholas rises to give a speech (as in 1917). But again and again his speech is "brought to the ground" by interruptions, and again Eleanor is disappointed by his not finishing. Nicholas, too, is about to speak of the need for a change, a different life for the human race, " 'which is now in its infancy, may it grow to maturity!' " (p. 426). But when he gets the words out at last, anticlimactically, and brings his glass down with a thump, the glass breaks.

The future in store for this infantine humanity is perhaps suggested in the mordant scene in which the two children of the caretaker—the children of the have-nots of earth—are brought "up from the basement into the drawing-room" and asked to sing. They sing a song of which "not a word was recognizable." "There was something horrible in the noise they made, it was so shrill, so discordant, and so meaningless" (p. 430). Yet—strange contradiction!—the faces of the children are "dignified" and "the contrast between their faces and their voices was astonishing" (p. 430). As usual, the perception is fragmented: "it was impossible to find one word for the whole" (p. 431).

We are left, as the sun rises, with the mixture, the bits, the pieces, the odd assortment: "in the mixture of lights they looked prosaic but unreal; cadaverous but brilliant" (p. 432). The men and women look "statuesque" for a moment, "as if they were carved in stone. ... Then they moved." But Eleanor, still seeing pattern in the flux, sees, in the last scene, that a taxi has stopped "in front of a house two doors down" (p. 434), as in 1880 Delia saw a cab stop "two doors lower down." And so Eleanor can only say, what Eugénie Partiger said after she had danced for her daughters, creating the symbol of eternity in the flux, "There! ... There!" The pattern is everywhere, life and death commingle, and the sun has risen as confirmation of the blessed vision of life in death.

Very beautiful indeed, then, is Woolf's integration of all the diverse parts of her novel. But even though we have established that there is poetic or thematic integration in the novel, we have not, of course, demonstrated that the novel is successful. And we must touch here upon a question having enormous importance in the analysis of much contemporary fiction and poetry: the question of the aesthetic effect of employing poetic integrations to replace plot as the major form of extended literary works. The question is prodigiously difficult, and I cannot hope to deal with it satisfactorily here. I would suggest, however, that Daiches's formulation of the problem raised by *The Years* is an excellent starting-point for further analysis. After remarking that *The Years* "appears to have an unnecessary expansion," Daiches asks: "Is a novel as good if increase of insight stops somewhere about the middle as it is when the insight continues until it ultimately floods the reader at the final resolution? This seems a reasonable criterion to apply, and by it *The Years* appears as a less adequate novel than the two masterpieces of her middle period." [14] To expand Daiches's criterion, may we not argue reasonably that works whose shaping principle is musical or thematic—works that state a theme and then explore the theme in an action whose organizing principle is "variations on a theme"—command attention only with difficulty for the simple reason that we realize very early, as we read, that the *fortunes* of the characters are scarcely involved; that hopes and fears are irrelevant; that not a dynamic but a static principle of composition is employed; that the work might continue endlessly, since no resolution of action but only a symbolic or musical resolution can be effected? Would it not be fair to argue that works which dispense with dynamic principles of composition—principles bringing into play our concern for the fates of the characters, our fears and hopes for them—do so only at very great peril?

Certainly the relatively greater concentration of the action of *Between the Acts,* and the greater intensity arising therefrom, would seem to suggest that Woolf is at her best when doing the lyric novel.[15] As E. M. Forster observed, she is essentially a poet. Her great gift is the presentation of the sense of life in immediacy—or in a short span of time. When she handles soliloquy in the "timeless present" of the lyrical poem, as in *The Waves,* she is superb. When, in *Between the Acts,* she concentrates on events occurring in a few hours on a summer afternoon, and finds a single, brilliant correlative of her sense of the tension between art and life, she brings the reader into the action as he is seldom brought into the action of *The Years.*

Her concern, in this last of her novels, is, again, the fragmentation of life. "Orts, scraps and fragments," says Isa Oliver, attempting to recall the words of the pageant she had witnessed at Pointz

Hall. And "orts, scraps and fragments" constitute the ineluctable reality of life—of life between the acts. If, for a short time, caught in the noose or ring of art, one feels somehow liberated from the great time-machine in which men are condemned to play the roles fate has assigned to them; if—under the spell of Miss La Trobe—one has ceased to be a mere fragment and has felt a liberating sense of wholeness, the mystic sense of the unity of things, past, present, and future, organic and inorganic—that sense of harmony is soon destroyed. "Dispersed are we," the record-player wails dolefully as the acts of the play come to an end. But when art ceases, fragmentation begins: life begins: and slavery. "They were all caught and caged; prisoners; watching a spectacle. . . . The tick of the machine was maddening." [16] The separate members of the audience, dispersed, must assume various roles, must play the parts that circumstance and fate and history have made inevitable. And must confront, bleakly, a reality in which whatever is pleasant is joined to the sinister.

The Manichean vision of life between the acts is so perfectly defined that there is not a scene or incident in the novel that is not informed by it. One sees it in the very first sentence: "it was a summer's night and they were talking, in the big room with the windows open to the garden, about the cesspool." The possible romance of the summer's night is inextricably linked with the symbol of corruption, the cesspool. But then, all lovely things are so linked to ugliness. The bird that sings sweetly bears "a coil of pinkish rubber in its beak" (p. 9). Mrs. Swithin, reading an *Outline of History* and remembering the age when the Continent was populated by "barking monsters," directs at the maid a "divided glance that was half meant for a beast in a swamp, half for a maid in a print frock and white apron" (p. 9). Then George Oliver, Isa's son, stooping to study the lovely flower that "blaze[s] a soft yellow," is suddenly frightened by a dog and by his grandfather, who has covered his face with a newspaper to play a trick on the boy. "Then there was a roar and a hot breath and a stream of coarse grey hair rushed between him and the flower. Up he leapt, toppling in his fright, and saw coming towards him a terrible peaked eyeless monster moving on legs, brandishing arms" (pp. 11–12).

The monster, the brute, the savage appear everywhere. And blood and corruption are pervasive. We are never far removed from sheer rapacity and utter malevolence. Even when the world seems most pleasant, the ominous or malignant shows:

> The light but variable breeze, foretold by the weather expert, flapped the yellow curtain, tossing light, then shadow. The fire greyed, then glowed. ... [P. 17]

> "The moor is dark beneath the moon, rapid clouds have drunk the last pale beams of even. ... I have ordered the fish," she said aloud, turning, "though whether it'll be fresh or not I can't promise." [P. 13]

> She had trotted after him as he fished, and had made the meadow flowers into tight little bunches, winding one long grass stalk round and round and round. Once, she remembered, he had made her take the fish off the hook herself. The blood had shocked her. ... [P. 21]

> Certainly the weather was variable. It was green in the garden; grey the next. Here came the sun—an illimitable rapture of joy, embracing every flower, every leaf. Then in compassion it withdrew, covering its face, as if it forebore to look on human suffering. [P. 23]

> They had met first in Scotland, fishing—she from one rock, he from another. Her line had got tangled; she had given over, and had watched him with the stream rushing between his legs, casting, casting—until, like a thick ingot of silver bent in the middle, the salmon had leapt, had been caught, and she had loved him. [P. 48]

Love and death, joy and sorrow commingle, and all is uncertain. And not only is experience "mixed" and "variable," but there is, ineluctably, a fragmentation arising from our subjective apprehension of things and from the necessity of assuming roles to deal with the exigencies presented by life. No one is free "to feel or think separately," for, as Mrs. Swithin observes, "We live in others. ... We live in things" (pp. 65, 70). Again: ' "When we wake" (some were thinking) "the day breaks us with its hard mallet blows." "The office" (some were thinking) "compels disparity. Scattered, shattered, hither thither summoned by the bell" ' (p. 119). Thus Isa is torn by the compulsion that she behave, at various moments, as wife, mother, poetess, "a good sort," a businesswoman, etc. "Prisoned," she must act out these various roles. Mrs. Manresa is "the wild child of nature"—unless she is all London artifice, a pure *femme du monde,* or an "old strumpet." As she says: "Tinker, tailor, soldier, sailor, apothecary, plough-boy ... that's me!" Mrs. Manresa's friend, William Dodge, is "an artist"—if he isn't "clerk in an office"; or he is a pervert, or just "William." Giles Oliver is a businessman, taking up "the pose of one who bears the burden of the world's woe, making money for [Isa] to spend" (p. 111); but, changing clothes, he becomes a cricketer. He is highly civilized, but "given the choice, he would have chosen to farm" (p. 47). Miss La Trobe's play, mirroring life, shows that the taking on of roles is the human story. But no matter what the role, it is certain that all human beings contain within themselves the savage, the beast, the wild dog. Even Isa, the dreamy poetess, would plunge a knife into Giles's breast (p. 113). And Giles, the killer of fish, also kills a snake that is choked with a toad in its mouth (p. 99).

Not only are people condemned to act parts. Their ruthlessly selective and abstractive sensibilities cause them to cut up reality into one-sided pictures. For example, there is Mrs. Sands: "She could see the great open door. But butterflies she never saw; mice were only black pellets in kitchen drawers; moths she bundled in her hands and put out of the window. Bitches suggested only servant girls misbehaving. Had there been a cat she would have seen it—any cat, a starved cat with a patch of mange on its rump opened the floodgates of her childless heart. But there was no cat" (pp. 100–101). There is old Cobbet, whose life centers on his plants and whose watch tells him when he must water them. There is Mrs. Swithin's faith; there is her brother's skepticism.

But art suggests wholeness, the opposite of life's fragmentation. If Miss La Trobe's pageant represents English history, the world driven by the time-machine, it also suggests the unchanging essences, the timeless uniformity. For all the scenes representing the past allude to the living men and women in the audience. Thus when the pageant represents the Elizabethan age, not only are the actors modern men and women, but a dozen phrases recall the modern scene. The cargo in the ships of "Hawkins, Frobisher, Drake" includes "ingots of silver" that bring to mind the hooked salmon Isa observes when she falls in love with Giles. The "cargoes of diamonds" remind us of Mrs. Manresa's jewels, as the reference to "the green wood, the wild wood" reminds us of the "wild child of nature." And all of the episodes awaken similar associations— remind us that, as Mr. Streatfield explains, "We act different parts; but are the same" (p. 192). The same story is enacted for ever and ever; the story "of love; and of hate" (pp. 48, 90). Thus, in the

Elizabethan era, the tale of "a false Duke" and of the love of the duke's daughter for Ferdinando both illustrates the Manichean nature of things and alludes to the present: the false duke reminds one of Giles's treachery, or perhaps of Mrs. Manresa's tainted background ("her grandfather had been exported for some hanky-panky mid-Victorian scandal"), while Carinthia's love for Ferdinando obliquely refers to Isa's love for Mr. Haines—or to the universal condition of falling in love.

In the eighteenth century, again, we see that "the earth is always the same" (p. 125) and that mankind timelessly acts out the tale of love and hate—the Manichean oscillation. Thus Lady Harpy Harraden calls to mind Mrs. Manresa, and the allusion to stinking fish ("the old hag stinks like a red herring") alludes to the fish that Isa has ordered that morning. Again, there is the recurrence of the story of the babe in the basket (pp. 130, 88) and the love of Valentine for Flavinda parallels that of Carinthia for Ferdinando—and of Isa for her husband (or for Mr. Haines). When Lady Harpy Harraden accuses Sir Spaniel Lilyliver of being faithless (p. 146), we are reminded of Isa's accusations of her husband (" 'Plunge blade!' she said. And struck. 'Faithless!' she cried" [p. 113]). So the scene from the eighteenth century ends appropriately with the summarizing observation: "The God of love is full of tricks" (p. 148). Mrs. Swithin's "God is love" is, as ever, undercut by a variant of her brother's ridicule.

In the Victorian age the exhibition of the "terrible mixture in things" continues. In 1860 Eleanor Hardcastle falls in love with Edgar, but Eleanor's mother wants the girl to marry a clergyman named Sibthorp. When Mr. Hardcastle prays, however, the "hind-quarters of the donkey, represented by Albert the idiot," become "active," and, we learn, "a titter drowned Mr. Hardcastle's prayer" (p. 171). There is always the beast, or the idiot, to rouse mockery and jeering. The God of love is full of tricks—if He *is* the God of love.

In the "Present Day" section, finally, the audience is compelled to behold itself in mirrors. It sees, of course, only fragments: "Here a nose. . . . There a skirt. . . . Then trousers only. . . . Now perhaps a face. . . . Ourselves? But that's cruel. To snap us as we are, before we've had time to assume. . . . And only, too, in parts. . . . That's what's so distorting and upsetting and utterly unfair" (p. 184).

Moreover, "the very cows" join in, "and the barriers which should divide Man the Master from the Brute" are "dissolved." The dogs join in too. And one beholds not only the mixture in things but also the oneness of things. One takes Mrs. Swithin's "circular tour of the imagination—one-making. Sheep, cows, grass, trees, ourselves —all are one" (p. 175).

But Woolf does not share Mrs. Swithin's serene faith. She sees that what men need is "a centre. Something to bring us all to- gether" (p. 198); she yearns for the integration of matter and spirit, nature and mind: "It's odd that science, so they tell me, is making things (so to speak) more spiritual. . . . There, you can get a glimpse of the church through the trees . . ." (p. 199). But the vision of unity lasts only for a time. Miss La Trobe, the "commander," may hold the audience in the noose of her art—for a time—but always they are ready to slip the noose (p. 180), and the artist feels she has failed. She, too, is neither free nor whole. She is "the slave of [her] audience"; and "the need of drink [has] grown on her" as well as "the horror and the terror of being alone" (p. 211).

What she envisions, then, as she drinks in solitude, is a scene in which two figures at midnight, near a rock, speak to each other. She sees, of course, the two human figures who both hate and love —two figures like Giles and Isa:

> Alone, enmity was bared; also love. Before they slept, they must fight; after they had fought, they would embrace. From that em- brace another life might be born. But first they must fight, as the dog fox fights with the vixen, in the heart of darkness, in the fields of night. [P. 219]

Woolf, like Conrad, like James, like Stevens, returns to the "heart of darkness" and to the "dwellers in caves . . . among rocks" (p. 219). She sees the monstrous; but she sees, also, love. Flowers and dogs commingle.

A. D. Moody has observed that in *Between the Acts* Woolf avoids both "scorn or cynicism or despair" and "the idealisms of art or the superego." Her "comprehension of life . . . accepts life as it is, contingent, limited, relative, even as it seeks for its fulfilment: it serves the best possibilities in human beings, but does not set itself above the world in which they exist and must act." [17] Woolf's acceptance of limitations and contingencies, her journey "beyond idealism," is thus much like Stevens's repudiation of "the false imagination" and his embrace of "things as they are." Like Stevens, she recognizes that there are no final solutions and no escape from fatal Ananke. But she also finds "beauty and joy" amid the "roaring and cursing," the "violence and unrest." She has been accused (again, like Stevens) of being a mere "aesthete." But her "aestheticism"—if the word applies at all—is scarcely an escape from reality; it is, on the contrary, a means of grasping the real in its total complexity, without seeking to convert the structure of things into a facile structure of ideas. She is a very great realist, far too intelligent to be satisfied with the partial perspectives of idealists or of materialists. And in her detachment, which she shares with the men whose work we have examined, in her ability to blend sympathy and irony, to balance positive and negative responses to life, she creates that rounded image of life which the artistic imagination inflamed by a Manichean vision discovers again and again to be the truest account of our human tenure on earth.

NOTES

1. Virginia Woolf, *Jacob's Room and The Waves* (New York: Harcourt, Brace & World, Harvest Books, 1959), p. 42. All other citations are to this edition.

2. Virginia Woolf, *Night and Day* (London: Hogarth Press, 1915), pp. 358–59.

3. David Daiches, *Virginia Woolf* (Norfolk, Conn.: New Directions Books, 1942), pp. 112–13.

4. Joan Bennett, *Virginia Woolf: Her Art As a Novelist* (Cambridge: At the University Press, 1945), p. 45.

5. Charles G. Hoffman, "Virginia Woolf's Manuscript Revisions of *The Years,*" *PMLA* 84 (January 1969): 88–89.

6. E. M. Forster, *Virginia Woolf* (New York: Harcourt, Brace & Co., 1942), p. 17.

7. E. M. Forster, *Howards End* (New York: Vintage Books, 1958), p. 269.

8. Ibid., p. 193.

9. Woolf, *The Years* (New York: Harcourt, Brace & World, Harvest Books, 1965), p. 392. All subsequent citations are to this edition.

10. The Partigers are so named, I suspect, because they are all "parts" of the whole and are all analogized to birds—partridges perhaps.

11. One minor similarity between *Howards End* and *The Years* is that in both the mother dies, the father is unfaithful, and a younger woman

takes the place of the dead mother. Eleanor Partiger is thus parallel to Margaret Schlegel, Rose Partiger to Ruth Wilcox.

12. In his *The Metamorphoses of the Circle*, trans. Carley Dawson and Elliott Coleman (Baltimore: Johns Hopkins Press, 1966), Georges Poulet traces a pattern in the thought of Coleridge that strikingly resembles Woolf's vision of reality. Poulet's book is of the greatest interest to any student of symbolism.

13. "οὗτοι συνέχθειν, ἀλλὰ συμφιλεῖν ἔφυν" (p. 414).

14. Daiches, *Virginia Woolf*, p. 113.

15. See Ralph Freedman, *The Lyric Novel* (Princeton: Princeton University Press, 1965), for a sensitive analysis of the lyricism of Woolf's fiction.

16. Woolf, *Between the Acts* (New York: Harcourt, Brace & World, Harvest Books, 1969), p. 176. All subsequent citations are to this edition.

17. A. D. Moody, *Virginia Woolf* (Edinburgh and London: Oliver and Boyd, 1963), p. 96.

V. "THE WAR
THAT NEVER ENDS"

Patterns of Proliferation
in Wallace Stevens's Poetry

THE OLD ANTITHESIS of idealism and materialism tempts the
critic to divide writers into two camps, tender-minded and tough-
minded: blue-eyed Emersons and Shelleys on one side, scowling
Hobbeses and Zolas on the other. It is a convenient division, reminiscent of the neat counting of Stevens's Canon Aspirin's sister
(who had "*two* daughters, *one* / Of *four*, and *one* of *seven*"), but the
simplification of the dichotomy has, until recently at least, blurred
our understanding of Stevens's views and our appreciation of their
sturdiness. For many years Stevens was relegated to the camp of
the idealists; his emphasis on the imagination and on poetry as "a
means of redemption," together with his apparent antagonism to
reason, stamped him as a champion of the spirit, a "Platonist," a fop
of fancy. There was thus a failure to see that the "idealism" in his
view of things is inseparable from his "materialism," and that, indeed, the modern symbolist movement of which Stevens was a part
was not, as Charles Feidelson, Jr., has pointed out, "an extreme
recurrence of the romantic method in reaction from naturalism, a
'second swing of the pendulum.' ..." [1] For while Stevens could
adopt, at times, an ironic solipsism, advising himself, in an outburst
of euphoric desperation, to be

> The unspotted imbecile revery,
> The heraldic center of the world
> Of blue, blue sleek with a hundred chins,[2]
>
> [*CP*, p. 172]

154

all this spiritual gluttony, this mental battening and bulging, signified, as Stevens well knew, no permanent victory of mind over matter. There still remained, ineluctable, that which "momentarily declares / Itself not to be I"—a physical stuff "out there" in a world whose "blunt laws make an affectation of the mind" (*CP*, pp. 171, 519). He saw, indeed, in his darker moods, a world of "machine within machine within machine,"

> a world
> That is completely waste, that moves from waste
> To waste . . .
> [*OP*, p. 49]

Let the idealist say what he will, he is subject to the irresistible operations and conditions of the world-machine. Matter, as Santayana observed, "is the matrix and the source of everything: it is nature, the sphere of genesis, the universal mother." This mother —Stevens's "Madame La Fleurie"—who seems so benignant at times, becomes "a bearded queen, wicked in her dead light," "the hating woman, the meaningless place" (*CP*, pp. 454, 507). Earth is like an "oppressor that grudges [men] their death, / As it grudges them the living they live" (*CP*, p. 173). Idealists may assert the ubiquity and dominance of the imagination, but though "life and death were not / Till man made up the whole, / Made lock, stock and barrel / Out of his bitter soul," that bitter soul "dare not leap by chance into its own dark." The only emperor is, not the imagination, but the emperor of the ice-cream-like flux. Or perhaps it is fairer to say that there are two emperors, and that Stevens's poetry perfectly reflects that sense of the "ambiguities," of "dualities in unities," that we have singled out as the essential feature of the Manichean vision.

Thus the tensions in Stevens's poetry are exactly the same as those one finds in Melville or in Conrad or Woolf. "The symbolist is a writer for whom the world, theoretically, is indeterminate," writes Charles Feidelson, Jr.,

> but who spends his life making a place for symbolism in a determinate world. His art treads a thin line between his theoretical premises and certain practical conditions which, if fully admitted, would render his premises null and void. Out of that tension comes

his awareness of universal paradox, his sense that "opposite or discordant qualities" are equally as real as the power of reconciliation. And out of the sense of paradox comes his characteristic subject matter, his tendency to seek his theme in the final paradox of his own activity.[3]

This, succinctly, is what Stevens's struggle between imagination and reality is all about.

Now *reality*, as the canons of a philosophy of symbolic forms would have it, is known only in language: man lives in a symbolic world. But *reality* as Stevens sees it—or postulates it—is also the noumenal world. What that world *is* one cannot say. "What is it that vibrates, moves, is changed?" Stevens asks, quoting C. E. M. Joad; and he answers: "There is no answer. Philosophy has long since dismissed the notion of substance and modern physics has endorsed the dismissal" (*NA*, p. 25). Whatever it is, though, the noumenal world is an inexplicable ugliness: "the space is blank space, nowhere, without color, and ... the objects, though solid, have shadows and, though static, exert a mournful power" (*NA*, p. 31). It is a world of "complete poverty," an "anonymous blank," extraneous, gratuitous, senseless in its expression of senseless laws, senseless samenesses. "Reality is a jungle in itself. As in the case of a jungle, everything that makes it up is pretty much of one color" (*NA*, p. 26).

Also, as in the case of a jungle, everything that makes it up is pretty ruthless. Those who stress Stevens's gaiety and his buoyant celebrations of matter in the early poetry sometimes forget the vision in "Domination of Black" of the terrifying concatenations of senseless matter:

> I saw how the planets gathered
> Like the leaves themselves
> Turning in the wind.
> I saw how the night came,
> Came striding like the color of the heavy hemlocks.
> I felt afraid.
> And I remembered the cry of the peacocks.
>
> [*CP*, p. 9]

Like Conrad's Kurtz, who also saw into this heart of darkness, Stevens might well have recoiled with the peacock-shriek, "The horror! The horror!"

And if there is horror in the concatenations of matter according to "crass casualty"—or crass causality—there is also a sort of horror in the modern world of business and industrialism, that warlike world in which "the employer and employee contend," the "hacked-up world of tools." Thus Stevens views the condition of man in "Oxidia, banal suburb, / One-half of all its installments paid," as a condition of war:

> To live in war, to live at war,
> To chop the sullen psaltery,
>
> To improve the sewers in Jerusalem,
> To electrify the nimbuses—
>
> Place honey on the altars and die,
> You lovers that are bitter at heart.
>
> [*CP*, pp. 173–74]

Reality in the twentieth century is "a state of violence"—so intense that there is pressure on man's consciousness "to the exclusion of any power of contemplation" (*NA*, pp. 20, 22). And Stevens knows that the war will never be ended, the red and the blue house blended. This world, the intolerable stone or rock that the imagination must somehow make tolerable, this antipoetic force that destroys all lovely integrations, the world in which "Frogs Eat Butterflies. Snakes Eat Frogs. Hogs Eat Snakes. Men Eat Hogs"—this volcano, this "dreadful sundry," this world of "the negro undertaker / Filling the time between corpses," this "nigger cemetery"—it is this that must be resisted. Thus "the poetry of a work of imagination," Stevens writes in a significant passage at the end of *Parts of a World*, "constantly illustrates the fundamental and endless struggle with fact. It goes on everywhere, even in periods that we call peace." There is always

> a war between the mind
> And sky, between thought and day and night. It is
> For that the poet is always in the sun,
>
> Patches the moon together in his room
> To his Virgilian cadences, up down,
> Up down. It is a war that never ends.
>
> [N. p.]

This war, the struggle between imagination and reality, cannot be ended because man lives in a world of change. The self changes—

splits up into a thousand selves, a "milleman": "Can one man think
one thing and think it long?"

> And yet what good were yesterday's devotions?
> I affirm, and at midnight the great cat
> Leaps quickly from the fireside and is gone.
>   [*CP*, p. 264]

Fictions change as the self, as feelings, change. Fictions, indeed,
originate in feeling, in the desire for the "exhilaration of changes,"
"the more than rational distortion." "Flicked by feeling," man
names and renames the world. But the world always eludes his
crystal, keeps turning, and the mind must continually renew its
struggle with fact. Thus Stevens is entirely serious when, apropos
of the war between imagination and reality, he speaks of "the
going round / And round and round, the merely going round,
/ Until merely going round is a final good. . . ." To see fact and
fiction, garden and angel, flying round is to apprehend the only
reality that we can ever know—the reality of a thoroughly human
world, created by a violently selective and transmuting nervous
system and the violently synthesizing and transformational faculties. (Stevens defines imagination as "the sum of our faculties.")
Poetry is "the interdependence of reality and imagination as
equals," and Stevens's aim is to present the endless struggle of the
two in such a way as to reveal that there is no victory, the mind's
resistance is equal to reality's. Thus Stevens seeks always to present
the "circulation" or "undulation" or "up down," the interweaving
of reality and the imagination, the admixture. Indeed, it is the
essence of healthy-mindedness to recognize this admixture. If the
interdependence of reality and the imagination is not recognized,
human beings succumb to the madness of mistaking their ideas for
the structure of things; or they fall into the idiocy of pure sensation. "How mad would he have to be to say, 'He beheld / An order
and thereafter he belonged / To it'?" (*CP*, p. 426). Poetry is "a cure
of the mind," a "health." And "The Good Man Has No Shape"
because he will not give allegiance to any fixed system of ideas
masquerading as the final truth about reality.

What we witness, in short, in the development of Stevens's
poetry is the realization of the vision we have already contem-

plated in Melville, Hawthorne, James, Conrad, and Woolf: we see the "dubious, uncertain, and refracting light" of experience. The skepticism is boundless; but the fictionalizing, the translation of feeling into fictions, is endless too. And symbolism is one of the chief devices by which Stevens causes us to see that reality and imagination interpenetrate at every moment of life. What he was bent on writing—as his career unfolds we see the determination manifesting itself in ever-closer approaches to his objective—was the poem in which *every line* would be expressive of the war between the mind and fact—the war and the truce, the momentary peace of correspondence. By developing an immense symbolic "poem within, and above, a poem," an immense symbolic scheme proliferating from the two great centers, the recalcitrant contraries, Stevens saw that he would be able to render in every experience in life the conjunctions of spirit and matter and of "bliss and bale." The poem of the act of the mind would be the creation of reality itself—the only reality the mind can know. Poetry would be, not rhetoric, but the human experience in immediacy, the process of living, temporary constructions and reconstructions of the data. Every "victory" would be a new beginning, the purpose would be the process itself, the merely going round and round, the establishing of an equilibrium and the destruction thereof, the discovery of supreme fictions—until the wind blows. *Living* is thus what Stevens's later poetry seeks to present: the act of living in the changes of matter and mind, the "never-ending meditation." The long poems Stevens wrote late in his career all issue from this same fundamental idea and are built upon the same pattern. The method may be summarized in a phrase appropriate to the age: splitting and fusion. Characteristically the poet begins with an attempt to drive a wedge between reality and the imagination, to contemplate each separately. Aloof, detached, both grave and witty, he is willing to accept what he can find to solve the dilemma he poses to himself, but as scholar ("poetry is the scholar's art," said Stevens) he wishes to overlook nothing—his scrupulousness permits no facile resolutions. Though he may for a moment be carried away by his desire, he always recognizes the romantic agony for what it is and resolves afresh to think nothing that is not true. Yet even as he struggles to make distinctions, to drive the wedge deeper, he discovers that the airy substance of life, like Miltonic angels, soon knits again; and yet he is aware that reality and imagination are distinct; and yet he is aware that they are one. Thus the opening lines of *An Ordinary Evening in New Haven:*

> Of this,
> A few words, an and yet, and yet, and yet—
> As part of the never-ending meditation. . . .
>   [*CP*, p. 465]

What emerges, then, is a poetry in which every line vibrates with doubling images and with the ambiguities of all the lines (all the lines in all of Stevens's poems) that precede it. Stevens's problem becomes analogous to that of neoclassical satirists who achieve final elegance in a verse which contains an antithesis in every line or couplet. The analogy extends also to the use of appositives by both the satirists and Stevens. The poetry becomes endlessly the same, endlessly different: "the one moonlight, the various universe."

Because it is in the building up of this gigantic symbolic system enabling him to present simultaneously the real and the imagined, both split and fused, in an atmosphere of purest skepticism, that Stevens most perfectly realizes his conception of poetry as "the interdependence of reality and imagination as equals," we had better take a close look at the construction of that symbolic scheme. Stevens worked it out over half a century, and at his death the symbolism had proliferated so richly, so subtly, that there was nothing under the sun or moon that he could not assimilate into his categories. Every object and experience was converted into a token of the vision that informed his work. Thus to study this great system is to trace the adventures of an intelligence that, in its patience and discipline, was able to create a model for all other symbolists to envy and to draw upon in the great effort to search out the reality of the human condition in this universe.

Analysis of a symbolism created by a vigorous imagination is never easy, however, and when, as in Stevens's poetry, symbolic patterns are developed deliberately over some fifty years, critics may find themselves so dazzled by the proliferations of the meanings—by what Marianne Moore has called the "interacting veins of life between his early and later poems"—that they may decide to content themselves either with very crude descriptions of the symbolic system or with the reflection that, after all, given the complexity of the system, no adequate description of it is possible. Criticism of Stevens's poetry, after some forty years of assiduous scholarship, today tends to rest satisfied with these two disturbing solutions to its difficulties. On the one hand we are told that

> when he [Stevens] is talking about "reality" the associated images he consistently gives us are: earth, rock, sun, day, green, north, winter, nature and body; when he is talking about the "imaginary," the associated images are: musical instruments, air, moon, blue, south, summer, art and mind.[4]

On the other hand we are told:

> Granted this degree of intricacy [an intricacy of ambivalent attitudes expressed in admixtures of imagery], the conclusion that no ready symbolic system will codify his work must inevitably follow. ... Moon does not always equal the transubstantial. Sun does not always equal actuality which then equals subman. Nor do seasons, places, peoples, and ideas present a permanent aspect: ideas of order do not catalogue an inflexible paradigm.[5]

But neither of these approaches to the symbolism is of much help to us if we would achieve a very full and subtle understanding of what Stevens is doing in his poems. In the first statement, *north, winter, south,* and *summer* somehow find their way into the wrong bins, and none of Stevens's subtlety in handling these symbols is suggested. In the second statement, the critic is so deeply impressed by subtlety that he dismisses the possibility of discovering the pattern of the symbolism and implies that any codification must needs be "ready," "inflexible," and "permanent." But why, one wonders, must it "inevitably" follow that highly intricate poetry cannot receive symbolic codification? And why must such codification be rigid? Surely it is possible for a poet to establish a basic symbolism in one group of poems, then to modify and adapt this symbolism, perhaps ironically, in a second group; and surely criticism ought to be sensitive enough to discern such procedures and to lay them bare. Eugene Paul Nassar's study of Stevens's symbolism demonstrates that sensitive classification can significantly enlarge our grasp of what Stevens is doing. But even Nassar, I think, does not go far enough; and a thorough study of the whole complex of Stevens's symbolism is obviously needed if we would grasp and appreciate the range and beauty of Stevens's vision.

The need for such a study is emphasized by the fact that some of Stevens's most frequently employed symbols continue to be interpreted as mere images—or as instances of Stevens's delight in ambiguity. The existing interpretations of "Life is Motion" are a case in point. Without exception critics have joined Elder Olson[6] in finding the poem about as simple as the thesis stated in its title: "An uncomplicated affair," writes one critic, a poem that "satirizes the ungainly frontier and its animal spirits as Bonnie and Josie celebrate the marriage (of flesh and air) in Oklahoma with an operatic 'Ohoyaho.'"[7] Even the critic who perceives that *air* is associated with the imaginary in Stevens's poetry concludes that in "Life is Motion" "we witness . . . a correspondence of person and place, and see how they are unified."[8] One may grant criticism the right to dispense with what Marius Bewley has called the "wide range of reference to the other poems" in Stevens's work,[9] but can one ignore that the "marriage of flesh and air" is but one more variation of the theme Stevens was fond of orchestrating throughout his life: the marriage of reality and the imagination? An insensitivity to the symbolic import of many of Stevens's most persistent images and epithets—*Negro, hill, serpent, bronze, point, round, tip, wood, dove, rise, fall,* etc.—continues to blur our awareness of what is going on in the poetry.

Consider the first word on our list, *Negro.* Now a title such as "Like Decorations in a Nigger Cemetery" makes a sort of sense on a nonsymbolic level, and Stevens himself did not bother, when questioned, to spell out the symbolic meaning of his title. Thus it seemed enough to conclude that "*Like Decorations in a Nigger Cemetery* is a sort of autumn journal in which [Stevens's] (frequently profound) moods of the season are given cryptic intimation, and mocked at in the title, which apparently means as oddly-assorted a collection of memorials as one finds in such cemeteries."[10] Another critic, writing ten years later, said that the poem, "as its gaudy title implies, revels in incongruity."[11] But it was not until such systematic studies as my "Wallace Stevens: His Theory of Poetry and its Application to his Poems" (1956) and Nassar's *Wallace Stevens: An Anatomy of Figuration* (1966) appeared, that understanding of the symbolism of this title became possible. It will be worthwhile to review the evidence that leads to an unambiguous interpretation of Stevens's "gaudy title" so as to suggest the powers and advantages of codification.

As early as 1916, in *Three Travelers Watch a Sunrise*, we find Stevens contrasting speechless Negroes with the articulate Chinese who discuss the "windless pavilions" of their court. In this symbolic play the Negroes are part of the mindless world, a blood-reality, which is the antithesis of the uninvaded "porcelain" which the Third Chinese prefers and advocates. They stand in fact very close to the First Chinese, a sensualist and a glutton, distinguished from the Negroes only by his power of speech. The action of the play discloses the attempt of the Second Chinese, "a man of sense and sympathy," to reconcile the worlds represented by the Negroes, the First Chinese, and the bloody hanging, with the world of the coldly abstracted Third Chinese.

The next appearance of the Negro occurs in a poem entitled "In the South," published in *Soil* in 1917. In this little lyric Stevens draws a contrast between the "black mother of eleven children" and the "frail princes of distant Monaco." The argument of the poem is that if the quilt which the black woman hangs under the pine trees is associated with *eleven* children, then the "paragon of a parasol" possessed by the princes of Monaco must disclose "at least one baby." For, as Stevens ironically suggests, even creatures as elegant and refined as these must have *something* of the physical about them.

Two poems which appeared in the first edition of *Harmonium* and an uncollected poem of the same period also associate the Negro with reality. In "Lulu Gay" (*OP,* p. 26) the poet creates an amused picture of a carefree girl who describes to a number of "eunuchs" her adventures among the "barbarians," apparently Negroes. The eunuchs are excited by Lulu's vivid colors and scents, and when she tells them of "how the barbarians kissed her / With their wide mouths / And breaths as true / As the gum of the gum-tree," the eunuchs cry out, "Olu . . . Ululalu" (*OP,* p. 26). Being what Stevens in a later poem calls "castratos of moon-mash," the eunuchs are tortured by their inability to make contact with a world of such opulent fleshiness.

In the *Harmonium* poems the picture is amplified. One of these, "Virgin Carrying a Lantern," contrasts the hot sensuality of a negress with the frigid piety of a maid. Observing the virgin with her lantern, the negress naturally supposes that the virgin will welcome physical embraces. In the other poem, "O Florida, Venereal Soil," the Negro acquires a slightly broader connotation. Florida, a realm of Darwinian do-or-die, is the appropriate habitat of the "negro undertaker," and it is the lasciviousness and death of the Negro's world that the poet seeks to escape by turning to a Florida of the imagination.

In *Ideas of Order* (1935) we find the Negro appearing as a symbol of reality in four poems, "Like Decorations," "Mud Master," and the companion-pieces "Nudity at the Capital" and "Nudity in the Colonies." In "Mud Master" the sun, because it is master of the realm of juicy fleshiness, is described paradoxically as "blackest of pickaninnies." In "Nudity at the Capital" the Negro's nudity is viewed ironically as a fictive covering over his "innermost atom," and in "Nudity in the Colonies" the poet observes, again ironically, that to be fully naked one must be stripped even of names— "anonymous." Then in *Owl's Clover* (1936) we encounter the Negro in his native habitat, Africa, a realm of "death without a heaven," which the imaginative angels from the North invade, seeking to conquer the lion- and jaguar-men.

In *Parts of a World* (1942) the Negro appears twice more in clusters similar to those already described. The rich magnolia, Solange, "a nigger tree with a nigger name," is viewed as a lush consolation for "the spirit left helpless by the intelligence" (in "The News and the Weather"), and the Negroes playing football in the park dispel the "intimations of winter" and of the "abstract" toward which the father walks in autumn (in "Contrary Theses II").

Stevens's last poems continue this symbolism. In "The Auroras of Autumn" (1948) the father, symbol of the imagination, fetches negresses to dance, as part of the barbarous reality he likes to transform into fictive patterns; and in "The Sick Man" (1950) a man listening to voices of "black men" from the South and to "voices in chorus" from the North, hopes to regain his health by achieving a "unison" of the two in "good hail of himself."

All of these poems point unmistakably to the conclusion that the Negro must be viewed as a symbol of reality in Stevens's poetry. But before accepting that conclusion, we must take into account two early poems in which the Negro appears to exhibit imaginative qualities. In "The Jack-Rabbit" we find the following:

> In the morning,
> The jack-rabbit sang to the Arkansaw.
> He carolled in caracoles
> On the feat sandbars.
>
> The black man said,
> "Now, grandmother,
> Crochet me this buzzard
> On your winding-sheet,
> And do not forget his wry neck
> After the winter."
>
> The black man said,
> "Look out, O caroller,
> The entrails of the buzzard
> Are rattling."
>
> [*CP*, p. 50]

Here the jack-rabbit is a creature of the South—therefore, by hypothesis, of reality; his carolings and caracoles appear to be manifestations of his *élan vital*, exactly the sort of animal exuberance that Stevens finds in, say, the jungles of Yucatan. Yet the enemy of this creature is the Negro, and he asks his grandmother to crochet an *image* upon her winding sheet. Is not the Negro a creature of the imagination, attempting to dominate reality? In the face of the contrary evidence gathered above, such an interpretation appears implausible, yet examination of "Some Friends from Pascagoula" gives it support. In that lyric Stevens, addressing the Negroes "Cotton" and "black Sly," asks them to describe an eagle's descent from the sky, a descent described as a "sovereign sight / Fit for a kinky clan." Apparently the eagle is just the sort of creature to win the admiration of people who live in a southern reality: the "kinky clan" finds its imagination satisfied in the mere description of an animal's flight.

It appears, then, that the Negro *may* function in Stevens's poetry as an imaginative creature. But we must notice that the Negro's imagination is only what one would expect in a creature of the flesh: it extends to buzzard-images and to descriptions of eagles, no further. So Stevens makes *ironic* use of the Negro-symbol in order to suggest that even the least imaginative of creatures do not see "things as they are." Similar ironies appear in "Nuances on a

Theme by Williams," in which an "old horse" and a "widow's bird" are viewed as "intelligences," and in "On an Old Horn," in which a bird is compared to a man because it is able to "tranquilize the torments of confusion" by singing from its "ruddy belly."

It is evident, then, that the title "Like Decorations in a Nigger Cemetery" can be read to mean "Like Decorations in a realm of gross fleshiness and death." But since the poem consists of a series of metaphors and similes by which the poet transforms this gross and ugly realm, "Like Decorations" very likely means "decorations by means of likeness"—that is, "metaphors and similes" applied to the brute flux. *Like* becomes an adjective instead of a preposition, and the whole title may be roughly translated "Imaginings in Reality." If such an interpretation seems forced, one has only to consider the many titles in Stevens's work which follow a similar pattern: "Hymn from a Watermelon Pavilion": a creation of the imagination issuing from a world of juicy vegetation—reality. "A Postcard from a Volcano": an imaginative creation, a poem, issuing from reality, a realm of violence and death. "The Dove in the Belly": the dulcet imagination in the grinding peristalsis of reality. "The Owl in the Sarcophagus": the owlish poet or imagination in the realm of death. "A Golden Woman in a Silver Mirror": the female, sunny earth reflected in the glass of the imagination. "Academic Discourse at Havana": an imaginative discourse in the lush physical world. "The Revolutionists Stop for Orangeade": poets in revolt, imaginative beings, stop for a drink from the juicy South, a drink of reality. "Nudity at the Capital": the absence of the imagination in the habitat of the imagination. "Angel Surrounded by Paysans": the imagination surrounded by reality. And so on!

Now the symbol of the Negro is not difficult to interpret, and even the most skeptical, confronted with the patterns of association, will acknowledge that *Negro*, whatever other meanings the term may have, functions chiefly as a token of sensuous reality. But such an interpretation is made possible only by studying its adventures in the entire body of Stevens's work, and the critic lacking knowledge of these adventures runs the risk of passing over many of the most interesting and evocative implications of Stevens's terms. That *Negro* may be employed ironically is an instance of the sort of insight permitted by a total description of the symbolic patterns. Of course the knowledge of these patterns must be applied judiciously. It is the primary illusion of life in a poem that determines meaning, and secondary meanings derived from outside the poem may be added only on condition that they do not conflict with, but on the contrary reinforce, the meanings implied by the primary illusion. But in reading the poems of a man whose work is all of a piece, we may certainly look for and expect the most remarkable kinds of subtleties. Before going on to catalogue the major patterns of Stevens's symbolism, I wish to stress—what cannot be stressed too strongly—the intricacy of Stevens's symbolic manipulations. A passage from "Notes toward a Supreme Fiction" illustrates the complexity of Stevens's later poetry:

> We say: At night an Arabian in my room
> With his damned hoobla-hoobla-hoobla-how,
> Inscribes a primitive astronomy
>
> Across the unscrawled fores the future casts
> And throws his stars around the floor. By day
> The wood-dove used to chant his hoobla-hoo
>
> And still the grossest iridescence of ocean
> Howls hoo and rises and howls hoo and falls.
> Life's nonsense pierces us with strange relation.
> [*CP*, p. 383]

In these lines we witness three related events: as the chanting Arabian imposes his astronomy upon the uncharted heavens, so the wood dove chants and the ocean howls. It is as if man, the lower animals, and the inorganic world were engaged in a common endeavor to sing the same song. (Samuel French Morse has said that the lines suggest "the universal existence of the poetic impulse." [12]) But students of Stevens's symbolism may also recognize that the poet is here disclosing, in line after line, the conjunctions of reality and the imagination—conjunctions so close that it becomes virtually impossible to sever the two or to say whether one is contemplating, at a given moment, the real or the imagined.

Stevens begins with pure imagination. The Arabian astronomer, like the astronomer in "A Candle A Saint," is one of "the sleepers" who make of the world a dream, a madman whose madness is woven of the same stuff as the madness of the night. He appears "at night" because that is the time for imaginative extravagance. His "damned hoobla-hoobla-hoobla-how" is an incantation of the imagination, a kind of magic, "damned" not only because it is amusingly infuriating but also because it is like the magic of salvation and damnation. Is the astronomer a scientist or a magician? Stevens means, of course, that he is both, since astronomy is but a kind of magic of the imagination. Yet for all the frenzy, the physical world does not dissolve into the Arabian's fictions: Stevens reminds us that the astronomy is inscribed upon an "unscrawled" future, a reality which is, after all, undifferentiated, unsymbolized, evading all fictive formulae.

The line "And throws his stars around the floor" requires very close analysis. That the Arabian throws *his* stars underscores the basic theme of Stevens's poetry, the theme of the interdependence of reality and the imagination, for the courses of the stars in the Arabian's astronomy are, ambiguously, the courses of the Arabian's fictions and the courses of the stars themselves, the *Ding an sich*. But why does he throw them around "the floor"? And why *around* the floor rather than *upon* it? Here a knowledge of the symbolic system is indispensable. A close study of *floor*[13] reveals that the word invariably meant, for Stevens, reality—the earth itself, on which man stands and from which he tries to rise. Close associates of *floor* are *hill* and *rock*, and when Stevens employs these terms he generally introduces also a submerged metaphor of varnishing: moonlight or paint or some other fictive varnish is applied to the bare floor, or a brilliant creature passes over the floor, thus metamorphosing the barren reality. As for the preposition *around*, it is one of the many terms of geometry (others are *line, point, ring, circle, cone, sphere, angle* and *ellipses*) that Stevens characteristically employs in order to stress imaginative ordering of the chaos of the material flux,[14] and a close study of Stevens's use of the preposition discloses that he had its symbolic meaning in mind when he was writing his earliest poems. Thus the line "And throws his stars around the floor" means (1) that the Arabian astronomer, in an act of extravagant imagination, imposes his fictions around—that is, in fictive patterns upon—reality; (2) that this creature of the imagination throws real stars in fictive patterns over reality; or (3) that the creature of the imagination throws real or fictive stars indiscriminately, profusely, in the fury of his imagining, over reality. In a poetry whose theme is the interdependence of reality and the imagination, such variety of interpretation is to be encouraged, not evaded.

We turn to the wood dove chanting his hoobla-hoo. Why "by day"? Why a dove? Or, why a wood dove? Why "used to"? If the creature of the pure imagination, the Arabian astronomer, chants "at night," time of the moon's and imagination's ragings, the wood dove, less imaginative, chants "by day." It is reality's time, as a number of Stevens's poems make clear.[15] For if the imagination is perforce associated with sleep and dream, reality is associated with the familiarity and ordinariness of daytime, as well as with the wakefulness of animals that must be alert in order to survive. As for the dove, it is, as close readers of Stevens will recognize, one of his most frequently employed symbols of the imagination; yet here Stevens calls it a "wood-dove"—the term *wood* symbolizing reality, which resembles a wood in its darkness and tangled disorder.[16] Thus *wood* stresses either that the habitat of the imagination is reality or that the bird belongs half to the reality of the wood, half to the imagination symbolized by *dove*. The dove chants her song, but by virtue of her limited imagination she is capable of only one hoobla-how to the Arabian's three, and she chants in the reality of "day" and of the "wood." Or rather, she "used to" chant, for another one of the strange relations that Stevens here perceives is the relation of events in the memory to events in immediacy: to bring past and present together is after all one of the chief occupations of the imagination as it constructs its fictive "descriptions without place."

We have, then, this much: as the Arabian, a figure of the imagination, imposes his fictions upon reality, so the wood dove, a creature half of reality and half of the imagination, performs a similar act. We move finally, on this scale of descending imaginative power, to the third member, the ocean, symbol of pure reality. If Stevens is amused by the first two instances of imaginative activity, his scrutiny of pure matter's poetic behavior is pure irony, as if he were to say, "Ho! Even the ocean imagining the world!"

That the ocean is a symbol of the material flux will be clear to readers of such well-known poems as "The Comedian as the Letter C" and "Sea Surface Full of Clouds." Close readers of Stevens will also note that he often characterizes reality as being wet, guzzly, juicy, flowing, dripping, or oozing, whereas the imagination, in contrast, is often dry and fixed. Here Stevens also stresses the ocean's materiality by employing the adjective *grossest.* Yet even this gross machine of ocean displays an "iridescence" that Stevens invariably associates with the imagination. As for the rise and fall of the waves, whatever that may signify on a nonsymbolic level, it is, as symbol, a deliberate rendering of a kind of imaginative ordering of reality.[17] The symbolic associates of *rise and fall* in Stevens's poetry are *up and down, to-and-fro,* and *undulation,* all of which are employed either to render the vital interdependence of reality and the imagination or to suggest the movement of the poet's rhythms. Moreover, *rising* and *falling,* taken separately, are almost invariably employed by Stevens to symbolize imaginative transformations, *rising* being associated with the poetic metamorphoses that enable to throw off the great weight of reality, and *falling* (as well as its associates *running down* and *descending*) referring to the descent of imaginative riches from heaven.

Small wonder, then, that Stevens concludes these lines with the statement "Life's nonsense pierces us with strange relation." The relation he is speaking of is obviously more than the presence of "hoo" in each of the three events. It is the presence in all three of the conjunction of reality and the imagination. And these events "pierce" us[18] in the sense that they awaken our awareness of the world: we experience the "momentary existence on an exquisite plane" that Stevens regarded as the characteristic effect of poetry.

Here we may return to the critic who writes that *moon* does not always equal the imagination. I grant that *moon* may on occasion symbolize more than imagination (and it can always be argued that the moon in a given poem is just the moon, as Blake's Tiger is, in a sense, just a tiger); but I have little doubt that *one* of the symbolic meanings of the word is always the imagination and I can find no evidence to refute that contention. It may be that the terms I have here been studying—*floor, around, wood, day, rise,* and *fall*—do not always equal what they equal in the passage I have explored. An image used as image in the early poetry sometimes does not appear as symbol until ten or twenty years later; moreover, the whole bent of Stevens's effort is to exhibit the interdependence of reality and imagination, and in consequence he creates, as I shall presently show, huge families of terms that symbolize *both* reality and imagination. But despite these intricacies, the major clusters of his symbolism are not difficult to isolate and codify (as I believe I have already shown), and it is only by means of codification that many of the problems presented by the poetry can be solved.

Stevens himself has provided an important clue to help us in our task of codification. In "Effects of Analogy," after discussing several kinds of analogy in poetry, he offers as his first major conclusion, "every image is the elaboration of a particular of the subject of the image," and goes on to say, "if this is true, it is *a realistic explanation of the origin of images*" (italics mine). In a closely related essay, "Three Academic Pieces," he writes that the proliferation of such analogies "extends an object" and intensifies the sense of reality, and that the intensified sense of reality creates, in turn, other resemblances, new analogies; the proliferation of resemblances, which is also a proliferation of images, might thus proceed indefinitely as long as the subject remains constant. Theoretically, given the subject and the first particular that enters the poet's mind, we should be able to infer all the images subsequently elaborated. If, for example, a writer's subject is Puritanism and his first particular a rock, we might expect images of hardness and coldness to proliferate from this particular, while images of softness, fluidity, and warmth might suggest an opposed attitude, less rigid and ascetic. Again, the rock is gray and we might expect a proliferation of other somber images, which would then elicit a host of opposed images of gaudiness. Since the images of color would breed still other images, the proliferations would continue until the poet had done with Puritanism as his subject.

In practice, of course, the proliferation of images is far more complicated than this illustration suggests. The imagination may uncover its richest images through associations so devious that the intellect can scarcely trace them. Stevens suggests as much when he writes:

> The point at which this process [proliferation] begins, or rather at which this growth begins, is the point at which ambiguity has been reached. The ambiguity that is so favorable to the poetic mind is precisely the ambiguity favorable to resemblance. [*NA*, pp. 78–79]

This being so, a poet's images can be traced to their source only with difficulty. Nevertheless, if "every image is the elaboration of a particular of the subject" and if, as Stevens asserts, this is "a realistic explanation of the origin of images," it should be possible to lay bare many of the associational patterns by which the poet comes to include any given image in his work.

Now in attempting to reconstruct the patterns of Stevens's images and epithets, we are exploring the workings of an imagination that conceives its

> voyaging to be
> An up and down between two elements,
> A fluctuating between sun and moon. . . .
>
> [*CP*, p. 35]

These two elements are *reality* and *imagination*. But we must remember Stevens's dictum in "Effects of Analogy": "Every image is a restatement of the subject of the image *in the terms of an attitude*" (*NA*, p. 128; italics mine). For Stevens there are basically two different realities—a posited objective world of matter in motion (a fearful world which is violent, ever-threatening, and destructive) and a subjective reality which is abundant, rich, sensuous, "green and gay." Also there are basically two different imaginations in his poetry—a false and a true, the former cold and artificial, closely related to the reason, the latter rich, vital, and productive. As Stevens's attitudes toward reality and the imagination shift, his imagery inevitably changes. If reality in one poem provides the poet with his deepest satisfactions, in the next it is a horror. If the imagination is often the bountiful patron and guardian angel, it sometimes provides nothing comparable to the satisfactions of a reality undissolved in mental categories, and when it is divorced from human experiences the imagination becomes as ugly and alien as brute fact. "Merely going round" *is* a final good in Stevens's work, and the symbolism subtly reflects his shifting moods.

When we understand, then, that Stevens's "up and down between two elements" is actually an up and down between four (or more), our next step is to identify the particulars from which the imagery seems inevitably to spring. The frequent occurrences in his poetry of *sun, moon, South* and *North, summer* and *winter* suggest that these are generative particulars, and we can derive from them virtually the whole body of the symbolism. Thus *sun*, whatever other connotations the word may have, is a symbol of reality, and associated symbols of warmth and vitality proliferate directly from it, along with contrasting symbols of coldness and lifelessness. Then, since the sun is red or golden, vivid colors come to be associated with reality, whereas the imagination is symbolized by the cold, pale hues of moonlight. Again, since *South* is a symbol of reality, whatever is contained in the South may also stand for reality; so there occurs a proliferation of symbols of southern countries, tropical zones, jungle animals, plants, and the like. These call up their opposites in the realms of the imagination: northern countries, civilized places, civilized creatures. And so Stevens's imagination proceeds, engendering new symbols of which each one, being consubstantial with the others in its family, may stand synecdochically for the entire realm of which it is part. In the end Stevens creates the vast system of symbols which, being "in harmony with each other," constitute "a poem within, or above, a poem" (*NA*, p. 78).

Since Stevens's chief concern in his poetry is to exhibit the incessant conflict between his two, or four, realms—that is, since "the poetry of a work of the imagination constantly illustrates the fundamental and endless struggle with fact" [19]—the relationships between the symbols may be viewed most clearly if we study the major antithetical patterns developed: remembering always that under the pressure of changes in attitude, the symbolic meanings must change. What we must try to do is in a sense to place ourselves inside the mind of the poet: to understand his ways of piecing the world together, to absorb his memory so that we may know how, having established a basic symbolism in the early poems, he is able, under the pressure of feelings of attraction and revulsion, to modify this symbolism, discovering new meanings in symbols whose use had once been limited. We have already seen how Stevens makes ironic use of the Negro-symbol to underscore the idea that even the least imaginative creatures imagine the world. But that process of extension, by irony, of symbolic meanings is not at all uncommon in his poetry, and we shall see repeated illustrations of it in the third section of this chapter.

What follows, then, is a catalogue of Stevens's symbolism as constructed under the pressure of his shifting moods: a record of the "felt thought" of a mind that moves, in its symbolic workings, sometimes along broad and well-marked paths, sometimes into uncharted, almost unchartable territory. What I have tried to do is to expose the *logic* of the symbolic system: to show why it was necessary, even inevitable, that Stevens employ the symbols he came to employ in rendering his vision of life. In effect, I say that the symbolism could not have been other than it is, given Stevens's habits of mind. But if the reader would prefer a quasi-statistical tabulation of Stevens's symbols, together with an indication of their meanings in thousands of passages, I refer him to the evidence in my doctoral dissertation, particularly to the lengthy appendix upon which this codification is based.[20]

REALITY'S CRUDITY, SHAPELESSNESS, GROTESQUERY; IMAGINATION'S REFINEMENT, PRECISION, AND DELICACY

Reality, being a purely physical, mindless world in which imaginative activities have no place or occur only as accidental by-products of the collocations of matter, is symbolized by those countries and places least invaded and transformed by man: tropical jungles, forests, thickets, and wildernesses, often physically opulent, often terrifying lands of death. Because physical abundance is greatest in the warm southern countries, the sun-countries, *Africa, South America, Cuba,* and the *southern United States* are invariably viewed as reality's lands. (*Florida,* with its romantic associations, is a special case, sometimes a land congenial to the imagination, sometimes a land of sensuality and death, world of the "negro undertaker.") Reality's formlessness is aptly represented by the *American Southwest.* Because reality "in itself" is an undifferentiated flux, a chaos, a "dreadful sundry," Stevens sometimes views it with abhorrence as a *dump,* an *abyss,* a *swamp,* a *waste,* a *delirium,* a *marsh,* a *slum.* Lacking the symmetries of the imagination, it is a grotesque and misshapen world: a *blob,* a *blotch,* a *blur, freakish, quirkish, eccentric, dwarfed* or *humped, tortured,* or *wry.* It has never been to school, this world, and has never learned manners or grace: it is *barbaric, boorish, crude, perverse, primitive, rough, rowdy, stubborn, peevish, sullen, vulgar, wild, gruff, free* and *casual.* It is full of such crudities as *sticks, stumps, weeds, slop, rags, peels, hunks,* and *thorns,* and its odors are *pungent* or *rancid, putrid* and *rank;* it is, indeed, no more than one vast *belly, craw, maw;* a great *trough* or *tub.* Its rude plain foods are the *cabbage, radish, turnip, cheese, taters,* and *sop.*

Imagination, because it does away with the blood-warmth of the physical world, abides in the white abstract purity of the *arctic.* Because it imposes form upon the undifferentiated flux, its natural habitat is the civilized countries of the *North,* of *Europe* and *America,* a world of cities and buildings, not of animals and vegetation. The imagination is particularly fond of *edifices* and finds its natural expression in such enlargements and elevations as *domes* and *pillars, pinnacles* and *porches, steeples, towers, porticos,* and *balconies.* It delights in geometric forms, in *arches, angles, circles, cones, spheres,* and *globes.* If reality is slovenly and sprawling, the imagination seeks precision and definition: prefers the *keen,* the *incisive,* the *sharp,* the *sure,* the *exact,* the *fine,* the *pointed,* the *edged,* the *piercing,* the *deft.* If reality is boorish, the imagination is *affected.* If reality is sloppy, the imagination is *elegant, suave, subtle, prim, debonair.* If reality maunders and slouches, imagination moves on *tiptoe, minces* or *promenades.* If reality is casual, imagination is *correct* and *gallant.* In contrast with the world of the belly is the world of eighteenth-century refinement, of *chandeliers* and *coiffures, parasols* and *tea, filaments* and *fillets* and *fans, demoiselles* and *French,* the *slender,* the *slight,* and the *slim.* In contrast with the huge and swollen plants of the jungle-reality are flowers of rare delicacy and sweetness—*jasmine, marguerite, coquelicot, eglantine.*

CREATURES

The creatures one finds in the jungles and swamps of the sun-countries or on the sprawling plains of the uncivilized Southwest are, as one might expect, simple and uncomplicated, entirely devoid of subtlety or delicacy: creatures such as the *ox* "with its organic boomings," the *bucks* that clatter over Oklahoma, the *dog,* the *frog,* the *bear,* the *donkey.* To this list we may add a number of human beings of a charming simplicity, directness, and candor: *children,* the *yeoman,* the *yokel,* the *ignorant man,* the *clown,* the *Johannisberger Hans,* the *Dane,* the *Russian,* the *peasant;* and we must not forget the naked *savages,* the *Negro* and the *negress, Eve,* and the *concubine* or *demimonde.* The cats are subtler, and some of them, such as the *firecat*, are so subtle and mysterious that they must be viewed as creatures of the imagination, delicate tasters of imagination's milk. The *swine* lies in the heat and torpor of a world unstimulated by the magical imagination. But reality, despite its mindless inertia, is also a wild and clamorous struggle for life, a struggle that begins when the sun rises and the *cock*, the *red bird*, crows, or as the *grackles* and *peacocks* utter their hideous cries. In this "poisoned wood" the *snakes* threaten, as do the *undertaker* and *Berzerk*; and because the conditions of existence are warlike, reality may be symbolized in the centurion, the soldier, the "butcher, seducer, bloodman, reveller."

If these are for the most part creatures of warm flesh and blood, the creatures of the imagination are of course "people in the air": *ghosts*, *phantoms* and *skeletons*, or the equally airy *astronomers*, *scholars*, *philosophers*, *Chinese*, *rabbis*, *Jews*, *doctors*. Then there are those with romantic dispositions, the truest lovers of phosphor, the *drunkard*, the *lover*, *young ladies about to be married*, *Cinderella*, the *nymph*, the *virgin*, the *Polish aunt*, the *widow*, the *youth*, the *ephebe*, the *musician*, the *poet*, *Ariel*. Because the imagination softens and sweetens the harsh and bitter reality, it becomes the rou-couing *dove*; because poetry is the scholar's art, imagination is the studious *owl*; and there are the immemorial *swan*, *nightbird*, and *thrush*.

In the exquisite edifices created by the imagination dwell the *monsieur* and the *lady*. And then there are the impressive ones, figures whom imagination has endowed with fictive nobility, potency, and sanctity: a host of unflinching heroes (*captain*, *major*, *general*, *chief*, *chevalier*, *paladin*); a courtful of aristocrats (*prince*, *king*, *queen*, *rodomontade*); and, to fill the cloudy domes and steeples of the imagination, a galaxy of religious figures (*bishop*, *cardinal*, *monk*, *priest*, *martyr*, *saint*, *angels*, *seraphim*). If we are mothered by reality, imagination is the *father*, *Adam*, the *parent* and *patron*. It is also, because of its amazing dexterity and command, the *entrepreneur*, the *impressario*, the *virtuoso*, the *master*, the *orator*, the *magistrate*. But imagination is not solely the possession of these exalted beings. Each creature pieces the world together according to its capacity, and in Stevens's poetry a surprising number of animals incapable of "imagining" in the ordinary sense of the word are discovered imposing their ardent fictions upon the world: the roaring *lion* "Reddens the sand with his red-colored noise" or the bird, singing from its belly, creates a "bird-world." A *horse* becomes an "intelligence" and *carpenters, tailors, shearsmen,* and *mechanics* raging for order are continually piecing, patching, stitching, and cutting reality into fictive patterns.

REALITY'S PHYSICAL ABUNDANCE AND VITALITY; IMAGINATION'S COLDNESS, REMOTENESS, NOTHINGNESS

In the hot moist countries of the sun, the vegetation is lush, green, and juicy, and Stevens delights in emphasizing its abundance, the succulence, the sheer "gobbiness" of physical being. Reality is a great scoop of *ice cream,* a *honeycomb,* a slough of oozing *mud,* a *watermelon pavilion, guzzly, juicy, moist, sopped, sprayed, wet, dripping* and *flowing.* Glutted on water and sun, it becomes *fat,* it *bulges,* it is *stuffed, packed, piled, rotund, copious.* And if it is a world of shameless eating and sleeping, it is also a land of shameless sexuality, a *venereal* soil, fantastically *fertile, concupiscent, lewd, lascivious, lusty, potent, virile, fecund;* a land of *births* and *blooms* and *blossoms,* a *nunnery* in the Elizabethan sense, a great *orgy,* one vast *seduction.* What energy is not consumed in sexual activity is given to the struggle for survival, which is waged by the *fierce,* the *robust,* and the *healthy.* The creatures who "anger to live" are *supple, tough, strong,* and the world for them is *fresh, big, breathing, spontaneous.* Because the competition for life is continuous in this reality of do or die, this world is also *awake* and *alert.*

But if the southern reality swarms thus with a vigorous life, imagination secretes itself in the cold and loneliness of the north. It prefers to be *alone,* to *meditate;* to be *clandestine, concealed, remote, secluded, secret, separate, sequestered, solitary.* It seeks the *far,* the *final,* the *furtive,* the *hidden,* the *high,* the *topmost,* the *distant.* It lives in a sexless arctic, *bleak, polar, stark, hard, icy.* Because it fixes and freezes the fluent mundo in its categories, it is properly represented by such materials as *bronze, marble, plaster,* and *porcelain.* Because it purifies a world which is tangled and muddy, washing away the dirt of reality, it is *clean, clear, immaculate, pure.* If reality is lewd, the imagination is *chaste.* If reality is squirmingly alive, the imagination is often *dead, dry, bloodless, emaciated, gaunt, lean, thin,* or *wasted.* Indeed, the world of the imagination, totally insubstantial, may be only a *cloud,* a *mist,* a *dew,* a *foam,* pure *air* or *space* or *ether,* a *blank,* a *vacancy,* a *nothingness.*

Colors

The hot sun of the South is *gold* and *red,* and its bold bright colors are everywhere symbolic of reality. The earth itself is *brown.* The jungle of reality is one overwhelming *green,* but because this jungle is a confusion, lacking the harmony that only the imagination can provide, its appropriate colors are also *piebald* and *motley.* Instead of a simplicity and perfection, one finds in reality objects *flecked, speckled, splashed, stained, streaked,* and *tinged.* And while this jostling diversity is often pleasant, Stevens never forgets that the *blackness* of death will dominate in the end.

From heaven and the moon the imagination takes its colors: the *whiteness* of abstraction, the *pallor,* the *paleness,* the *phosphor,* the *silver,* the *alabaster,* the *ivory,* the *opalescence;* from the sky the *blue,* the *azure,* the *transparence.* Imagination, never point-blank or obvious, prefers the subtle *hues* and *tints* and tincts. It flees from the sun and retreats into *shadows,* the *dark,* the *dim,* the *dusky,* into the romantic *indigo, lavender, iris,* and *heliotrope.* Yet imagination is also a furious fire, and its ragings may be so intense as to be indistinguishable from those of the sun; we must consider ambiguities in the color symbolism later.

Reality's Turmoil, Violence, Vigor; Imagination's Peacefulness and Repose

Before the fury of the material flux and the violence of the struggle for survival, the imagination often seems impotent. The world is one vast *dizzle-dazzle,* a *golden fury,* a *concussion,* a *convulsion,* an *apocalypse,* a *tempest,* a *bubbling turbulence,* a *volcano,* a *war.* Reality's winds *blow* and *bluster* and *whirl,* in *gales* and *gusts;* oceans *batter* and *heave* and *plunge;* in the jungles animals *claw, grapple, peck, jostle, leap, stalk,* and *squirm.*

The imagination, however, shrinks from all this frenzy and would *tranquilize* the torments of confusion: desires *accords,* a *calm,* a *douceur.* For the wounds inflicted by reality it brings *ointments* and *mercy,* it *nurses, placates, quiets, soothes, smooths, blends, softens,* and *solaces.* To sweeten reality's bitterness it brings *cake, confection, honey, sugar.* If the world is a violent abyss, the imagination reposes in that which is *complete, final, fixed, motionless, solved, still, total, whole.*

Yet here, too, there is a sense in which the imagination cannot be distinguished from reality: for it, too, is swift and violent, as furious in its leapings as the animals of the crashing jungles; ambiguities will be considered later.

REALITY'S CACOPHONY: IMAGINATION'S EUPHONY

One aspect of the "angering to live" is the frightful noisiness of the competitors. They *blare* and *blatter* and *belch, clatter* and *crash, growl* and *grunt, grind* and *gnash, halloo* and *harangue* and *hiss* and *howl, jingle* and *jangle, rattle* and *roar, shriek* and *skritter* and *snarl* and *squawk.* It is all one maddening *rattapallax,* a *boo-ha,* an immense *wordiness.*

Imagination, on the other hand, delights in *breathings* and *exhalations, hummings* and *purlings, sibilance* and *whisperings, murmuring* and *mewing.* Instead of uncontrolled belly-sounds, it provides *rhapsodies, serenades, fugues,* and the *chants* chanted by its many *choirs* and *choruses.* Yet sometimes the imagination, in its fury, produces sounds strikingly similar to those of reality, even indistinguishable from reality's loud twangings; these, too, will be considered later.

REALITY'S NAKEDNESS AND SIMPLICITY; IMAGINATION'S ELABORATIONS, DEVIATIONS, AND MAGIC

Because objective fact is not invested with human interpretations, it is *naked,* and because it is incapable of imaginative trickery or distortion, it is *direct, frank,* and *true.* Lacking complexity or fictive embellishment, it is also *simple* and *small;* and being purely material and senseless, it is *ignorant.*

Imagination, on the other hand, transforms this naked simplicity into astonishingly elaborate patterns. Especially prominent in Stevens's poetry are the clothes with which imagination dresses the naked reality, the *hats* and *crests* and *turbans, cloaks* and *capes, bands, belts, buckles, hoops, plumes, ribbons, sashes, scarves, tufts, tassels, boots* and *slippers.* If these do not sufficiently convert reality into the fictive, there are always the jewels and cosmetics, *diamonds, emeralds, rubies, sapphires, topaz, baubles* and *trinkets, pearls* and *paste, perfume* and *powder* and *rouge.* Then, because imagination cuts the world to a pattern, it is often viewed as a tailor whose activities spawn another cluster of symbols: *stitching, knotting, patching, cutting, braiding, threading, twisting, weaving,* and *embroidering.* Again, imagination is a painter who *gilds* or *gilders, lacquers, varnishes,* or *covers* reality with his fictions. Or it is a sculptor or an interior decorator, *arranging* or *posing* and *carving* reality. In any event, it adds something to the real. "The commonest idea of an imaginative object is something large," Stevens writes in "Imagination as Value" (*NA,* p. 143), and he has created a great family of symbols that stress fictive enlargements, additions to the bare, empty reality. Thus the imagination *elongates, elevates, embellishes, magnifies, enlarges, extends, humps, increases, quickens,* and *deepens.* Its works are *voluminous, voluble, dense,* a *plural,* a *dissertation.* If reality is an emptiness and a poverty, the imagination stretches up *colossal:* its fictions are *enormous, prodigious, gigantic, huge, humped, large, lofty, long, massive, plenteous, portly, stretched, swollen, tall, vast.* The mind itself is a *mountain,* a *monster,* a *giant,* a *boon,* which gluts and gorges itself and will never be satisfied. But here we must note, once again, that Stevens sometimes views reality in an almost identical way, and we shall consider later on many interesting overlappings.

The imagination also "divests reality of its propriety," introducing a quirkish novelty with hundreds of deviations from reality's undeviating course: thus reality's simplicity becomes *blotted, blobbed, blotched, blurred.* Fictive things go *slanting, tilting, diverging;* are *eccentric, elliptical, oblique;* are *strange, queer, aberrant, evasive, distorted.* One huge family stresses the magical powers of the imagination, which *conjures* and *enchants, haunts, hypnotizes,* and *hallucinates.* Closely related are the symbols associated with theater and make-believe: the *mask, masquerade, juggler, actor, farce;* and finally, in contrast with reality's alert and wide-awake habits, there is imagination's deep *sleep,* its *coma,* its *doze,* its *dream.*

REALITY'S COLDNESS, INERTIA, INDIFFERENCE, EMPTINESS;
IMAGINATION'S VITALITY AND QUICKNESS

If Stevens sometimes contrasts the fecundity and vitality of the real world with the coldness and blankness of the imagination, he may invert this contrast and view reality as an empty, inert world, lacking the furious energy and potency of the imagination. In the heat of the south, reality lies in a *drowse, inert, lazy, lax, lethargic, somnolent.* So deep is this inertia, so unresponsive is reality to the demands of the imagination, that Stevens sometimes thinks of it as a world totally impoverished—*beggared, haggard, indigent, weedy.* Being an "anonymous blank," reality gives nothing to the spirit; threatens, rather, to crush the soul with its ruthless indifference and coldness. Thus it is nothing but *slate, steel, lead, stone, cast iron, a rock,* a *desert,* a heap of *cinders.* Because it works according to remorseless laws, it is a *machine,* a *clock,* a *mechanism.* It is *arid, ascetic, austere, barren, bleak, colorless, contracted, empty, hollow, inanimate, mute, vacant, stern, rigid.* It is a *zero,* a *void,* a *no* to the imagination's yes. Especially as the juice and joy of summer are destroyed by cold, and the world slides into the desolation of autumn and winter, Stevens views with disgust and fear the "nothing that is." Reality at these times is *cadaverous,* a *sepulcher,* a *limbo,* a world of *darkness* and *cold,* of *bones* and *rot* and *rust, shrivelled, lessened, weathered, boarded up, bleached.*

But in this unresponsive world, the imagination rises up to assert itself with astonishing vigor. The spirit *leaps* "from heaven to heaven"; it *dances* and *darts, soars* and *speeds, strides* and *spreads sail, plunges* and *spins.* It *fidgets* and is *captious* or *fitful.* It is *furious, turbulent, violent.* It is *lithe* and *nimble,* it *sizzles* and *seethes* as it circulates. From the fountain of inspiration the fictions come *pouring, foaming, frothing, spouting, spraying, streaming, sprinkling,* in a *torrent* that *drowns.* And if reality is sexually vigorous, the spirit, creating new metaphors and new worlds, also displays a remarkable potency: is *fertile, virile, prolific; seduces, conceives,* bears its *broods* and *births; engenders, breeds, rejuvenates,* delights in *honeymoons* and *weddings,* is *eager, trembles,* says *yes.* It is, above all, a masculine force, exhibiting a masculine authority: *arrogant, brave, capable, dauntless, ferocious, fierce, gallant, haughty, heroic, proud,* and *strong.*

REASON'S COLDNESS, IMPOTENCE, RIGIDITY

Because the reason is closely associated with what Stevens called the "false imagination"—the imagination severed from reality—the symbolism of the reason is not entirely separate from some of that already set down under such headings as "Imagination's Coldness,

Remoteness, Nothingness." But reason can be isolated as a discrete faculty in Stevens's poetry, particularly in his first two books, and to round out this map of the symbolic geography we may chart briefly the major categories. Like the categories of reality and imagination, they exhibit harmony by virtue of their derivation from a few generative terms, and the entire family may be viewed as a simple proliferation from Stevens's conception of the rationalist as a "snow man," a sterile and mechanical creature standing outside the "radiant and productive atmosphere" of the poet and outside the voluptuousness of sensation.

The places associated with the reason are, inevitably, small and confined: the *cabin*, the *cell*, the *parish* or *village*, or the inland *lake* and the insular city like *Geneva*, which is contrasted with the overwhelming power and disorder of reality in the form of the Pacific Ocean. It is a world of caution and tidiness: of *breakfast, lunch, salads, parasols, quilts, gelatin, promenades, curtains,* and *ribbons*. It is *dull, flat, "historic," inhibited, journalistic;* it *drones* and produces *dissertations*. But if it does not seem dangerous, this *snug* and *sealed* world, one may remember the *crevice* in which a serpent-like intelligence hides; and there is always *Moscow*, city of the logical lunatic.

In these confined and uninspired places appear creatures coldly rational, oblivious of the external world, intent on their categories and definitions. Because they abjure poetry and sensual pleasure, they are *ascetics, beggars, misers,* and *invalids, bald, barren, bloodless, cadaverous, neuter* or *sterile, castrated, dry, emaciated, gaunt, haggard, lank, lean, skinny* or *thin, morbid, sleepless,* in need of *aspirin*. They *scowl* and *glare*. Because their thought is cold and rigidly logical, they are *calipers, botanists, doctors, lexicographers, scholars, "dark" rabbis*. Because to live in the mind is to be insane and dangerous, they are *assassins, lunatics, nihilists, scorpions, serpents, witches*.

Their dress, as one might expect, is severe and puritanical. Rationalists wear *square hats* (never sombreros), *stiff cuffs,* dark *cloaks, mantles,* and *homburgs;* the rigidity and falsity of their thought is symbolized by such materials as *chalk, granite, lead, marble, papiermâché, paste, porcelain, powder, slate, steel, stone, tinsel,* and *wax*. The mechanical nature of the reason is symbolized by such instruments as *cameras* and *clocks* and by the sounds of machinery: *click-clack* and *clank*. The reduction of the fluent mundo to geometry is suggested in such symbols as *angles, lines, spheres, triangles,* and *volumes*. Inevitably the products of the reason lack spontaneity—are *applied, arranged, set, stiff, rigid, bony, taut*. And as for the mind, it is appallingly crude and awkward: a *mountain*, a great *boon* that *maunders, bulks, clambers*, in no way exhibiting grace or subtlety. Finally, this world, because it excludes both the real and the fictive, is empty and cold—a *void*, an *anonymous blank*, a world of *death* and *poverty, destitute, colorless, dank, dark, flat, harsh, hollow, icy, musty, pale, remote, severe, stark*, and *vapid*.

Having sketched in these simple patterns of Stevens's basic symbolism, I should not wish the reader to infer that I would reduce Stevens's poetry to mere oppositions between reality and the imagination. Yet here it may be necessary to insist, once again, upon the importance of establishing these categories. Passages that have steadfastly resisted explication will be found to yield up their meanings readily once a few of the basic symbolic antitheses are understood and the reader forms the habit of viewing every term in the company of its associates. Moreover, it is only when one understands what Stevens has created as his symbolic foundation that one is able to appreciate his delicate and ironic elaborations and projections of his symbolic counters in the later poetry. Indeed, one of Stevens's more impressive accomplishments in his later work is that by exerting ironic pressure on symbols established in the early poetry he forces them to absorb some of the meanings of their antitheses. Reality-symbols come to acquire imaginative connotations; symbols of the imagination come to connote reality. In this way Stevens is able to stress the central paradox of his poetry: that fact equals fiction, reality the imagination.

Stevens is slow to create a considerable body of straddling symbols, but of course some synthesizing terms appear in the earliest poetry. An illustration is *blue*. As the sky's color *blue* symbolizes the imagination and is naturally contrasted with the earth-colors; but as the color of the sea—a sea which in "Sea Surface Full of Clouds" is viewed as "a body, wholly body," a "gross machine"—*blue* may also be the color of the watery reality. Hence a phrase like "the blue ocean" may well mean either the imagined reality or the reality of the ocean as "fact." A similar straddling symbol is *red*. In "On the Adequacy of Landscape," in which the "blood-red-

redness of the sun" is contrasted with the barrenness of "the people in the air," *red* is obviously a symbol of reality. But in "Disillusionment of Ten o' Clock," the old sailor who "catches tigers / In red weather" does his hunting in a weather of furious imagination. By the time Stevens came to write "The Red Fern," however, he was able to employ *red* as a straddling symbol, and the opening of the "red fern" of reality is analogized to the opening of imagination's "red fern":

> The large-leaved day grows rapidly
> And opens in this familiar spot
> Its unfamiliar, difficult fern,
> Pushing and pushing red after red.
>
> There are doubles of this fern in clouds,
> Less firm than the paternal flame,
> Yet drenched with its identity,
> Reflections and off-shoots, mimic-motes
>
> And mist-mites, dangling seconds, grown
> Beyond relation to the parent-trunk:
> The dazzling, bulging, brightest core,
> The furiously burning father-fire. . . .
>
> [*CP*, p. 365]

The "large-leaved day" is both reality and the poem, written on "large" leaves of paper. The rapid growth is the growth of the sunrise and the growth of poetic resemblances—the proliferations from a generative particular. The "furiously burning father-fire" is the fire of the sun and the fire of the imagination. In a poet whose "intimidating thesis" is that "absolute fact includes everything that the imagination includes," one is not surprised to find a whole series of symbols that render not oppositions but coalescences.

These considerations lead directly to the question of how images which double for reality and imagination may be distinguished from those which do not. In the illustration of the red fern, we have seen that the symbolism of the imagination fuses with that of reality. Such fusions obviously do not occur in all of Stevens's poems, and when they do, they occur only when the context is "open"—that is, when the poem *invites* the reader to seek out correspondences or "the ambiguities." Thus, as we have seen, the term *blue* in "Sea Surface Full of Clouds" may symbolize both reality and the imagination because the poem celebrates the miraculous fusion of the two contraries. But in the passage quoted earlier from *The Man with the Blue Guitar*, in which the poet, in his gay desperation, is tempted to become "The unspotted imbecile revery, / The heraldic center of the world / Of blue, blue sleek with a hundred chins," the context is obviously "closed": it does not permit us to discern ambiguity in the symbol *blue*.

Now there are, as we find, four major categories of straddling symbols that may refer, in open contexts, to the admixture of reality and the imagination. Because the two contraries have in common the properties of brilliance, fecundity, size (or power), and sound (or noise), Stevens can employ symbols drawn from any of these four categories whenever he wishes to render the synthesis of reality and imagination.

(1) His employment of straddling symbols of brilliance occurs chiefly in his later poetry. We have already observed his practice in "The Red Fern," and a single additional illustration will indicate his characteristic handling of such fusing symbols. In "The World as Meditation" the brilliance of the sun corresponds to a fictive glow within the spirit. As the "form of fire" approaches, it becomes impossible for Penelope to know whether she is gazing at the sun or at the fictive hero:

> But was it Ulysses? Or was it only the warmth of the sun
> On her pillow? The thought kept beating in her like
>   her heart.
> The two kept beating together. It was only day.
>
> It was Ulysses and it was not.
>
> <div align="right">[<i>CP</i>, p. 521]</div>

The sun is an "heroic" appearance tantamount to a vision of Ulysses —a reality so brilliant that it is the equivalent of the imagined.

(2) That there is a parallel between reality's fecundity and that of the imagination has already been made clear in our analysis of the basic antithetical patterns. Stevens's procedure in effecting the synthesis of reality and imagination is almost exactly the same as that employed in "The Red Fern," and again we may note that the best illustrations of the synthesis appear in the later poetry. In "The Rock" Stevens again puns upon the word *leaves:*

> And yet the leaves, if they broke into bud,
> If they broke into bloom, if they bore fruit
>
> And if we ate the incipient colorings
> Of their fresh culls might be a cure of the ground.
>
> [CP, p. 526]

The cure for the barrenness and bitterness of "the ground"—objective reality—is not only the rich fertility of the earth itself but also the making of poems, whose budding and blooming converts the rock into "a thousand things."

(3) The stature and might of reality also have their analogues in the imagination, and such terms as *mountain, giant, huge,* and *tall* may easily, in open contexts, symbolize a fusion of the two realms. Thus in section 26 of *The Man with the Blue Guitar* the contest between earth and heaven is resolved in a synthesis based upon the shared property of enormous size:

> The world was a shore . . .
> . . . a bar in space,
>
> Sand heaped in the clouds, giant that fought
> Against the murderous alphabet:
>
> The swarm of thoughts, the swarm of dreams
> Of inaccessible Utopia.
>
> A mountainous music always seemed
> To be falling and to be passing away.
>
> [CP, p. 179]

The word *mountainous* may refer either to the world or to the mind, and a "mountainous music" is both a music about the mountain of reality and such music as the mountain-minded Hoon characteristically produces. In a similar passage in "Study of Images I" the adjectives *big* and *vast* perform a doubling function:

> Ah, bella! He [man] is, we are,
> Within the big, blue bush and its vast shade
>
> At evening and at night.
>
> [CP, p. 463]

The bush is big because it is both "blue"—that is, imagined—and "of day"—that is, of reality. The shade is "vast" because the bush casts just such a shadow and because the human spirit, the ghost or shade, interprets the reality. (4) Finally, reality and the imagination are both noisy. Although, as we have indicated, the imagination is often associated with euphony, Stevens also thinks of its creations as being mere sound and fury, and its musical instruments are clawed and strummed with a passionate ferocity in the great rage for order. (Stevens's repertory of imagination's noises includes *bing* and *ding*, *clash* and *clatter*, *hip-hip* and *honky-tonk*, *hoo* and *hoobla-how*, *hoot*, *hullaballoo*, *jingle* and *jangle*, *rattle*, *repeat*, *resound*, *rub-a-dub*, *rumble*, *shoo-shoo*, *ting-tang*, *toot*, *tinkle*, *tum-tum*, *whiroo*, and *whistle*.) The noises of reality are generally produced by such creatures as the grackles, who "crack their throats of bone," whereas the imagination generally employs musical instruments: *bassoons*, *bells*, *bugles*, *cornets*, *cymbals*, *fiddles*, *gongs*, *guitars*, *lutes*, *mandolins*, *pianos*, *saxophones*, *tambourines*, *trombones*, *tubas*, *zithers*. But in some few instances reality also employs a *banjo* or *bassoon*, *drums*, *cymbals*, and *trumpets*, and in open contexts the noises of the imagination may of course symbolize reality. An illustration of the characteristic procedure is a passage from "Things of August":

Nothing is lost, loud locusts. No note fails.
These sounds are long in the living of the ear.
The honky-tonk out of the somnolent grasses
Is a memorizing, a trying out, to keep.
[*CP*, p. 489]

Honky-tonk here refers both to the noises of reality's creatures, the locusts, and to the poet's "tink and tank and tunk-a-tunk-tunk." Again, in part 3 of "A Thought Revolved," Stevens fuses a number of opposites:

Winter devising summer in its breast,

Summer assaulted, thundering, illumed,
Shelter yet thrower of the summer spear.
[*CP*, p. 186]

The "thundering" of summer is both the sound of the *Ding an sich* and the furious poems, the "thunderings" of the "earthly leader" imposing his imagination upon reality.

In addition to these four major categories of straddling terms there are a number of symbols less easily classified. *Air*, for example, may stand either for what we breathe or for the sounds and symbols of the imagination. *Twilight* combines reality's darkness and imagination's light (or reality's day and imagination's night),[21] and *shadow* may refer either to the shade cast by an object or to the spirit. In a poem like "Ghosts as Cocoons" the term *spring* symbolizes both the season itself and the imagination; and of course no reader of Stevens needs instruction in regard to *blue-green*. It is enough, for the present, to suggest the adroitness and sublety of Stevens's marriages of reality and the imagination.

We may turn then to two fascinating questions that the study of the symbolism inevitably presents. First, how does Stevens employ this vast system in building up passages of particular poems and in fashioning the total structure of his poems? Second, what changes in his handling of the symbolism can be observed from his earliest poems to his latest, and what do these changes tell us about Stevens's development as a poet and about his success in creating the sort of poetry that would accomplish the purposes he describes in his essays dealing with poetic theory?

Stevens's essays supply some valuable clues to help us answer the first question. As he speaks in "Three Academic Pieces" of the way in which "a strand of a child's hair brings back the whole child and in that way resembles the child" (*NA*, p. 75), so he understood clearly that any member of a symbolic family, because it resembles the other members, is able to bring back the whole family. This capacity of the part to evoke the whole and to proliferate in many directions—the biologist's term *cladogenesis*, or branching evolution, is apt—becomes the subject of an extended discussion in "Three Academic Pieces," a discussion illustrated in the tour de force that follows the essay, "Somebody Puts a Pineapple Together." Part 3 of that poem is an excellent place to begin a study of Stevens's methods of handling his symbols, for it displays the breeding or proliferation of resemblances in a pure, an "academic" form.

After presenting twelve different views of a pineapple, Stevens goes on to say:

> These casual exfoliations are
> Of the tropic of resemblance, sprigs
> Of Capricorn or as the sign demands,
>
> Apposites, to the slightest edge, of the whole
> Undescribed composition of the sugar-cone. ...
>   [*NA*, pp. 86–87]

In these lines the vocabulary is drawn from three different kiths. *Exfoliations*, a member of the plant or generative family, proliferates *sprigs* in line two. *Tropic*, an image of place, proliferates *Capricorn*. And *edge*, an image of geometry or precision, proliferates *cone*. In the next few lines these exfoliations continue:

> Shiftings of an inchoate crystal tableau,
>
> The momentary footings of a climb
> Up the pineapple, a table Alp. ...
>   [P. 87]

The words *shiftings* and *momentary*, proliferating from *casual*, are part of an imagery of exploration. *Inchoate*, referring, like *sprigs*, to beginnings, derives from the family of generative images; and *footings* comes partially from the same source, for it refers to the imagination's capacity to extend reality beyond itself, to proliferate *feet*.[22] Also *footings* derives from the phrase *slightest edge*, which in the poet's mind has come to resemble the steps hacked by a mountain climber in the ice. *Climb*, like *footings*, springs from both the imagery of mountain-climbing and that of generation. And *table* may spring, by an association of sound, from *tableau*. *Alp*, of course is derived from the imagery of mountain-climbing, "slightest edge" and "crystal tableau."

The poem continues:

>   ... and yet
> An Alp, a purple Southern mountain bisqued
>
> With the molten mixings of related things,
> Cat's taste possibly or possibly Danish lore,
> The small luxuriations that portend
>
> Universal delusions of universal grandeurs.
>   [P. 87]

In these lines *Southern* is engendered by the epithets of place, *tropic* and *Capricorn; mountain* springs from *Alp;* and *mixings* picks up the imagery of addition which began in *footings. Bisqued* introduces a new cluster of images, but, like *molten mixings,* a phrase which suggests the fusing power of the imagination, it is derived from the imagery of addition—the idea that the imagination puts things together and blends them in a rich soup. The richness of the mixture is further suggested in "Cat's taste" (the imagination's savorings) and in "Danish lore" (the lore, or collected imaginings, supplied by simple, "Danish" reality).

Here we may pause to observe that the interrelations of the images have become so intricate that it is difficult to determine the precise meaning of any image taken by itself. In the phrase "a purple Southern mountain," for example, although *Southern* clearly refers to the abundant physical zone from which the pineapple springs, *purple* may refer either to the imagination or to reality, and *mountain* may mean either the pineapple or the gigantic fictions which the mind has made of the pineapple. We find ourselves in that atmosphere of ambiguity which Stevens termed favorable to resemblance—an open context in which images not specifically limited may easily straddle the poles of reality and imagination. And we have a concrete illustration of Stevens's notion that "the total artifice reveals itself as the total reality."

The poem ends with these lines:

> The small luxuriations that portend
> Universal delusions of universal grandeurs,
> The slight incipiencies, of which the form,
> At last, is the pineapple on the table or else
>
> An object the sum of its complications, seen
> And unseen. This is everybody's world.
> Here the total artifice reveals itself
>
> As the total reality. Therefore it is
> One says even of the odor of this fruit,
> That steeps the room, quickly, then not at all,
>
> It is more than the odor of this core of earth   ·
> And water. It is that which is distilled
> In the prolific ellipses that we know,

In the planes that tilt hard revelations on
the eye, a geometric glitter, tiltings
As of sections collecting toward the greenest cone.

Here all the images are derived from the preceding lines. *Luxuriations* and *incipiencies* are produced by the images of generation, *exfoliations* and *sprigs*, which also produce *small* and *slight*. *Sum* proliferates from *footings* by picking up the idea of adding quantities to reality. *Steeps* probably springs in part from the images of mountain-climbing. *Distilled* is the offspring of *bisque* since it continues the idea of a highly concentrated mixture. *Prolific* stems from the generation-cluster. *Ellipses, planes, sections* and *cone* stem from the imagery of geometry. *Tilt* is derived from the earlier image of deviation, *shiftings;* and *collecting* springs from *sum, mixings*, and *footings*.

The metamorphoses of the images are easy to follow, of course, for the poem is an exercise in proliferation, but the method of the exercise—piling up appositives, each new term being generated by its predecessors—is characteristic of much of Stevens's poetry. Indeed, it is not only one of the chief methods by which Stevens develops his subjects; it is one of his principal devices for *organizing* his poems. For, as Kenneth Burke has pointed out in *The Philosophy of Literary Form,* prolonged exposure to any single impression tends to generate a desire for the relief that an opposite impression can provide. In Stevens's poetry, prolonged exposure to reality's heaviness generates the desire for imagination's light leapings; reality's ugliness engenders imagination's beauty; ordinariness calls up nobility; darkness, light; flux, fixity; savagery, refinement; discord, harmony; the north, the south; and in short, by the logic of qualitative form, each realm begets its opposite. In the early poetry, the symbols proliferate in relatively unmixed series or blocks, one block of symbols calling forth an antithetical block. It was not until some twenty years after *Harmonium*'s publication that Stevens was able to write the meditative lyric in which the circulations between reality and the imagination are incessant and appear in virtually every line.

The early qualitative form may be illustrated by a few lyrics from *Harmonium* that treat of the desire for imaginative fulfillments in a reality oppressively ugly. The speaker, appalled, disgusted by the scene confronting him, turns to the world of the imagination for release and succor. He may or may not succeed in gratifying his desires. In "Banal Sojourn" he fails:

> Two wooden tubs of blue hydrangeas stand at the foot of the
>   stone steps.
> The sky is a blue gum streaked with rose. The trees are black.
> The grackles crack their throats of bone in the smooth air.
> Moisture and heat have swollen the garden into a slum of
>   bloom.
> Pardie! Summer is like a fat beast, sleepy in mildew,
> Our old bane, green and bloated, serene, who cries,
> "That bliss of stars, that princox of evening heaven!" reminding
>   of seasons
> When radiance came running down, slim through the bareness.
> And so it is one dams that green shade at the bottom of the
>   land.
> For who can care at the wigs despoiling the Satan ear?
> And who does not seek the sky unfuzzed, soaring to the
>   princox?
> One has a malady, here, a malady. One feels a malady.
>   [*CP*, pp. 62–63]

The poem's movement is a simple shift from reality to the imagination. Finding himself confronted by a physical grossness which sickens him, the speaker cries out for "radiance ... slim through the bareness." But failing to attain such bliss, he falls back into torpor and weary disgust: "One feels a malady."

Of course many variations of the qualitative method are possible. In "Stars at Tallapoosa" (the imagination in reality) the speaker first contemplates the purity and perfection of mind in its apprehension of the stars:

> The lines are straight and swift between the stars.
> The night is not the cradle that they cry,
> The criers, undulating the deep-oceaned phrase.
> The lines are much too dark and much too sharp.
>
> The mind herein attains simplicity.
> There is no moon, on single, silvered leaf.
> The body is no body to be seen
> But is an eye that studies its black lid.
>   [*CP*, p. 71][23]

In stanza three this "simplicity" is contrasted with the crudity and complexity of the world:

> Let these be your delight, secretive hunter
> Wading the sea-lines, moist and ever-mingling,
> Mounting the earth-lines, long and lax, lethargic.
> These lines are swift and fall without diverging.
>
> [CP, p. 72]

If the lines between the stars are "straight," the "sea-lines" are "moist and ever-mingling"; if the star-lines are "swift," the earth-lines are "long and lax, lethargic." The image of moisture then begets "melon-flower" and "dew" at the beginning of stanza four: "The melon-flower nor dew nor web of either / Is like to these." But in the same stanza the star-imagery is restated, and the poem ends with a joyous contemplation of the stars' stirring effects:

> But in yourself is like:
> A sheaf of brilliant arrows flying straight,
> Flying and falling straightway for their pleasure,
>
> Their pleasure that is all bright-edged and cold;
> Or, if not arrows, then the nimblest motions,
> Making recoveries of young nakedness
> And the lost vehemence the midnights hold.
>
> [P. 72]

Slightly more complicated than this is the movement of "Gubbinal," in which a dialogue or an "oscillation" between two views of reality is presented:

> That strange flower, the sun,
> Is just what you say.
> Have it your way.
>
> The world is ugly,
> And the people are sad.
>
> That tuft of jungle feathers,
> That animal eye,
> Is just what you say.
>
> That savage of fire,
> That seed,
> Have it your way.

> The world is ugly,
> And the people are sad.
>
> [CP, p. 85]

The first speaker argues that reality may be metamorphosed according to the beholder's wishes: he states the claim of the imagination. The second speaker, resisting metaphor as a means of redemption, states the claim of an antipoetic reality. The poem is similar in structure to Yeats's "A Dialogue of the Self and Soul," and the reader, recognizing the claims of both disputants, is led finally to a qualified acceptance of one of the arguments over the other.

The method of such a poem is not unusual in lyric poetry, but in Stevens's early work it is employed so deliberately that one is sometimes tempted to reduce the structure of the poem to the structure of the image-blocks. In the later poetry, however—as I have indicated—the usual development of a subject is not by means of images in blocks but rather by means of a *continuous* to-and-fro, a kind of incessant shuttling and exchange between the poles. A passage from "An Ordinary Evening in New Haven" will illustrate:

> He preserves himself against the repugnant rain,
> By an instinct for a rainless land, the self
> Of his self, come at upon wide delvings of wings.
>
> The instinct for heaven had its counterpart:
> The instinct for earth, for New Haven, for his room,
> The gay tournamonde as of a single world
>
> In which he is and as and is are one.
> For its counterpart a kind of counterpoint
> Irked the wet wallows of the water-spout.
>
> The rain kept falling loudly in the trees
> And on the ground. The hibernal dark that hung
> In primavera, the shadow of bare rock,
>
> Becomes the rock of autumn, glittering,
> Ponderable source of each imponderable,
> The weight we lift with the finger of a dream,
>
> The heaviness we lighten by light will,
> By the hand of desire, faint, sensitive, the soft
> Touch and trouble of the touch of the actual hand.
>
> [CP, pp. 475–76]

Here the image of "repugnant rain" calls to mind its opposite, "rainless land." Then "rainless land" evokes "heaven," which in turn promptly elicits "earth." "Repugnant" engenders "gay," and "gay tournamonde" is contrasted with "hibernal dark." *Hibernal,* however, may refer to the wintry coldness of the imagination as well as to the season, and "hibernal dark" may thus be read either as "imagined reality" or simply as "cold reality." But *dark* is picked up by *shadow,* and since *shadow* may mean spirit, the phrase "the shadow of bare rock" may be read "the imagination of reality"— in apposition with "hibernal dark." (*Dark* would then refer to the dark cabin of the mind.) Furthermore, *hibernal,* if taken to refer to the imagination, elicits its opposite, *primavera,* or reality.

At this point such terms as *earth, falling, ground, hung* and *rock* engender the terms of heaviness or inertia—*ponderable, weight,* and *heaviness.* At the same time *wings, heaven* and *shadow* evoke *imponderable, lift, dream, lighten,* and *light,* a fusion of the images of insubstantiality and brilliance. The passage is indeed a "counterpoint" of symbols, and may be converted—outrageously, I grant, but according to a strict logic—into "balancing equations" of reality and the imagination, thus:

> The imagined reality that hung
> In reality, the imagination of reality,
>
> Becomes the reality of reality, imagined,
> The real source of the imagined,
> The reality changed by the imagination,
>
> The reality imagined by the imagination.

Such a poetry, with its incessant oscillations, its "going round and around," might become—as some critics in the thirties and forties charged—the sterile finger-exercises of an aging epistemologist. But it is a poetry capable of achieving nobility too—as in "The Auroras of Autumn," in which all of the most powerful elements of Stevens's vision converge. In "The Auroras" there is a superb depiction of the human condition—of man dwelling in the flux and of the human family, its members clinging to one another in their instinctive need and in their fear of the destructive forces of nature. There is the deep pathos of impending death and, simultaneously, there is the fictive glory of the brutal machine of the material universe, displayed in some of Stevens's most magnificent imagery. There is, above all, the vision of man struggling to make of the alien world a home—a vision suffused with tenderness though remaining detached and unsentimentalized. The "poem of the idea" here builds to the poet's discovery of a sustaining attitude for man in face of the annihilating flux. "The poem of the words," meantime, continues Stevens's rich and various counterpoint of symbols, and every word, issuing from the "miraculous multiplex" of the reality- and imagination-equations, flashes with the light of its associates. But only close examination of the poem will enable us to appreciate its richness and power.

Stevens begins "The Auroras of Autumn" with a depiction of the elemental context of human existence. We feel the sheer *strangeness* of the planet as the scene of human life:

> This is where the serpent lives, the bodiless.
> His head is air. Beneath his tip at night
> Eyes open and fix on us in every sky.
>
> [*CP*, p. 411]

The serpent is physical reality—the death-dealing god of Africa, upon whose throne "Death, only, sits" (as we learn in *Owl's Clover*); or is merciless Ananke, in whom "the sense of the serpent" resides (as we find in "Like Decorations in a Nigger Cemetery"). But this fatal, poisonous god of a hostile reality is, paradoxically, "bodiless. / His head is air." The god of death is also the imagined god of the redemptive air. (For *air* is one of Stevens's oldest symbols of the imagination, a symbol opposed to such tokens of physical reality as "Oklahoma," "the sea," and the "blood-red-redness of the sun.") Thus the poem begins with an idea that Stevens was to develop in "Metaphor as Degeneration": the idea that "being / Includes death and the imagination."

The god of this world both kills and saves. Moreover, all of his parts exhibit the duality of the real and the imagined. His "tip" may be the venomous head, but the word *tip*, like its associates *point* or *peak*, is a symbol of imaginative heightening or perfecting. (*Tip* is symbolic in a score of Stevens's poems; thus: "Tomorrow / will be an appearance . . . not quite the fluid thing, / A little changed by tips of artifice"; or thus: "Each man himself [becomes] a giant, / Tipped out with largeness.") The "night" in which the serpent appears may be the night of fear (as in "Domination of Black") or it may be the night of imagination (as in *Owl's Clover*, where "night and the imagination" are "one"). The stars—those "eyes that open and fix on us in every sky"—seem cold, distant, implacable in their staring, yet they are also tokens of the redemptive imagination. And the term *fix* brings to mind a host of Stevens's poems in which imagination "fixes" or "freezes" the fluid mundo of reality—creating, for example, "the lark fixed in the mind," "an order most Plantagenet, most fixed," or causing the flow of "watery grasses" to appear "fixed as in a photograph."

In the next three lines Stevens develops the paradoxes implicit in his view of the serpent. Perhaps, he asks, the god of being is *pure* imagination, pure fiction?

> Or is this another wriggling out of the egg,
> Another image at the end of the cave,
> Another bodiless for the body's slough.
>   [*CP*, p. 411]

But here too the conjunction of the physical and the metaphysical is pervasive. "Wriggling out of the egg" suggests a purely physical process, the creative evolution of life; but of course the line also alludes to Plato's myth of the egg, and the term *egg* is often employed by Stevens to denote the mind or "egghead" of the intelligence. (Thus: "We make, although inside an egg, / Variations on the words spread sail"; "And the egg of the earth lies deep within an egg.") The "image at the end of the cave" is of course the appearance of reality of which Plato spoke; yet the cave may be either Plato's cave, or the serpent's, or the mind itself. (Stevens often thinks of the mind as a cell—"our accustomed cell"—or as a room, and the association of the serpent with the cave of the mind is developed in a number of his poems.) In any case, the lines are paradoxical: the "bodiless" contains the body—the serpent and his "body's slough." And confronted again with paradox, the poet turns, as if to end all questioning, to indubitable fact:

> This is where the serpent lives. This is his nest.
> These fields, these hills, these tinted distances,
> And the pines above and along and beside the sea.

Apparently a bare description of the solid *donnés*. But the *donnés*, apparently untampered with, here testify ironically not merely to

the presence of naked fact but also to that of elaborate fiction.
"Tinted distances" are observations shaped and colored by the
imagination. (The word *tint,* as employed by Stevens—as in "a
beautiful tableau tinted and towering"—invariably betokens the
imagination's presence; and *distances*—in such phrases as "the topmost distances" of "icy Elysée," "the distances of sleep," or "clouds,
benevolences, distant heads"—betokens the imagination in its abstractive bent, its penchant to convert close and concrete reality
into a remote fiction.) Moreover, the last line, with its insistent
prepositions—"And the pines *above* and *along* and *beside* the sea"
—suggests the prolific constructive powers of the imagination,
which may discover limitless relationships among the phenomena
to which it attends. So the solid world of the serpent's "nest" is
revealed, ineluctably, as a fictive world.

The fourth and fifth tercets thus contemplate the possibility of
a total transformation of the given by the imagination: they contemplate, that is, the serpent's metamorphosis—"Skin flashing to
wished-for disappearances / And the serpent body flashing without the skin"—and his ultimate apotheosis as supreme fiction in a
completely resolved world:

> These lights may finally attain a pole
> In the midmost midnight and find the serpent there,
>
> In another nest, the master of the maze
> Of body and air and forms and images,
> Relentlessly in possession of happiness.

The imagination, in its "midmost midnight," may "find" the serpent
of reality as its supreme fiction. But the next line—"This is his
poison: that we should disbelieve / Even that"—punctures that vision of a happy resolution. Whatever our supreme fiction may be,
the world remains (as Stevens reminds us in other poems) "a poison
at the winter's end," a "poison in the blood," a "poisoned wood."
And the deadliest poison of the world is that man is condemned
to doubt his fictions—to disbelieve *even in the serpent* as lord of
reality. The vision concocted in midmost midnight collapses, and
Stevens returns again to the sun-reality of which he can be sure:

His meditations in the ferns,
When he moved so slightly to make sure of sun,

Made us no less as sure.
[*CP*, pp. 411-12]

But here, once again, there are gleams of irony and ambiguity. While the lines state that man, like the serpent, is "sure" of the sun —of a reality beyond all fictions—the ironic "meditations" suggests a qualification; and the serpent's slight movement is exactly the sort of delicate, fine activity that Stevens likes to associate with imagination's sleight of hand (as in a poem like "Jouga," for example, where Stevens contemplates "beasts that one never sees, / Moving so that the foot-falls are slight and almost nothing"). The serpent's movement to make sure of the sun is thus, paradoxically, a movement testifying to the ubiquity of the imagination. And in the final lines of the first section of the poem, it is the admixture of reality and imagination that is rendered—in a series of wedded contrarieties:

We saw in his head,
Black beaded on the rock, the flecked animal,
The moving grass, the Indian in his glade.
[*CP* p. 412]

Here *black* is a symbol of reality (generally, in Stevens, of reality's horror), *beaded* is a jewel-image of the imagination, *rock* is a symbol of earth or reality, *flecked* is an image either of reality or of imaginative metamorphosis (cf. "hats of angular flick and fleck"; "thought ... Salt-flicker"), and *animal* is of course a reality-image. "Moving grass" certainly appears to designate the fluid mundo, but we may also think of *moving* in the sense of "highly affecting." "Indian in his glade," finally, refers to the "Indian" of the imagination and the "glade" of reality. So the stanza ends with a series of antithetical equations.

Such equations occur throughout the poem, and further illustration is unnecessary. The major form of the poem is repetitive: in each section (or in two related sections) Stevens entertains the possibility of a metamorphosis of the real by the imagination—the possibility of a world endowed with fictive glamor and significance; but after each such effort he returns to a recognition of the limits of the imagination and to an acknowledgement that "fortune" and "fate," the serpent's beauty and the serpent's poison, commingle. Thus in part 2, the frigid, killing northland of reality is also the symbolic (and magnificent) "north" of the imagination. In part 3 the wind that knocks "like a rifle-butt against the door," threatening the mother and the family, also "spread[s] its windy grandeurs round" (p. 414). In parts 4 and 5 the father's efforts to build a self-contained fictive world—his music and his theater, his ardent etherealizations—are seen as comic or pathetic in face of the flux which undercuts all pretensions of the imagination. In part 6 Stevens presents a vivid picture of that flux, a world in which "fire's delight" is "splashed side-wise because it likes magnificence" —but the spectacular "Arctic effulgence" also inspires fear.

In part 7, again, Stevens considers the possibility of a supreme fiction, the imagination "enthroned" and determining the just and the unjust; but this mystical projection fails to yield satisfaction in the life of men on this earth, the fantastic drama of sin, redemption, and final justice is dismissed, and in parts 8 and 9 the picture of the human condition on earth is rounded out by the limiting notion of "innocence." Men "partake" of the "innocence of the earth." Death is only "part of innocence," "almost . . . the tenderest and the truest part."

Throughout, the poet never disguises the harshness and fatality of the flux.

> Shall we be found hanging in the trees next spring?
> Of what disaster is this the imminence:
> Bare limbs, bare trees and a wind as sharp as salt?

But a fictive grandeur attends the march toward death:

> The stars are putting on their glittering belts.
> They throw around their shoulders cloaks that flash
> Like a great shadow's last embellishment.

Thus the poem concludes with the recognition that the poet-rabbi, skeptical priest of the imagination, addressing "an unhappy people in a happy world," helps men to live their lives by revealing "the full of fortune and the full of fate"—the fictive blaze, the fire of reality's straw:

> In these unhappy he meditates a whole,
> The full of fortune and the full of fate,
> As if he lived all lives, that he might know,
>
> In hall harridan, not hushful paradise,
> To a haggling of wind and weather, by these lights
> Like a blaze of summer straw, in winter's nick.
>
> [*CP*, pp. 420–21]

The conclusion is as paradoxical as the beginning. Yet the poem has not merely repeated itself. Eliminating false imagination—an imagination of life divorced from bitter fact—it has arrived at an acceptable definition of the human condition. It has moved from the most general view of things to a limited statement of the poet's mission. Ostensible repetition is here a whittling away, a gradual focusing, the achievement of satisfaction in precision and limitation. The poem never ceases to evoke pity and wonder simultaneously. The equilibrium Stevens achieves is that of a man stubbornly resisting self-pity or sentimentalism, yet viewing the tragicomic human situation with genuine tenderness. Compassion exists, but tempered by wit, by delight, by appreciation. "The serpent is our god," Stevens says in effect. "But realize that he's beautiful as well as deadly." In the end a sober joy emerges—a joy made possible by the fierce energy of Stevens's symbolism, which permits him, in its subtlety, to render everywhere "the full of fortune and the full of fate"—the "whole" of experience.

The poem in which symbols of reality balance those of the imagination in every line is, as we have seen, an achievement toward which Stevens worked steadily from the beginning of his career. It is anticipated in *Harmonium*. In *The Man with the Blue Guitar* Stevens set out deliberately to display the conjunctions of things as they are and things imagined, and reality and imagination engage in a protracted struggle for possession of the guitar, now one, now the other succeeding. But the technique is not perfected until the appearance of *Notes toward a Supreme Fiction*. By the time Stevens wrote "The Auroras of Autumn" the yoking of reality and the imagination in straddling symbols and by hundreds of deft cross-combinations and shuttlings between the symbolic families was apparently more than a triumph of technique: it amounted to a habit of Stevens's mind. His virtuosity had become so great that he was able to express his Manichean vision of the admixture of reality and imagination whenever he wanted to. Almost every word springing to his pen had a place in the vast scheme, the vast poem, that he had been working out in his head for fifty years. If the symbolic meanings of his images and epithets escaped many readers, the poet himself must have looked with delight on the astonishing combinations, the "miraculous multiplex" of poems fertilizing one another—like "rubies reddened by rubies reddening." He had done what he had set out to do: had displayed the interdependence of reality and the imagination *as equals*, balanced in every line. And because in "The Auroras of Autumn" he had carried his technique of incessant straddling and shuttling as far as it could be carried, he was ready, in the fifties, for the directness and clarity of his last poems.

NOTES

1. Charles Feidelson, Jr., *Symbolism and American Literature* (Chicago: University of Chicago Press, 1953), p. 51.
2. References to this and to other works by Stevens are to *The Collected Poems of Wallace Stevens* (New York: Alfred A. Knopf, 1954); *Opus Posthumous: Poems, Plays, Prose by Wallace Stevens*, ed. with intro. by Samuel French Morse (New York: Alfred A. Knopf, 1957); and *The Necessary Angel: Essays on Reality and the Imagination* (New York: Alfred A. Knopf, 1951). Hereafter these books will be cited respectively as follows: *CP, OP*, and *NA*.
3. Feidelson, Jr., *Symbolism and American Literature*, p. 174.
4. Robert Pack, *Wallace Stevens* (New Brunswick, N.J.: Rutgers University Press, 1958), p. 194.
5. John J. Enck, *Wallace Stevens: Images and Judgments* (Carbondale, Ill.: Southern Illinois University Press, 1964), pp. 141–42.
6. Elder Olson, "The Poetry of Wallace Stevens," *English Journal* 44 (April 1955): 191–98.
7. Enck, *Wallace Stevens*, p. 53.
8. Pack, *Wallace Stevens*, p. 68.
9. Marius Bewley, *The Complex Fate* (New York: Grove Press, 1953), pp. 171–92.
10. Olson, "The Poetry of Wallace Stevens," p. 197.
11. Enck, *Wallace Stevens*, p. 111.

12. Samuel French Morse, "An Examination of the Practice and Theory of Wallace Stevens" (Ph.D. diss., Boston University, 1952), pp. 217–18.

13. See Appendix.

14. See Appendix.

15. See Appendix.

16. See Appendix.

17. See Appendix.

18. See Appendix.

19. Wallace Stevens, *Parts of a World* (New York: Alfred A. Knopf, 1951), p. 183.

20. Daniel J. Schneider, "Wallace Stevens: His Theory of Poetry and Its Application to His Poems" (Ph.D. diss., Northwestern University, 1956).

21. As Bernard Heringman noted in "The Poetry of Synthesis," *Perspective* 7 (Autumn 1954): 167–74.

22. With *footings* compare *inchings* and *ouncings*, all signifying imagination's additions or elaborations.

23. In the description of the *criers* Stevens seems to have had Whitman's "Sea-Drift" in mind.

VI. THE SYMBOLIC SYSTEM AND THE AUTHORITY OF THE LITERARY WORK

SYMBOLIC SYSTEMS GROW BY ACCRETION, and often very slowly, over several decades. The symbolist's first transmutations of images and metaphors into symbols are often hesitant, stiff, self-conscious. The writer, having discovered a few expressive symbols, is not yet aware of the possibilities of his symbolism; the manifold extensions, the interlacings and crossbreedings, are yet to occur. But after two decades of working, the artist's basic symbols may spawn a huge progeny. Often the most prolific and useful symbols are generated unexpectedly, having multiplied in the back-hills of the mind, strange kiths possessed of a queer vitality. Weddings have occurred in secret that the artist himself could not have foreseen. Some of the imagination's offspring are as grotesque as they are numerous. But all, by virtue of their origins, seem part of a single clan and constitute what Stevens calls a "central poem":

> The central poem is the poem of the whole,
> The poem of the composition of the whole,
> The composition of blue sea and of green,
> Of blue light and of green, as lesser poems,
> And the miraculous multiplex of lesser poems,
> Not merely into a whole, but a poem of
> The whole, the essential compact of the parts,
> The roundness that pulls tight the final ring.
> . . . .
> It is a giant, always, that is evolved,
> To be in scale, unless virtue cuts him, snips
> Both size and solitude or thinks it does,
> As in a signed photograph on a mantelpiece.

But the virtuoso never leaves his shape,
Still on the horizon elongates his cuts,
And still angelic and still plenteous,
Imposes power by the power of his form.

[CP, pp. 142–43]

This central poem, which is, in one sense, the great poem of the
whole race, is also, in another sense, the poem that Stevens himself
wished to write for "the universal mind." The "miraculous multiplex of lesser poems" of which he speaks is not merely the collection of lesser contributions by all members of the race (each
according to his fated eccentricity) but also Stevens's own collected poems, oscillating continually between the blue and the
green, the sea and heaven. And, as we have seen, Stevens, in developing this great "poem within, and above, a poem," "never leaves
his shape," but, continually reworking his subject, "elongates his
cuts" as he proceeds, developing all the possibilities latent in his
early work, returning again and again to the symbols established
in his first poems, building upon them, evolving the giant of the
whole.

Now there can be no doubt that, as Stevens says, the virtuoso
who never leaves his shape is in possession of tremendous power,
the power of his prolonged patience and concentration, his tena-
cious commitment to the development of his "central poem." As
Stevens wrote in a letter to William Carlos Williams, "My idea is
that in order to carry a thing to the extreme necessary to convey
it one has to stick to it . . . to fidget with points of view leads always
to new beginnings and incessant new beginnings lead to sterility.
. . ." [1] But while departure from a fixed point of view may lead to
sterility, there are dangers in the working out of a symbolism with
such single-minded persistence, and it will be worthwhile for us to
examine some of these, together with some of the arguments usually adduced to praise or denigrate the practices of symbolists. A
great deal of opinionating still mars discussions of literary symbolism; a great many received opinions having to do, especially, with
the evaluation of symbols have blurred our understanding of the
merits of many a literary work. And if there has been too much
facile negative criticism, there has also been too much ill-consid-
ered admiration. So we may offer, by way of rounding out this
study of Manichean symbolism, a few observations on the relative

effectiveness of the symbolism employed by the writers who have engaged our attention.

The great danger for the symbolist—as Stevens's poetry illustrates, and as we find also in some of the work of Conrad, James, and Woolf—is that the symbolic scheme, in its proliferation, may become so importunate, so insistently pervasive, that the symbols tend to drive out the sense of life itself, the freshness and irregularity, or one might say the unexpectedness, the surprise, of life as felt. The danger, in other words, is that *dianoia* will dominate at the expense of character, action, "felt life." For as there is, in novels (as E. M. Forster has pointed out), a sort of war between the characters and the plot—the characters wishing to take control and do what they want to do, while plot wishes to bully them, force them into submission to the plan, the idea—so we may speak of a contest between symbolism (which is a form of the idea) and life itself.

The danger of allowing a symbolic system to assume too great control of one's writing is strikingly illustrated in Stevens's poetry. The charge that Stevens's poetry is, all too often, merely fanciful rather than imaginative, that it is sometimes mechanical and full of lifeless repetitions, seems sometimes to have originated in a desire to convert Stevens's "poem of the act of the mind" into the sort of lyric that one associates with Keats, Hopkins, Dylan Thomas. There are many poems in which Stevens *wants* to be fanciful— *wants* to call attention to the constructive activity of the mind, to the mental fabrications, the artifice. Indeed, by 1942 Stevens had virtually purged his poetry of plot and personae; the situations tend toward abstraction or, when concrete, are given highly stylized treatment. Abstract composition—the elboration of the poetry by means of symbolic counters abstracted from specific occasions—has become a habit. The scene of his poems has shifted from Florida and the Carolinas to the world itself, the wind and stars and sea and mountains that constitute the world of Everyman. The poetry is all artifice—as if to emphasize the queerness of the mental universe, the fantastic metamorphoses accomplished by the mind, the normal madness of perception and apperception. But while all this is true, there are innumerable occasions when Stevens seems to *stop thinking* and to allow his endlessly elaborating symbolism simply to take over, to proliferate as if out of habit, without significantly enriching the illusion of life or without significantly deepening the reader's apprehension of the arbitrary, schematizing nature of the mind. This tendency to allow symbols simply to breed, without ensuring that all of them are functioning at maximum power and expressiveness, is manifest, for example, in the "Africa" section of *Owl's Clover*, in which Stevens repeats what he had already done splendidly in "The Comedian as the Letter C":

> But in Africa
> The memory moves on leopards' feet, desire
> Appoints its florid messengers with wings
> Wildly curvetted, color-scarred, so beaked,
> With tongues unclipped and throats so stuffed with thorns,
> So clawed, so sopped with sun, that in these things
> The message is half-borne.
>
> [*OP*, p. 57]

One is glad that Stevens wrote the passage. It is good in itself. But it contributes little to the poem, and the block of harmonious symbols is developed almost for its own sake. Or consider:

> ... the black sublime,
> Toward which, in the nights, the glittering serpents climb,
> Dark-skinned and sinuous, winding upwardly,
> Winding and waving, slowly, waving in air,
> Darting envenomed eyes about, like fangs,
> Hissing, across the silence, puissant sounds.
>
> [*OP* p. 55]

There is a vast difference, D. G. James has observed, between expressing feeling and contemplating it. Stevens, in this passage, does neither: he simply lets the imagery take over and proliferate at its own pleasure. The passage is purple—reminiscent of the Tennyson of the "Lotus-Eaters."

It has been pointed out that Stevens tends to employ a rhetoric of appositives and to circle in upon his subject in repeated efforts to formulate precisely his state of mind. Obviously such a technique is very useful to a poet who would, without oversimplifying, "catch from that Irrational moment its unreasoning." If one would present the incessant conjunctionings of imagination and reality, the marshaling of antithetical images side by side can suggest, by virtue of the grammatical parallelism, the identity of opposites; and the proliferating appositives can give the effect of a mind continually struggling to find its way through the immense disorder of experience, trying again and again to reach some solid point at which it can rest and say: "That's it." Thus in "Romanesque Affabulation," part 2 of *A Thought Resolved:*

> He sought an earthly leader who could stand
> Without panache, without cockade,
> Son only of man and sun of men,
> The outer captain, the inner saint,
>
> The pine, the pillar and the priest,
> The voice, the book, the hidden well,
> The faster's feast and heavy-fruited star,
> The father, the beater of the rigid drums,
>
> He that at midnight touches the guitar,
> The solitude, the barrier, the Pole
> In Paris, celui qui chante et pleure,
> Winter devising summer in its breast,
>
> Summer assaulted, thundering, illumed,
> Shelter yet thrower of the summer spear,
> With all his attributes no god but man
> Of men whose heaven is in themselves,
>
> Or else whose hell, foamed with their blood
> And the long echo of their dying cry,
> A fate intoned, a death before they die,
> The race that sings and weeps and knows not why.
>
> [*CP*, pp. 185–86]

Having released himself from the confinement of a concrete situation, Stevens is able here to employ his symbols freely, allowing them to interact and proliferate on their own terms, so long as they fulfull the conditions of the system. After separating his opposites in the first two lines, he proceeds to join them in line four, where the secular and religious symbols mingle. In line five, the reality-symbol *pine* is followed by two imagination-symbols, *pillar* and *priest. Priest* is then made to rhyme with its opposite, *feast,* and the remainder of the stanza also consists of opposites, the *star* being the antithesis of *heavy-fruited,* and *the father,* a symbol of the imagination, being the antithesis of *the rigid drums,* which deliver reality's death-roll. The first two lines of the third stanza contain only imagination-symbols, but in the last line of the stanza imagination

and reality join in *winter-summer;* and the rest of the poem fuses
the opposites *shelter* and *thrower, god* and *man, heaven* and *hell.*
Stevens makes increasing use of this grammatical tool as he goes
along: and indeed the later poems sometimes appear to be nothing
more than catalogs of appositives, mechanically constructed antitheses and fusions. In "Things of August," for example, Stevens
begins the fifth section with the line: "We'll give the week-end to
wisdom, to Weisheit, the rabbi," and then he ticks off the following:

> The thinker as reader reads what has been written.
> He wears the words he reads to look upon
> Within his being,
>
> A crown within him of crispest diamonds,
> A reddened garment falling to his feet,
> A hand of light to turn the page,
>
> A finger with a ring to guide his eye
> From line to line, as we lie on the grass and listen
> To that which has no speech,
>
> The voluble intention of the symbol,
> The ghostly celebrations of the picnic,
> The secretions of insight.
>
> [*CP,* p. 492]

Since the thinker as reader is transformed, "ennobled" by his reading, the symbolism of royalty is not inappropriate: yet since Stevens might easily have used another pattern of symbols to depict
the reader's transformation, (for example, symbolism of the hero,
or impressario, or priest), the catalog seems contrived. It does not
issue from a deep apperception of the subject. The method of
piling up appositives is thus dangerous because it invites mechanical repetition of the imagery.

Closely related to the difficulties caused by the use of the rhetoric of appositives is the weakness we may describe as "illustrating"
—instead of presenting—a subject matter. By *illustration* I mean
the development of the subject by means of symbols (which may
be inseparable from characterization, action, etc.) which do not
interest the writer in themselves but are interesting to him only as
expressions or developments of something else. Illustration in literary art is almost invariably a confession that the subject matter has

ceased to be significant as experience, as life, and has become, for the artist, mere conception, mere idea, mere development of his theme. An example is the characterization of Jewel in *Lord Jim*. Has Jewel any character? Or is she simply the "extraterrestrial animal," the butterfly, the ideal to which Jim weds himself? Conrad, stout man, does all that his work requires. He works out his idea. But what a price he pays for willing, for imposing his meanings upon the second half of his novel! How mechanical, how *forced* the whole second half of Lord Jim is! The symbolism is certainly "organic" and springs from the "matrix of the story"; but the logical or organic development of a symbolism does not in itself make for the vitality of a work of art, as some critics seem to hold.

Now Stevens, in his later poetry especially, runs into a similar difficulty, in *forcing* himself to illustrate his ideas. That is to say, he creates works which, requiring for their proper rounding out, rather full and impressive development, demand very remarkable powers of invention. But when invention falters, as in extended works it will, illustration takes over, if only to supply a proper weight and "dignity" to the part. An analogy from sculpture will clarify. We may imagine a sculptor doing a statue of a woman and requiring, to complete his work, only to carve the left forearm and hand. But his model vanishes at the moment when he has reached the elbow. The sculptor cannot suspend operations. He does the best he can, drawing upon memory and technique, perhaps on technique alone, to shape the stone from elbow to fingertips. That is illustrating. It is working from an emptiness within, devising by association instead of consulting vital sources within the self, within experience.

The sixth section of "An Ordinary Evening in New Haven" exhibits a typical kind of illustrating in Stevens's work:

> Reality is the beginning not the end,
> Naked Alpha, not the hierophant Omega,
> Of dense investiture, with luminous vassals.
>
> It is the infant A standing on infant legs,
> Not twisted, stooping, polymathic Z,
> He that kneels always on the edge of space
>
> In the pallid perceptions of its distances.
> Alpha fears men or else Omega's men

Or else his prolongations of the human.

These characters are around us in the scene.

[*CP*, p. 169]

And so on, for another eight lines. Yet the attempt to dramatize the notion that reality is from beginning to end a verbal construction depends upon the heavy pun upon "characters," and the development of the idea exhibits not ingenuity but a kind of forcing: "the infant A standing on infant legs," etc. The poet's associations do not deepen our understanding of the idea nor invest the idea with feeling, but simply elaborate the idea, illustrate it. Stevens stops thinking, *stops valuing the idea as experience,* and falls back upon what he himself condemns: reason's click-clack. What the poetry requires here is a rich representation not merely of the paradox that the beginning is verbal but of the sense of the *miracle* of reality's being both "infant" and "infant A."

The vice of illustration may be described in another way as a failure to dramatize. And most weak uses of symbolism occur, I believe, not necessarily because the symbols are not fresh, but because the illusion of life in the work as a whole has failed. The symbolism of *The Nigger of the Narcissus* is, much of it, rather obvious, even banal. White and black are woven in a very simple design. But the image of life in that novella is so powerfully established, so complete and so convincing, that the symbols themselves, even when banal, are expressive: they deepen and enrich all the meanings and emotions which the story seeks to present. Stevens's symbolism, by the same token, is expressive when his poems are successful as poetic wholes; but when the action of the poem, the movement of the mind, goes dead, the symbols too are dead.

Perhaps, then, it is a mistake to speak of symbols good in themselves or *intrinsically* powerful. Criticism ever since Goethe's time has distinguished between nonvital (or artificial or arbitrary) symbolism and vital or genuine. As Goethe said:

> There is a great difference, whether the poet seeks the particular for the general or sees the general in the particular. From the first procedure arises allegory, where the particular serves only as an example of the general; the second procedure, however, is really the nature of poetry: it expresses something particular, without thinking of the general or pointing to it.

> True symbolism is where the particular represents the more gen-
> eral, not as a dream or shadow, but as a living momentary revelation
> of the Inscrutable.[2]

And there are, it goes without saying, compelling reasons to support Goethe's view—the sort of reasons that have impelled critics
like Tate to distinguish between a poetry of the imagination and
a poetry of the will; or have impelled Henry James to attack the
"importunate" symbolism in Hawthorne and to express his prefer-
ence for a fiction immersed in a sense of the particular. The argument has indeed become standard: true poetry is associated with
the vital, the dynamic, and the intrinsic, while allegory (false or bad
poetry?) is viewed as the static, extraneous, willed, and univalent.
Even the distinguished *Norton Anthology* ratifies the prejudice
against the univalent symbol, the a priori procedure of allegory. In
the prefatory note to *Everyman*, E. Talbot Donaldson remarks that
while the onlooker of the play

> takes a good deal of intellectual satisfaction in watching the nice
> operation of the allegorical equations ... one might object that
> allegory, when so neatly handled, sacrifices for a kind of mathemati-
> cal regularity the suggestiveness that inheres in the far looser alle-
> gory of such a work as *Piers Plowman*, which stimulates the
> imagination more than it satisfies the intellect. Nevertheless, when
> it is well staged and well acted, Everyman, despite its uncompromis-
> ing didacticism, is a powerful drama.[3]

Powerful *despite* its uncompromising didacticism and despite its
sacrifice of imaginative symbolism! But one would have thought
that *Everyman* is powerful *because* it is uncompromisingly didactic
and *because* it imposes its univalent meanings rigorously, with *un-
mistakeable clarity*, and thus succeeds in teaching its lesson. The
symbols of *Everyman*, I would suggest, are perfect—for *Everyman*.
They would not be perfect for the fiction of Joseph Conrad or
Henry James.

The contention that symbolism ought to proceed a posteriori—
its meanings arising in particulars in the organic life of a poem or
story—does not, then, hold for works "uncompromisingly didactic." But the attack on a willed or forced symbolism, a symbolism
which is obtrusive, "dependent upon explicatory pointers," and
arbitrary, may certainly be just when applied to mimetic works,

such as those of the great realistic novelists we have studied. Consider Henry James's description of Charlotte Stant:

> ... he knew above all the extraordinary fineness of her flexible waist, the stem of an expanded flower, which gave her a likeness also to some long loose silk purse, well filled with gold pieces, but having been passed, empty, through a finger-ring that held it together. It was as if, before she turned to him, he had weighed the whole thing in his open palm and even heard a little the chink of the metal.[23:47]

What is offensive in this passage is, indeed, the reliance on "explicatory pointers" (to use Henry H. H. Remak's phrase) and the forcing of Charlotte to participate in patterns of relationships that she seems not inevitably to embody. She is a money-girl, all right, and all her parts are valuable, are for sale, are gold. But she doesn't *look* like that silly purse—at least one hopes she doesn't! And James, as a lover of the image of life, had no business forcing her to look like one. So there is here the sort of "analogical baiting" that Edwin Honig has described—the use of an analogy that "simply dangles before the reader like an artificial bait," in contrast with the "analogy that fully engages him in a lively interplay between fact and fantasy"—this latter being termed by Honig "the allegorical waver," "an oscillating movement continually held in balance between two levels of correspondence—one realistic, the other symbolic."[4] Perfectly right, I should say—as criticism of a work like *The Wings of the Dove*; but not as criticism of *Everyman*.

There is, finally, the problem of the psychological and philosophical penetration of symbols. Do they give us insight? Are they, or are some of them, "cognitive"? Or are they to be considered solely as components of the literary work, having aesthetic but not cognitive functions? This was the question we touched upon in our first chapter, when we observed that for Dylan Thomas symbols have an extraliterary significance because they arise in life itself, and, presumably, give definition to life. Flanders Dunbar, in his study of Dante and medieval symbolism, distinguishes among three types of symbol—the arbitrary or extrinsic, the descriptive or intrinsic, and the interpretive or insight symbol. The arbitrary symbol arises through a mental association based on contiguity, the intrinsic through an association based on resemblance; but the insight-symbol is an "embodiment or revelation of the infinite."

Quoting Caroline Spurgeon's observation on mystics', "passionate belief in continuity of essence through ever-changing form," Dunbar points out that the grasp of essence through ever-changing form was made possible, in the Middle Ages, only through the insight symbol.[5] "Medieval ontology demanded that a study of things-as-they-are begin and end in a study of the eternal infinite expressing itself in time and space."[6] The symbol is esemplastic; it permits one to see a given fact in its relation to a pattern, and the pattern in relation to a totality, a comprehensive scheme of things.

Now without insisting upon the existence of a pattern of patterns or on any hierarchical structure of things from lowest to highest, we may observe that the process of generalization made possible by the employment of symbols is often just such an attempt to grasp an underlying law as one finds in a scientific work. Nietzsche's first grasp of the idea of the *Wille zur Macht* occurred when he observed an embodiment of that will—a symbol: Prussian officers riding past in their splendid regalia, proud, exulting in their puissance, fit for the fray, complete as gods. The symbol said plainly: "This is what men live for—to have this sense of power, to taste the joys of dominance." If Nietzsche had written novels, he might have developed a symbolism much like that of Henry James: an intricate pattern of warfare, seizure, imperialism, conquest, a comprehensive vision of the instinct of territoriality, a vision that, proliferating into all corners of life, everywhere enlarges our understanding of human behavior.

Or consider Wallace Stevens's man with the blue guitar, "a shearsman of sorts," or his Remus ploughing North America, ploughing on Sunday. It is as if, in a moment of inspiration, Stevens saw embodiments everywhere of the rage for order. Every human act became for him an expression of the determination to piece the world together—to cut it and stitch it and sew it so as to satisfy an insatiable imagination. The Canon Aspirin's sister, explaining that she has "two daughters, one / Of four, and one of seven," the farmer ploughing his field on Sunday, bringing order into the slovenly wilderness, the tailor cutting his cloth—all are only doing what poets do; everyman is a poet, and the whole race creates its skeleton of ether.

Or consider, again, the proliferations from the symbol of the jungle in Conrad's *Heart of Darkness*. What Conrad saw in the

Congo was the embodiment of all he feared, a nightmare made visible, madness triumphant. But it was only a step from that to a view of the entire world as embracing "intoxication," and the symbolism of jungle madness and disorder spreads out in his work until it touches every corner of life.

This spreading out of symbolism into every corner of experience—this process of generalization—is the cognitive aspect of art that the great realists have always insisted on.[7] It was not enough for the naturalist to collect notes. The notes were important, to be sure; as James said, the artist could never collect enough of them; but the subsumption of the notes under a single law, the discovery of pattern in the multitude of apparently unrelated facts, was the great object. It was the most highly generalizing minds that created the works valued today as the finest expressions of the realistic and naturalistic movements. These minds, determined to see life steadily and whole, were able to integrate thousands of unassimilated facts in symbolic patterns.

At the same time they were too intelligent to allow a single pattern to masquerade as the whole truth. The error of much nineteenth century science was to affirm that the material world of particles jostled and jostling is the only world, the sole reality. The Manichean symbolists carefully avoid that "genetic fallacy": the reduction of complex wholes to simpler elements. James, for example, does not *reduce* life to a Nietzschean will to power. If the insights of a Nietzsche are dissolved into the symbolic patterns of James's work, we find also such insights as those of Hobbes and Machiavelli, Veblen and Marx, Adler and William James, Darwin and Konrad Lorenz. But what emerges finally in the fiction is not ideas but a complex image of life that transcends the myth of isolation. And it is James's mastery of the "art of complete representation"—that mastery he so deeply admired in Balzac—that enables him to draw as close as possible to the whole truth about experience.

The employment of a mixed symbolism is, of course, but one of the means used by the Manicheans to grasp the whole truth of experience. We have noted other means from time to time: the employment, as a "reflector" of the action, of a consciousness capable of transcending the limitations of partial perspectives, a consciousness "subject to fine intensification and wide enlargement";

the avoidance of neat endings and of plot; the effort (in James especially) to "do" the subject thoroughly, developing the whole pattern of causation and interconnectedness arising from the *donnés;* the multiplication of perspectives so as to present a plurality of truths. Behind all of these devices, however, stands the Manichean artist, impersonal, detached, possessed of a mind so fine that no idea can violate it. Where there is no ax to grind, where there is no personal stake in the outcome of one's reflections, we may look for significant extensions of our grasp of reality. The whole truth about experience may be accessible only to an infinite mind; but the artist, if he is detached, if he is a free man, can so enlarge his views of things, so multiply his perspectives, so open himself to the ambiguities of experience, that it becomes entirely meaningful to speak, with Whitehead, of his passing beyond mythology and the myth of isolation. In the work of artists like James, Conrad, Woolf, and Stevens, the beauty of the complex symbolization of the ambiguities is finally inseparable from its truth.

NOTES

1. William Carlos Williams, *Kora in Hell: Improvisations* (Boston: The Four Seas Co., 1920), pp. 17–18.

2. Quoted in René Wellek, *A History of Modern Criticism* (New Haven: Yale University Press, 1955), 1:211.

3. *The Norton Anthology of English Literature*, 2 vols. (New York: W. W. Norton, 1962), 1:282.

4. Edwin Honig, *Dark Conceit* (New York: Oxford University Press, Galaxy Books, 1966), pp. 129, 127.

5. Flanders Dunbar, *Symbolism in Medieval Thought*, (New York: Russell and Russell, 1961), p. 23.

6. Ibid., p. 31.

7. Cf. Emerson: "The metamorphosis of Nature shows itself in nothing more than this, that there is no word in our language that cannot become typical to us of Nature by giving it emphasis. The world is a Dancer; it is a Rosary; it is a Torrent; it is a Boat; a Mist; a Spider's Snare; it is what you will; and the metaphor will hold, and it will give the imagination keen pleasure. Swifter than light the world converts itself into that thing you name, and all things find their right place under this new and capricious classification" (*Journals*, 6:18). But the classification need not be capricious; science, in its origin in the imagination, consists precisely of such hunches or intuitions, and when a hunch is confirmed by the

observations and predictions it makes possible, it becomes ontologically true. For an illuminating discussion of the whole problem, the reader is referred to Phillip Wheelwright's *The Burning Fountain* (Bloomington: University of Indiana Press, 1968).

APPENDIX: SOME OBSERVATIONS ON WALLACE STEVENS'S SYMBOLISM

THE FULL MEANING of Stevens's symbols is disclosed only by a study of their adventures through poems written over a period of fifty years. The meanings of *floor, round, day, wood, rise and fall,* and *pierce* emerge clearly from scrutiny of a generous sampling of the passages in which the words appear.

Floor. In "Sea Surface Full of Clouds" the speaker sees "blooms - / Of water moving on the water-floor" (*CP*, p. 100)—reflections of the clouds, imaginative reflections, traversing the floor of reality. Similarly, in "Le Monocle de Mon Oncle," the red bird that flies "across a golden floor" is an imaginative, romantic bird flying over the sun-colored floor of the earth (*CP*, p. 13). Sometimes it is the moonlight that casts its fictive glamor over the floor of earth, as in "The Ordinary Women," in which "The moonlight / Rose on the beachy floors," or as in "Academic Discourse at Havanna," in which the poet's speech causes "sleepers in their sleep" to "Waken, and watch the moonlight on their floors" (*CP*, p. 145). Again, in "Less and Less Human, O Savage Spirit" (*CP*, p. 327) the argument is that the spirit should not listen to the "human" but rather should be part of "the mass / Of which we are too distinctly a part": let the spirit not distort reality, rather let it move "silently" "as the sunlight moves on the floor, / Or moonlight," revealing the floor of reality as sunlight reveals objects or, ironically, as the fictive moonlight reveals them. Closely related is a passage in "The Creations of Sound," in which the syllables accumulated by the poet's sensibility are described as "syllables that rise / From the floor, rising in speech we do not speak" (*CP*, p. 311)—rising, that is, not from the human spirit but from an unconscious, prelogical self dwelling in the "dirty silence," the "floor" of the material mass. In another group of poems *floor* appears in conjunction with the death-dealing flux: thus in "Farewell to Florida" the poet rejects the South in which the snake has "left its skin upon the floor" and turns for fulfillment to an imaginative North (*CP*, pp. 117–18); in "The Bouquet" (*CP*, p. 453) the vase of flowers, after being toppled by the soldier who symbolizes the violence and brutality of the flux, lies "on the floor," an object no longer adulterated by fictions. In "The Auroras of Autumn" the wind blowing "the sand across the floor" is once again the flux dispelling the fictive arrangements of the speaker (*CP*, p. 412), and in "The Plain Sense of Things" the decay of autumn and the encroachment of death are described in these words (*CP*, p. 502): "The great structure [nature] has become a minor house. / No turban walks across the lessened floors. / The greenhouse [earth] never so badly needed paint." All of these passages suggest that *floor* refers to the earth itself, the rock or mat on which man stands, and behind most of them is the submerged metaphor of varnishing.

Round. In "Anecdote of the Jar" (*CP*, p. 76) the round jar causes nature, the slovenly wilderness, to rise up and sprawl "around, no longer wild": sprawling "around" is acquiring a geometrical shape at the dictates of the imagination. Somewhat less obvious is the connotation of the word in "The Bird with the Coppery, Keen Claws," but when we note that the "parakeet of parakeets" that prevails "above the forest of parakeets" is much like the jar that prevails over the wilderness of Tennessee, the line "The rudiments of tropics are around" comes to mean not only what it says but also that the primitive earth has acquired geometric form under the influence of the parakeet. In "Life is Motion," in which Bonnie and Josie dance "around a stump," the dancing is obviously part of the ceremony by which the stump of reality is transformed and the flesh of reality is married to the air of the imagination. In "Some Friends from Pascagoula" the eagle's "slowly-falling-round / Down to a fishy sea" is said to be a "sovereign sight" to the Negroes, who describe it "with deepened voice / And noble imagery." (And indeed every image of the eagle's flight has imaginative connotations, the imagery of geometric definition occurring

not only in *round* but also in *point, edging* and *sovereign rings.*) The
moon of the imagination, too, is *round,* and in "God is Good. It is
a Beautiful Night" (*CP,* p. 285) is told to "Look round"—"Look
round you as you start to rise." Again, in "Description without
Place" (*CP,* p. 342) when the poet sees "the sun of Nietzsche
gildering the pool," the "swarm-like manias" move "In perpetual
revolution, round and round." And in "An Ordinary Evening in
New Haven" the "wandering mariners" look upon "big women,
whose ruddy-ripe images / wreathed round and round the round
wreath of autumn" (*CP,* p. 486). Further illustration is probably
unnecessary.

Day. In "Evening without Angels" Stevens writes that we live
in the physical world, not in a fake of the imagination: "Let this
be clear that we are men of sun / And men of day and never of
pointed night" (*CP,* p. 137). The "people in the air" may avoid "the
keenest diamond day / Of people sensible to pain," but in choosing
the imagining owl to the crowing cock, the airy people reveal a
sterile escapism ("On the Adequacy of Landscape," *CP,* pp. 243–
44). Of "the two dreams, night and day," Stevens chooses day,
reality, the "feme . . . leaf-green, / Whose coming may give revel /
Beyond revelries of sleep" ("Hymn from a Watermelon Pavilion,"
CP, pp. 88–89). And because it appeals to the mindless, to those
who prefer reality, "Day is the children's friend" ("The Prejudice
against the Past," *CP,* pp. 368–69).

Wood. "In the woods of the dogwoods" there are no fictions, no
"large white horses" ("Forces, the Will & the Weather," *CP,* pp.
228–29). Mankind lives in a "poisoned wood" ("The Pastor Cabal-
lero," *CP,* pp. 379). And the man "white as marble" sitting "in a
wood, in the greenest part," is the imagination sitting in reality
("Metaphor as Degeneration," *CP,* p. 444).

Rise and Fall. In "The Comedian as the Letter C," Crispin,
assaulted by the brute flux, discovers a

> Triton incomplicate with that
> Which made him Triton, nothing left of him,
> Except in faint, memorial gesturings,
> That were like arms and shoulders in the waves,
> Here, something in the rise and fall of wind
> That seemed hallucinating horn.
>
> [*CP,* pp. 28–29]

More than twenty years later Stevens employs a similar irony when, in part 2 of "Two Versions of the Same Poem," he turns his attention to "the sea, insolid rock," and notes how the human imagination transforms this bare matter into "The human ocean ... rising and falling," an "ocean of watery images." And in "Page from a Tale," Hans, by his drift-fire on the shore, is reminded of the lines from "The Lake Isle of Innisfree" that rise and fall in his mind: "*Of clay and wattles made* as it ascends / And *hear it* as it falls *in the deep heart's core.*" Here we may remark, too, an interesting association of *rise and fall* with *up and down*, established in the early "The Curtains in the House of the Metaphysician," where the speaker marvels at how the curtains, like the rhythms of poetry, "Up-rising and down-falling, / Bare the last largeness, bold to see." And a number of poems continue this symbolism, employing *up and down* to mean the poet's rhythms and the vital to-and-fro of imagination and reality. Thus in "The Comedian as the Letter C" Crispin's "fluctuating between sun and moon," reality and imagination, is described as an "up and down between two elements." In "Homunculus et La Belle Étoile" the light of the imagination, symbolized by the evening star, falls upon several imaginative creatures and conducts "the thoughts of drunkards, the feelings / Of widows and trembling ladies, / The movement of fishes," which by starlight proceed in "many directions / Up and down." Even the submarine, part of the harsh reality of war in "Examination of the Hero in a Time of War," behaves poetically, its journey "up the great sea and downward" being associated with imaginative "Chopiniana." And at the end of "Notes toward a Supreme Fiction," the up and down of the pacing soldier becomes the up and down of the imagination when Stevens instructs his soldier that "the poet is always in the sun, / Patches the moon together in his room / To his Virgilian cadences, up down, / Up down."

Generally speaking, *rising* is associated with metamorphoses: in half a dozen poems the moon rises and, at its rising, reality is transformed; or a figure rises above the others, noble and mighty, as in "The Candle a Saint" and "Thunder by the Musician." The killdeer "rise / At the red turban / Of the boatman," surrogate of the poet (in "The Load of Sugar-Cane," *CP*, p. 12), or the mind, in defiance of a drowsing, torpid reality, "Rose up besprent and sought the flaming red" (in "Hibiscus on the Sleeping Shores," *CP*,

p. 22). Again, the "dweller in the dark cabin of the mind is urged to experience the revelry of awakening to a world as glorious as any fictive realm: "Rise, since rising will not waken, / And hail, cry hail, cry hail" ("Hymn from a Watermelon Pavilion," *CP*, p. 89). Or again, the poet finds that after a period of despair, "a bright red woman will be rising / And, standing in violent golds, will brush her hair" ("Debris of Life and Mind," *CP*, p. 338).

Falling, commonly referring to the descent of beneficent imagination from heaven, is strikingly illustrated in "Anecdote of the Prince of Peacocks," in which the moonlight comes "Falling there, / Falling / As sleep falls / In the innocent air." In "Banal Sojourn" the speaker dreams of seasons when "radiance comes running down, slim through the bareness," and in "Ghosts as Cocoons," the speaker invokes the season of the imagination, spring, as "season / Excelling summer, ghost of fragrance falling /On dung." The lines of the stars, in "The Stars at Tallapoosa," are "swift and fall without diverging," like "A sheaf of brilliant arrows." In "Two at Norfolk" we find: "the music of the boy fell like a fountain." And in "Some Friends from Pascagoula" there is the eagle's "slowly-falling-round / Down to a fishy sea," his "Dropping in sovereign rings / Out of his fiery lair." This basic symbolism continues into the later poetry, from which we may select one illustration: In "An Ordinary Evening in New Haven" a "recent imagining of reality" is likened to "a new resemblance of the sun, / Down-pouring, up-springing and inevitable." The diligent will find dozens of instances in which Stevens handles *falling* and its associates with absolute confidence respecting their symbolic meanings.

Pierce. The poet, in "Mozart, 1935," strikes "the piercing chord." The moon's song "pierces / The fresh night" (in "God is Good. It is a Beautiful Night"). The bouquet strikes its beholder, not as one of the "choses of Provence, growing / In glue," but as a thing "transfixed, transpierced" (*CP*, p. 449). And the fire of the sun, if seen freshly (and not merely taken for granted), would "pierce the vision that beholds it" ("Questions are Remarks," *CP*, p. 462).

A SELECTIVE BIBLIOGRAPHY

Anderson, Quentin. *The American Henry James.* New Brunswick, N.J.: Rutgers University Press, 1957.

Bachelard, Gaston. *The Psychoanalysis of Fire.* Translated by Alan Ross. Boston: Beacon Press, 1964.

Baines, Jocelyn. *Joseph Conrad: A Critical Biography.* London: Weidenfeld and Nicolson, 1960.

Balakian, Anne. *The Symbolist Movement: A Critical Appraisal.* Gloucester, Mass.: Peter Smith, 1968.

Barzun, Jacques. *Darwin, Marx, and Wagner.* New York: Doubleday & Co., Anchor Books, 1958.

Beach, Joseph Warren. *The Method of Henry James.* New Haven: Yale University Press, 1918.

————. *Obsessive Images: Symbolism in Poetry of the 1930's and 1940's.* Minneapolis: University of Minnesota Press, 1960.

————. *The Twentieth-Century Novel: Studies in Technique.* New York: Appleton-Century-Crofts, 1932.

Bennett, Joan. *Virginia Woolf: Her Art As a Novelist.* Cambridge: At the University Press, 1945.

Benziger, James. *Images of Eternity: Studies in the Poetry of Religious Vision from Wordsworth to T. S. Eliot.* Carbondale and Edwardsville: Southern Illinois University Press, 1968.

Bewley, Marius. *The Complex Fate.* New York: Grove Press, 1953.

Black, Max. *Models and Metaphors.* Ithaca, N.Y.: Cornell University Press, 1962.

Blackall, Jean Frantz. *Jamesian Ambiguity and "The Sacred Fount."* Ithaca, N.Y.: Cornell University Press, 1965.

Bodkin, Maud. *Archetypal Patterns in Poetry: Psychological Studies of Imagination.* London: Oxford University Press, Oxford Paperbacks, 1960.

————. *Studies of Type Images in Poetry, Religion and Philosophy.* London: Oxford University Press, 1951.

Boroff, Marie, ed. *Wallace Stevens: A Collection of Critical Essays.* New Brunswick, N.J.: Rutgers University Press, 1963.

Bowden, Edwin T. *The Themes of Henry James.* New Haven: Yale University Press, 1956.

Bradbrook, M. C. *Joseph Conrad: Poland's English Genius.* Cambridge: At the University Press, 1941.

Brewster, Dorothy. *Virginia Woolf's London.* London: G. Selen & Univin, 1959. New York: New York University Press, 1960.

Brown, Ashley, and Haller, Robert S. *The Achievement of Wallace Stevens.* Philadelphia: J. B. Lippincott Co., 1962.

Campbell, Joseph. *The Hero with a Thousand Faces.* Bollingen Series no. 17. New York: World Publishing Co., Meridian Books, 1956.

Canby, Henry Seidel. *Turn West, Turn East: Mark Twain and Henry James.* Boston: Houghton Mifflin Co., 1951.

Cargill, Oscar. *The Novels of Henry James.* New York: Macmillan Co., 1961.

Cassirer, Ernst. *An Essay on Man.* New York: Bantam Books, 1969.

Conrad, Joseph. *Chance.* New York: Doubleday & Co., 1923.

_____. *Lord Jim.* New York: Random House, Modern Library, 1931.

_____. *The Secret Agent.* New York: Doubleday & Co., Anchor Books, 1953.

_____. *Under Western Eyes.* New York: Doubleday & Co., Anchor Books, 1963.

_____. *The Works of Joseph Conrad.* 20 vols. London and Edinburgh: John Grant, 1925.

Daiches, David. *The Novel and the Modern World.* Chicago: University of Chicago Press, 1939.

_____. *Virginia Woolf.* Norfolk, Conn.: New Directions Books, 1942.

Damon, S. Foster. *A Blake Dictionary: The Ideas and Symbols of William Blake.* New York: Dutton, 1971.

Doggett, Frank. *Wallace Stevens' Poetry of Thought.* Baltimore: Johns Hopkins Press, 1966.

Dunbar, Flanders. *Symbolism in Medieval Thought and its Consummation in the Divine Comedy.* New York: Russell and Russell, 1961.

Dupee, F. W. *Henry James.* New York: William Sloane Associates, 1951.

_____, ed. *The Question of Henry James.* New York: Holt, Rinehart & Winston, 1945.

Edel, Leon. *Henry James: The Untried Years, 1843–1870.* Philadelphia: J. B. Lippincott Co., 1953.

_____. *The Conquest of London, 1870–1881.* Philadelphia: J. B. Lippincott Co., 1962.

_____. *Henry James: The Middle Years, 1882–1895.* Philadelphia: J. B. Lippincott Co., 1962.

_____. *Henry James: The Treacherous Years, 1895–1901.* Philadelphia: J. B. Lippincott Co., 1969.

_____, ed. *Henry James: A Collection of Critical Essays.* Englewood Cliffs, N.J.: Prentice-Hall, 1963.

Eliade, Mircea. *Cosmos and History: The Myth of the Eternal Return.* Translated by Willard R. Trask. Bollingen Series, no. 46. New York: Harper & Row, Harper Torchbooks, 1959.

_____. *Images and Symbols.* Translated by Philip Mairer. New York: Sheed & Ward, 1969.

_____. *Myth and Reality.* Translated by William R. Trask. New York: Harper & Row, Harper Torchbooks, 1963.

_____. *Rites and Symbols of Initiation: The Mysteries of Birth and Rebirth.* Translated by William R. Trask. New York: Harper & Row, Harper Torchbooks, 1963.

Ellmann, Richard. *Yeats: The Man and the Masks.* New York: Dutton, 1958.

Feidelson, Jr., Charles. *Symbolism and American Literature.* Chicago: University of Chicago Press, 1953.

Fletcher, Angus. *Allegory: The Theory of a Symbolic Mode.* Ithaca, N.Y.: Cornell University Press, 1964.

Ford, Ford Maddox. *Joseph Conrad: A Personal Remembrance.* Boston: Little, Brown & Co., 1924.

Forster, E. M. *Virginia Woolf: The Rede Lecture.* Cambridge: At the University Press, 1942. New York: Harcourt, Brace & Co., 1942.

Foss, Martin. *Symbol and Metaphor in Human Experience.* Princeton: Princeton University Press, 1949.

Frazer, Sir James G. *The New Golden Bough.* Edited by Theodor H. Gaster. New York: New American Library, Mentor Books, n.d.

Freedman, Ralph. *The Lyric Novel.* Princeton: Princeton University Press, 1965.

Freud, Sigmund. *On Creativity and the Unconscious: Papers on the Psychology of Art, Literature, Love, Religion.* New York: Harper & Row, Harper Torchbooks, 1958.

_____. *On Dreams.* Edited and translated by James Strachey. New York: W. W. Norton & Co., Norton Library, 1962.

_____. *General Selection from the Works of Sigmund Freud.* Edited by John Rickman. New York: Doubleday & Co., Anchor Books, 1957.

_____. *The Interpretation of Dreams.* Translated by James Strachey. New York: Avon Books, 1965.

Fromm, Erich. *The Forgotten Language: An Introduction to the Understanding of Dreams, Fairy Tales, and Myths.* New York: Grove Press, Evergreen Books, 1957.

Frye, Northrop. *The Anatomy of Criticism: Four Essays.* Princeton: Princeton University press, 1957.

_____. *Fables of Identity: Studies in Poetic Mythology.* New York: Harcourt, Brace & World, Harbinger Books, 1963.

_____. *The Return of Eden: Five Essays on Milton's Epics.* Toronto: University of Toronto Press, 1965.

_____. *T. S. Eliot.* New York: Barnes & Noble, 1963.

_____, Knights, L. C., et al. *Myth and Symbol: Critical Approaches and Applications. Fifteen Essays.* Omaha: University of Nebraska Press, Bison Books, 1963.

Fuchs, Daniel. *The Comic Spirit of Wallace Stevens.* Durham, N.C.: Duke University Press, 1963.

Gale, Robert L. *The Caught Image: Figurative Language in the Fiction of Henry James.* Chapel Hill: University of North Carolina Press, 1964.

_____. *Plots and Characters in the Fiction of Henry James.* Hamden, Conn.: Archon Books, 1965.

Gordon, John Dozier, *Joseph Conrad: The Making of a Novelist*. Cambridge: Howard University Press, 1940.

Graver, Lawrence. *Conrad's Short Fiction*. Berkeley and Los Angeles: University of California Press, 1969.

Graves, Robert. *The White Goddess: A Historical Grammar of Poetic Myth*. New York: Farrar, Straus & Giroux, Noonday Press, 1966.

Guerard, Jr., Albert. *Joseph Conrad*. Cambridge, Mass.: Harvard University Press, 1958.

Guetti, James. *The Limits of Metaphor: A Study of Melville, Conrad, and Faulkner*. Ithaca, N.Y.: Cornell University Press, 1967.

Hafley, James. *The Glass Roof: Virginia Woolf as Novelist*. Berkeley: University of California Press, 1954.

Hardison, Jr., O. B., ed. *The Quest for Imagination*. Cleveland and London: Press of Case Western Reserve University, 1971.

Hay, Eloise Knapp. *The Political Novels of Joseph Conrad*. Chicago: University of Chicago Press, 1963.

Holder-Barrell, Alexander. *The Development of Imagery and Its Functional Significance in Henry James's Novels*. Cooper Monographs, no. 3. Bern: Francke Verlag, 1959.

Holland, Laurence B. *The Expense of Vision: Essays on the Craft of Henry James*. Princeton: Princeton University Press, 1964.

Honig, Edwin. *Dark Conceit: The Making of Allegory*. New York: Oxford University Press, Galaxy Books, 1966.

Jacobi, Jolande. *Complex, Archetype, Symbol in the Psychology of C. G. Jung*. Bollingen Series, no. 57. New York: Random House, Pantheon Books, 1959.

———. *The Psychology of C. G. Jung*. Translated by Ralph Manheim. New Haven: Yale University Press, 1963.

James, Henry. *The Art of the Novel: Critical Prefaces by Henry James*. Edited by Richard P. Blackmur. New York: Charles Scribner's Sons, 1934.

———. *The Complete Tales of Henry James*. Edited by Leon Edel. 12 Vols. London: Rupert Hart-Davis, 1961–64. Philadelphia: J. B. Lippincott Company, 1962–65.

———. *French Poets and Novelists*. London: Macmillan & Co., 1878.

———. *Henry James: Autobiography*. Edited by F. W. Dupee. New York: Criterion Books, 1956.

———. *The Letters of Henry James*. Edited by Percy Lubbock. 2 vols. London: Macmillan & Co., 1920. New York: Charles Scribner's Sons, 1920.

———. *The Middle Years*. London: William Collins Sons & Co., 1917. New York: Charles Scribner's Sons, 1917.

———. *The Notebooks of Henry James*. Edited by F. O. Matthiessen and Kenneth B. Murdock. New York: Oxford University Press, 1947.

———. *Notes of a Son and Brother*. New York: Charles Scribner's Sons, 1914. London: Macmillan & Co., 1914.

———. *Notes on Novelists with Some Other Notes*. London: J. M. Dent & Sons, 1914. New York: Charles Scribner's Sons, 1914.

_____. *The Novels and Tales of Henry James.* 26 vols. New York: Charles
Scribner's Sons, 1907–17.
_____. *Partial Portraits.* London and New York: Macmillan & Co., 1888.
_____. *The Question of Our Speech. The Lesson of Balzac: Two Lectures.*
Boston and New York: Houghton Mifflin Co., 1905.
_____. *A Small Boy and Others.* New York: Charles Scribner's Sons, 1913.
London: Macmillan & Co., 1913.
_____. *Within the Rim and Other Essays.* London: William Collins Sons &
Co., 1919.
Jean-Aubry, G. *Joseph Conrad: Life and Letters.* 2 vols. New York: Double-
day & Co., 1927.
_____. *The Sea Dreamer.* New York: Doubleday & Co., 1957.
Johnstone, J. K. *The Bloomsbury Group.* London: Seker and Warburg, 1954.
Jung, Carl G. *The Archetypes and the Collective Unconscious.* Translated by
R. F. C. Hull. Vol. 9, pt. 1 of *Collected Works.* Edited by G. Adler et
al. 17 vols. Princeton: Princeton University Press, 1968.
_____. *Man and His Symbols.* New York: Dell Publishing Co., 1968.
_____. *Psyche and Symbol.* Edited by Violet S. de Laszlo. New York:
Doubleday & Co., Anchor Books, 1958.
_____. *Symbols of Transformation: An Analysis of the Prelude to a Case of
Schizophrenia.* Vol. 5 of *Collected Works.* 2 vols. New York: Harper &
Row, Harper Torchbooks, 1962.
Krieger, Murray. *The Tragic Vision.* New York: Holt, Rinehart & Win-
ston, 1960.
Krook, Dorothea. *The Ordeal of Consciousness in Henry James.* New York:
Cambridge University Press, 1962.
Laing, R. D. *The Divided Self: An Existential Study in Madness.* Baltimore:
Penguin Books, 1970.
Lesser, Simon O. *Fiction and the Unconscious.* New York: Random House,
Vintage Books, 1962.
Leyburn, Ellen Douglass. *Strange Alloy: The Relation of Comedy to Tragedy
in the Fiction of Henry James.* Chapel Hill: University of North Carolina
Press, 1968.
Marks, Robert. *James's Late Novels: An Interpretation.* New York: William-
Frederick Press, 1960.
Matthiessen, F. O. *Henry James: The Major Phase.* New York: Oxford
University Press, 1944.
Meyer, Bernard C. *Joseph Conrad: A Psychoanalytic Biography.* Princeton:
Princeton University Press, 1967.
Moody, A. D. *Virginia Woolf.* Edinburgh and London: Oliver and Boyd,
1963.
Moore, Harry T. *The Intelligent Heart: The Life of D. H. Lawrence.* London:
William Heinemann, 1955.
Moser, Thomas. *Joseph Conrad: Achievement and Decline.* Cambridge, Mass.:
Harvard University Press, 1957.
Nassar, Eugene Paul. *Wallace Stevens: An Anatomy of Figuration.* Philadel-
phia: University of Pennsylvania Press, 1965.

Neumann, Erich. *Art and Creative Unconscious: Four Essays.* Bollingen Series, no. 61. Princeton: Princeton University Press, 1959.
———. *The Great Mother. An Analysis of the Archetype.* Bollingen Series, no. 47. Princeton: Princeton University Press, 1964.
Olson, Elder. *The Poetry of Dylan Thomas.* Chicago: University of Chicago Press, 1954.
Pack, Robert. *Wallace Stevens.* New Brunswick, N.J.: Rutgers University Press, 1958.
Piaget, Jean. *Play, Dreams and Imitation in Childhood.* Translated by C. Gattegno and F. M. Hodgson. New York: Norton, 1962.
Pippett, Aileen. *The Moth and the Star: A Biography of Virginia Woolf.* Boston: Little, Brown & Co., 1955.
Poirier, Richard. *The Comic Sense of Henry James: A Study of the Early Novels.* New York: Oxford University Press, 1962.
Poulet, Georges. *The Metamorphoses of the Circle.* Translated by Carley Dawson and Elliot Coleman. Baltimore: John Hopkins Press, 1966.
Putt, S. Gorley. *A Reader's Guide to Henry James.* Ithaca, N.Y.: Cornell University Press, 1969. London: Thames and Hudson, 1966.
Rehder, Helmut, ed. *Literary Symbolism: A Symposium.* Austin and London: University of Texas Press, 1965.
Riddel, Joseph N. *The Clairvoyant Eye: The Poetry and Poetics of Wallace Stevens.* Baton Rouge: Louisiana State University Press, 1965.
Rosenfield, Claire. *Paradise of Snakes: An Archetypal Analysis of Conrad's Political Novels.* Chicago: University of Chicago Press, 1967.
Royce, Joseph R., ed. *Psychology and the Symbol: An Interdisciplinary Symposium.* New York: Random House, 1965.
Schneider, Daniel J. "Wallace Stevens: His Theory of Poetry and Its Application to His Poems." Ph.D. dissertation, Northwestern University, 1956.
Sears, Sally. *The Negative Imagination.* Ithaca, N.Y.: Cornell University Press, 1968.
Seward, Barbara. *The Symbolic Rose.* New York: Columbia University Press, 1960.
Slote, Bernice, ed. *Myth and Symbol.* Lincoln: University of Nebraska Press, 1963.
Stern, Herbert J. *Wallace Stevens.* Ann Arbor: University of Michigan Press, 1966.
Stevens, Wallace. *The Collected Poems of Wallace Stevens.* New York: Alfred A. Knopf, 1954.
———. *Letters.* Edited by Holly Stevens. New York: Alfred A. Knopf, 1966.
———. *The Necessary Angel: Essays on Reality and the Imagination.* New York: Alfred A. Knopf, 1951.
———. *Opus Posthumous: Poems Plays, Prose by Wallace Stevens.* Edited by Samuel French Morse. New York: Alfred A. Knopf, 1957.
Stevenson, Elizabeth. *The Crooked Corridor: A Study of Henry James.* New York: Macmillan Co., 1940.

Symons, Arthur. *The Symbolist Movement in Literature.* New York: E. P. Dutton & Co., 1958.

Taupin, René. *L'Influence du symbolisme Français sur la Poésie Americaine.* Paris: H. Champion, 1929.

Tuve, Rosemund. *Allegorical Imagery: Some Medieval Books and Their Posterity.* Princeton: Princeton University Press, 1966.

Van Ghent, Dorothy. *The English Novel: Form and Function.* New York: Rinehart & Co., 1953.

Vendler, Helen Hennessy. *On Extended Wings: Wallace Stevens' Longer Poems.* Cambridge, Mass.: Harvard University Press, 1969.

Vivas, Eliseo. *D. H. Lawrence: The Failure and the Triumph of Art.* Evanston, Ill.: Northwestern University Press, 1960.

Ward, Joseph A. *The Imagination of Disaster: Evil in the Fiction of Henry James.* Lincoln: University of Nebraska Press, 1961.

――――. *The Search for Form: Studies in the Structure of James's Fiction.* Chapel Hill: University of North Carolina Press, 1967.

Weinberg, Bernard. *The Limits of Symbolism: Studies of Five Modern French Poets.* Chicago: University of Chicago Press, 1966.

Weston, Jessie L. *From Ritual to Romance: An Account of the Holy Grail from Ancient Ritual to Christian Symbol.* New York: Doubleday & Co., Anchor Books, 1957.

Wheelwright, Phillip. *The Burning Fountain.* Bloomington: Indiana University Press, 1968.

White, John J. *Mythology in the Modern Novel.* Princeton: Princeton University Press, 1971.

Whitehead, Alfred North. *Adventures of Ideas.* New York: New American Library, Mentor Books, 1955.

――――. *Modes of Thought.* Cambridge: At the University Press, 1938.

Wiley, Paul L. *Conrad's Measure of Man.* Madison: University of Wisconsin Press, 1954.

Wilson, Edmund. *Axel's Castle.* New York: Charles Scribner's Sons, 1931.

Wimsatt, W. K., and Beardsley, Monroe C. *The Verbal Icon.* Lexington: University of Kentucky Press, 1954.

Woolf, Virginia. *Between the Acts.* New York: Harcourt, Brace & World, Harvest Books, 1969.

――――. *Jacob's Room and The Waves.* New York: Harcourt, Brace & World, Harvest Books, 1959.

――――. *Night and Day.* London: Hogarth Press, 1915.

――――. *The Years.* New York: Harcourt, Brace & World, Harvest Books, 1965.

Wright, Walter. *Romance and Tragedy in Joseph Conrad.* Lincoln: University of Nebraska Press, 1949.

Yeats, William Butler. *The Collected Poems of William Butler Yeats.* London: Macmillan & Co., 1950.

INDEX

Abrams, M. H., 12
Anderson, Quentin, 63

Barzun, Jacques, 4
Baudelaire, Charles, 16
Beach, Joseph Warren, 91
Bennett, Joan, 123
Bewley, Marius, 162
Blake, William, 18, 32
Brontë, Emily, 75
Brooks, Cleanth, 10
Brown, Norman O., 21
Burke, Kenneth, 23

Cassirer, Ernst, 30
Chase, Richard, 62
Coleridge, S. T., 1, 32
Comte, Auguste, 1, 2
Conrad, Joseph, 123, 155, 156,
   206, 214–15; denial of free
   will, 9; emphasis on truth and
   detachment, 34–35; emphasis on
   will to power, 42–43;
   pessimism, 7–9; symbolism of
   appearance and reality, 20;
   symbolism corresponding to
   Stevens's, 60–61; symbolism in
   his works: *Lord Jim*, 44–55; *The
   Nigger of the Narcissus*, 42–44;
   Nostromo, 58–59; *An Outcast of*

the Islands, 40–42; *Under
   Western Eyes*, 56–58; use of
   Marlow as "reflector," 59–60
Crane, Hart, 4, 15

Daiches, David, 13, 22, 123, 146
Determinism: influence on
   Conrad, 8–9; significance for
   symbolists, 2, 3. *See also*
   Mechanistic determinism
Dunbar, Flanders, 32, 33, 213–14

Eckhardt, Meister, 32
Eliade, Mircea, 32
Eliot, T. S., 15, 17, 18, 118–19
Emerson, Ralph Waldo, 1, 4, 6,
   31

Feidelson, Jr., Charles, 5, 154,
   155–56
Fitzgerald, F. Scott: symbolism in
   The Great Gatsby, 17, 22, 71
Flaubert, Gustave, 10
Forster, E. M., 18, 124, 146;
   Howards End, 124–26
Frisch, Max, 21
Frye, Northrop, 22; his
   classification of images, 11–13;
   possible limitations of his
   approach, 13–14

233